The Information Edge

THE
INFORMATION
EDGE

N. DEAN MEYER
MARY E. BOONE

McGraw-Hill Book Company

New York St. Louis San Francisco Auckland Bogotá
Hamburg London Madrid Mexico Milan New Delhi
Panama Paris São Paulo Singapore Sydney
Tokyo

Copyright © 1987

Gage Educational Publishing Limited

ISBN 0-07-041782-2

Originally published in 1986 by Holt, Rinehart and Winston of
Canada, Limited

Printed in the United States of America.
    4 5 6   91 90 89 88

To Dr. Douglas C. Engelbart, whose vision established and still guides the office automation profession, and to Larry Day, who exemplifies the art of translating vision into practice.

The **Converging Technologies Series** is designed to help today's managers lead and control the profound technological tide now sweeping the traditional workplace; dramatically improve organizational performance; and improve the quality of work life.

Under the Consulting Editorship of Don Tapscott, an international authority in the field of integrated office systems, the **Converging Technologies Series** draws on the proven experience and insights of industry experts.

Other books in this series:

People and Productivity: A Manager's Guide to Ergonomics in the Electronic Office

The Ergonomics Payoff: Designing the Electronic Office

The Information Edge

"The authors present a rich basis of case studies to defend their premise that the strategic use of information technology can be quantified and they offer pragmatic methods for identifying value-added applications. I appreciate the way the book is organized to zero in on a specific systems issue or business problem for any particular executive or office automation implementor."

Albert B. Crawford
SENIOR VICE PRESIDENT, SYSTEMS , AMERICAN EXPRESS TRS COMPANY

"**The Information Edge** will trigger creative sparks in the minds of our executives, and will focus our systems staff on high-return business opportunities. Meyer and Boone's approach is essential as we integrate business and computer systems in our corporate strategy."

Jacob H. Waller,
VICE PRESIDENT, ADMINISTRATION, COCA-COLA FOUNTAIN DIVISION

Contents

Foreword

In the past two decades, computer- and communications-based tools
have become commonplace on the desks of secretaries and clerks. The
remarkable productivity gains resulting from these administrative
support tools make them relatively easy to justify. In the 1980s, the
information industry has shifted its attention away from administration to help executives, managers, and professionals — the "knowledge workers" — achieve the objectives of their organizations. Research
began as early as 1960, and commercial products have been available
for over a decade. The popularization of the personal computer that
began in 1980 made many of these new tools readily available, and
built widespread awareness of the innovative use of information
tools. Now, in the mid-1980s, approximately 20 per cent of the
knowledge workers in large businesses use some form of office
information tools. Personal computers sit on the desks of between 15
and 20 per cent of white-collar workers. Even in smaller organizations, office information tools are commonly available.

The industry now faces its next hurdle. In large businesses, extending these capabilities to the remainder of the white-collar work force
will require a tremendous investment. Meanwhile, advanced users
are demanding more powerful tools, necessitating investments in
departmental computers, networks, and interactive access to large
mainframe computers. New tools, such as teleconferencing, offer
great potential returns but demand even greater investments in capital and support staff.

The potential investment in office automation in the next few
years is likely to match all that has been spent on it to date, and by the
end of the decade may rival the amount spent on corporate data
processing. Executives are naturally demanding clear explanations
of the return on their already significant investments before further
expenditures are authorized.

In less progressive firms, office information tools have not yet spread so far. Here too the obstacle to progress is often the inability to present a clear justification for investing a firm's limited capital in tools for thinking rather than tools for production. These more conservative executives join the ranks of the early risk-takers who authorized expenditures "on faith" and now question the value of office automation.

The industry has struggled for some time with the challenge of measuring the return on investments in information tools for knowledge workers. For secretaries and clerks, it was relatively easy. Their work is structured and measurable, so productivity measures were straightforward. Managers, however, are not paid to process papers or answer telephones. Their outputs are not measurable. (Do you know how much money you made for your company last week?) Nor are inputs measurable; it is virtually impossible to determine what bits of time and experience go into the making of a decision. While time savings on some managerial tasks can be captured, it is unclear where the time saved will be spent and unlikely that staff will be reduced as a result. It is also uncertain whether an additional few minutes "saved" in a day will have any impact on corporate profits. Productivity measures do not seem to apply to managers and professionals.

In this book, we use the term "value-added" to mean benefits counted in terms of effectiveness rather than efficiency. This use of the term, originally applied to office automation by Larry Day and Jeff Rulifson in 1977, has come into use throughout the information industry. Similarly, many people talk about the "strategic value of information," implying a link between information tools and corporate profits.

On closer inspection, one often finds that these phrases are being used only to disguise old-fashioned productivity studies. Decision makers have every right to remain suspicious of the stopwatch approach applied to people whose jobs involve creativity and judgment.

Even when the term "value-added" is defined, it is often a source of frustration. Information professionals often equate value-added with "intangible" benefits, implying that it is impossible to measure the impact on profits of information tools for knowledge workers. If this were true, user organizations would be hard-pressed to invest further in office automation, and vendors would be hard-pressed to continue to expand the size of the marketplace.

Fortunately, value-added benefits *can* be measured. Our experience and research have uncovered hundreds of creative people who are putting information tools to work on problems of strategic significance. They are having tangible impacts on the bottom lines of their organizations. This book includes over 60 cases in which value-added benefits were measured.

A value-added focus should lead the industry away from replacing people with computers, and toward applying tools to make people more effective. By providing a number of examples of how much each office information tool can really contribute, the cases should stimulate thinking and help to identify new and more meaningful opportunities to apply office information tools.

We wrote this book to help lift the focus of the computer and communication industry out of the realm of marginal gains in administrative efficiency and into the mainstream of business. Our goal is to help these tools, and the information staff groups that support them, claim their proper role as a strategic asset to the organization. We hope this book will help executives to understand the strategic importance of investments in the intelligence of their knowledge workers; we hope it will help information staff groups to direct their efforts toward the high-payoff applications that are most relevant to their users; and we hope it will help vendors justify proposals to sell tools that can help people to be more creative, clever, and collaborative.

Acknowledgments

Over a year of intensive research went into the preparation of this book. This consumed an enormous amount of time and expense. The authors are grateful to Craig Zamzow of Digital Equipment Corporation, whose financial and moral support helped initiate this research; any organization would benefit from people like Craig who seek new ideas and bring them to bear on corporate practice. We also thank Holt, Rinehart and Winston of Canada for its contributions to the research, and especially Jocelyn Klemm for her guidance throughout the preparation of the book.

We are indebted to Don Tapscott of DMR and Associates Ltd. for encouraging us to document the concept of value-added in the form of this book, and to Dick Rossi, who contributed a great deal to the decision analysis techniques used throughout the book.

In addition to all of those mentioned in cases throughout the book, we are grateful to a number of people who helped identify and report value-added cases: Tom Almus, Rodney Armitage, Pete Daks, Larry Day, Robert A. Frankel, Steve Gelb, Eugene A. Gilchrist, Elliot Gold, Charlie Reed, Ward D. Ring, and Shirley Singletary. We also thank the numerous people who took time to explore with us cases that do not appear in the book.

Introduction

To some, office automation (OA) is a way to gain extraordinary returns on investments and improved competitive edge. To others, it seems to be an unjustifiable increase in corporate overhead. The key difference is in the uses to which the tools are put. Companies experiencing low returns have either focused on low-payoff applications or sold technology for technology's sake. Those who have turned OA to their competitive advantage have taken a strategic, business-driven approach.

To us, OA covers the broadest range of technologies and tools that are relevant in the office. We do not limit its scope arbitrarily (for example, to common tools such as word processing and electronic mail). Rather, we consider OA to include the whole range of "tools for thinking." Our intent is to encourage collaboration among the various staff groups that support OA, so that office systems can be built that are comprehensive and well-integrated toolkits.

This book focuses on applying these tools in ways that help an organization make money or achieve its mission. It is designed to help organizations find the rewarding path toward strategic, value-added applications of OA. Its purpose is to assist people in the twin challenges of finding and measuring value-added applications of office automation—to unleash the creativity of both implementors and users.

By broadening awareness of the many OA tools that are available, and by describing the wide range of possible benefits, this book will help readers to identify high-payoff applications. By describing a range of evaluation methodologies, this book will help readers develop meaningful measures of gains in business effectiveness.

Part 1 is fundamental to understanding the research and its results. Chapter 1 defines terms and concepts used throughout the book, and introduces a framework that defines the scope of OA and provides a perspective on the many OA tools. Chapter 1 defines two distinct types of benefits—cost-displacement and value-added—that can result from applications of office information tools. Chapter 2 surveys the literature on value-added applications and the strategic value of information. It traces the history of concepts of measuring information tools and provides a historic context for the research that went into the making of this book.

We have found that there is no single "correct" way to measure value-added benefits. The cases in Part 2 demonstrate that it is possible and profitable to do so, and that meaningful performance metrics can be defined for information systems based on business objectives. Chapters 3 through 9 analyze the impact of office automation in over 60 case studies. Each case demonstrates the potential contribution of OA tools to seven categories of business objectives.

The seven chapters in Part 2 address the major critical business success factors faced by most of today's organizations: generating revenue through sales and marketing; producing products through efficient operations, people management, and financial control; getting new products to market; and winning negotiations. This is not intended as a comprehensive taxonomy of business issues, since this book is about office automation and is not a primer on management. The business-oriented framework for this book is chosen to illustrate the wide range of applications of OA tools.

Part 3 looks in greater depth at two leading-edge applications of OA. Chapter 10 describes the use of OA tools by executives, who are by far the most difficult users to measure; before we attempt to do so, we need to know a great deal more about the relationship of tools to the executives' work. Chapter 10 begins that exploratory process by describing their use of the tools.

Chapter 11 describes a new frontier in the application of OA tools— augmenting meeting effectiveness. It outlines the concept of an augmented meeting, some of the experiences of the pioneers, and the benefits in meeting dynamics. Chapter 11 closes with practical suggestions for implementing augmented meeting support in today's organizations.

Part 4 is written for OA implementors, those staff managers and professionals who implement OA for others within their organization. Chapters 12 through 14 close the book with pragmatic methodologies for pursuing value-added applications. Chapter 12 describes a methodology for identifying very high-payoff applications, a process that is quite different from traditional systems analysis. In chapter 13, we describe our research methodology for defining meaningful measures of the kinds of benefits that used to be considered "intangible." Chapter 14 discusses the changes involved in adopting the value-added perspective.

The appendixes are also intended for OA implementors. Appendix A offers guidelines for conducting a value-added user interview as a replacement for traditional industrial engineering and systems analysis approaches to needs assessment and measurement. Appendix B discusses techniques for understanding subjective judgments.

Together, chapters 12 through 14 give implementors the methodologies they need to direct their OA efforts toward improving their organizations' bottom line. The approaches are not mechanistic—they are not cookbooks that can be followed without thought. Furthermore, there is no guarantee of success. The likelihood of value-added benefits depends on the centrality of the user and the business understanding of the implementor.

The index is an important part of this book, and is intended for all audiences. The structure of the book allows readers with a particular type of business problem to select the most appropriate chapter in which to look for ideas. The index provides other views of these case studies. For example, an executive may wish to look at cases in a particular industry. A vendor may wish to look at the applications of a particular tool. Internal OA staff may wish to find examples of a particular measurement technique. The index is designed to provide the reader with customized perspectives on the body of evidence.

We have written the book in business rather than technical terms in hopes that it will encourage participation from executives, managers, and users of computers at all levels of the organization. Without the active involvement of executives and line managers, there is little likelihood of finding strategic opportunities for office automation. With a common view of the bottom line, OA staff and line managers can work together on the challenge of improving office performance.

THE CONCEPT OF
VALUE-ADDED BENEFITS

Part 1 specifies the common terms used throughout the book. Chapter 1 defines terms such as "office automation" and "management information systems," and differentiates between two types of benefits: cost-displacement and value-added. This distinction is fundamental to the premise of the book. Chapter 2 describes a genealogy of concepts as they were developed and applied to office automation. This context sets the stage for the research reported in the remainder of the book.

Office Automation, Productivity, and Success

Can office automation really improve managerial and professional productivity?[1] Can computers become part of a business strategy? Can new technology have a significant impact on a corporation's bottom line? The answer to these questions is an unqualified "yes!" But perhaps you have heard these claims before — assertions about the "strategic value of information" and pleas to accept "intangible" benefits as justification for the investment of tangible dollars. Executives have reason to be skeptical of such claims, and are justifiably concerned about the payoff from investments in personal computers and office information networks.

Our research has grounded such claims in fact. We have developed methodologies for measuring the impacts of OA on profits, and have examined actual uses of the tools with new rigor. In this book you will find cases in which

- a spreadsheet made $75 million for a chemical company;
- electronic mail got a telecommunications product to market two months early, with a return on investment of 1,000 per cent;
- a $600 search of public information data banks made a material difference in an $18 million law suit;
- an internal database brought in $60 million of additional revenue for a real estate firm.

In this book we describe over 60 cases in which OA measurably enhanced profits. We have found that returns on investments (ROI) in OA frequently exceed 200 per cent, and payback periods are often less than one year. When well implemented, OA easily passes corporate capital-investment hurdles. In fact, information tools in the office may offer the most lucrative capital-investment opportunities available to today's organizations.

The challenge goes even further. As organizations evolve toward high-productivity systems, OA will make computers a critical part of business strategy. These tools are providing an "information edge" — a competitive advantage gained through improving the "intelligence" of an organization. Today, leading organizations are winning competitive battles through their use of OA. Tomorrow, organizations will either invest in the effectiveness of their knowledge workers or lose their place in internationally competitive markets.

The direct impacts of OA tools on success are only beginning to be explored, and many applications with above-average returns on investments remain untapped. These opportunities are the subject of this book.

This presents two challenges for business managers. First, we must train ourselves to find (and see) value-added opportunities for technology in a wide variety of business settings. Second, we must develop skills for measuring the profit impacts of OA, both to justify investments and to evaluate results. By presenting case experiences along with concepts and methodologies, we hope that this book will be helpful in enabling you to meet both challenges.

Framework of Office Automation Tools

As a foundation for the book, we must begin by defining a few terms. First, the term "office automation" is used throughout this book and throughout the world, yet its definition is often unclear. If it is defined too narrowly, opportunities will be missed and the various office systems will lack needed integration. If it is defined too broadly, its unique focus will be lost amid the many large projects relating to existing systems.

We differentiate three major application domains of computing and communications: data processing and management information systems, process control, and office automation.

Data processing (DP) handles routine operational business transactions. This "information factory" results in databases that document the historic performance of the organization; these are generally termed "management information systems" (MIS). Process control applications, such as automated factories and warehouses, imbed the computer in a larger machine. We define OA as "computer- and communications-based tools for thinking."

OA is distinguished from MIS in three important ways. First, OA provides tools to individuals and groups of users, who then operate the tools themselves. MIS operates a centralized resource on behalf of the entire organization. Second, OA applies to unstructured knowledge work, while MIS processes routine, well-structured transactions. Third, OA tools work with data that belong to the users, while MIS processes organizational data.

These three distinctions define both the scope of OA and the boundaries of our research. If an information service is interactive, operated by and at the discretion of a user, it is considered part of the domain of OA. Note that component technologies such as networks and time-sharing computers may be provided by service bureaus in an MIS staff department. Nonetheless, we consider any interactive thinking tool to come within the scope of this book.

The overlap between MIS and OA is in interactive access to corporate data. These systems are usually managed by the same staff groups who operate the MIS systems. The ability to access data interactively from individuals' work stations classifies data query as an OA tool, however. Furthermore, selected data must then be merged with other desktop tools to "massage" them, think about their implications, communicate conclusions to others, and act on them. Thus, access to MIS data is considered one of the many tools of OA.

OA and artificial intelligence (AI) also overlap. AI is a powerful technology that can be applied to build or enhance interactive office information tools. To date, AI has appeared in the office primarily in the form of expert (decision support) systems. AI may also be applied to a variety of other areas of data processing and process control, such as factory automation. These applications, while related, are outside the domain of this book.

Throughout this book, the term "tool" is used in a special way. A tool is a set of information capabilities (commands) that together are applied by users to a business function. Tools are made up of technologies, each of which is useless alone. For example, an electronic mail system is a tool that is made up of technologies such as computers, digital networks, telephones, and terminals. In most cases, the user is primarily concerned with the capabilities of tools, not with the technologies that comprise them. The framework of OA tools shown in Figure 1.1 will be used throughout this book.

The various OA tools have been developed by different types of technical professionals, including data-processing, administration, telecommunications, management science, and library science experts. By integrating them into a single tool kit, OA offers systems that are of interest to managers and professionals as well as to administrative staff.

Including the entire range of tools within our purview is essential to a business-oriented approach. For one, there are no simple ways to

Figure 1.1.   Framework of OA Tools
(copyright © 1984 N. Dean Meyer and Associates Inc.)

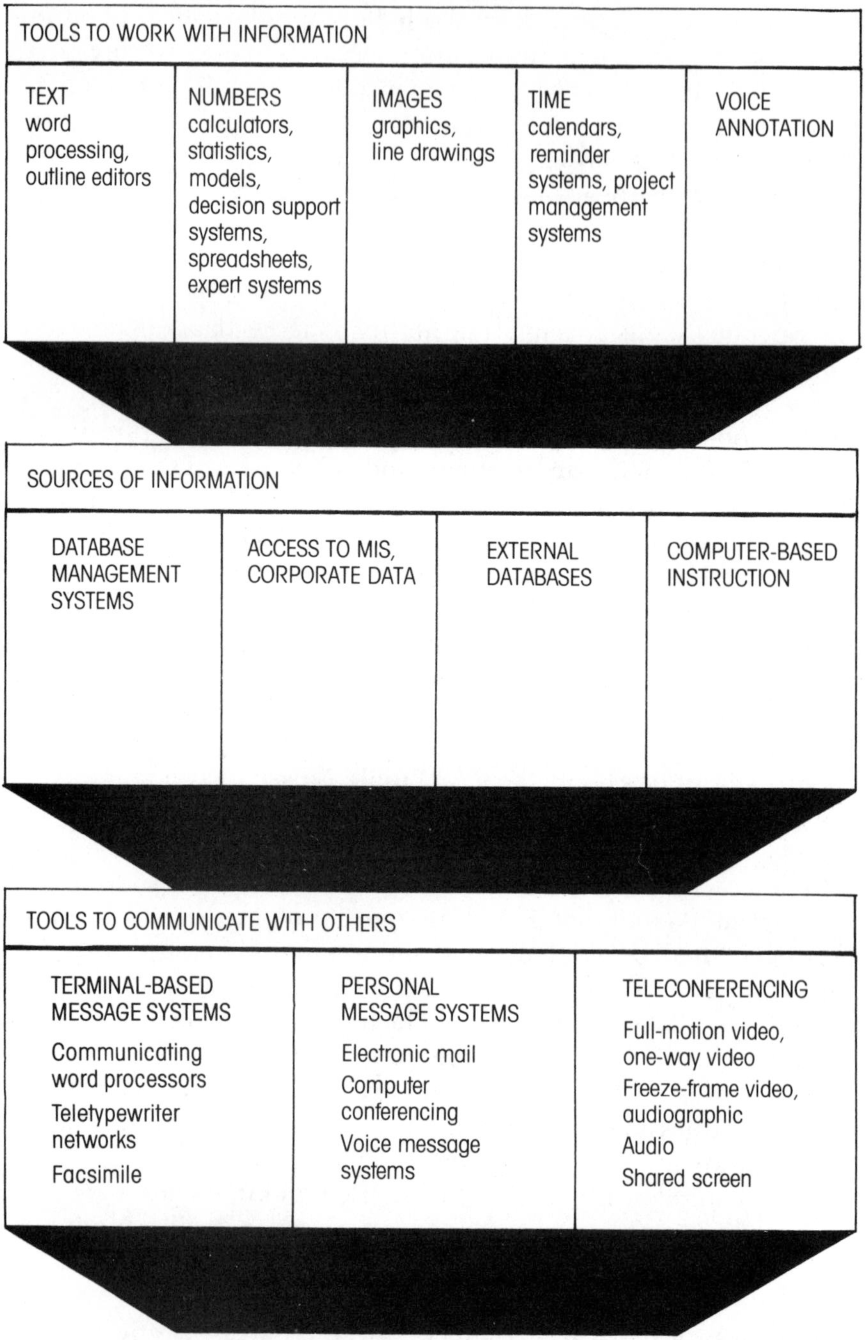

TOOLS TO WORK WITH INFORMATION

TEXT word processing, outline editors	NUMBERS calculators, statistics, models, decision support systems, spreadsheets, expert systems	IMAGES graphics, line drawings	TIME calendars, reminder systems, project management systems	VOICE ANNOTATION

SOURCES OF INFORMATION

DATABASE MANAGEMENT SYSTEMS	ACCESS TO MIS, CORPORATE DATA	EXTERNAL DATABASES	COMPUTER-BASED INSTRUCTION

TOOLS TO COMMUNICATE WITH OTHERS

TERMINAL-BASED MESSAGE SYSTEMS	PERSONAL MESSAGE SYSTEMS	TELECONFERENCING
Communicating word processors	Electronic mail	Full-motion video, one-way video
Teletypewriter networks	Computer conferencing	Freeze-frame video, audiographic
Facsimile	Voice message systems	Audio
		Shared screen

anticipate the users' needs. Thus, the implementor must be prepared with a broad "kitbag" of tools rather than a single system in search of a user. When the toolkit is limited, the implementor becomes a technology salesperson rather than a business problem-solver.

Furthermore, all of these tools should eventually be integrated so as to be able to work together. Consider the content of managerial work. Organizations develop products and services, market and sell them, deliver and bill for them, and account for the results. To develop a plan, one might extract from a database, develop and run a model, graph results and merge them with a written document, distribute the document to colleagues for comments, update and restructure the document, publish it, distribute it, and file it in the organization's library.

Thus, the business process must integrate many different information tasks. Because the tasks are interdependent, efficiency in any one of them may not help the organization achieve its overall mission.

By imagining the integration of all of the OA tools, one can envision the office of the future. Consider using a work station at home or in the office to check your in-basket for messages that arrived by telephone or via the computer-based electronic mail system. In the process, you might be reminded of events and appointments. You might brainstorm, structure your thoughts into documents or action plans, communicate with people either interactively or by message, prepare for decisions by gathering information from a variety of sources internally and externally, and consider the consequences of courses of action before choosing a direction. This image of an integrated tool kit can help us creatively seek the many opportunities available from the application of today's tools.

Two Types of Benefits

Measuring the payoff of OA is is very important both before and after each implementation project. Before implementation, an understanding of the benefits is necessary to identify and focus on high-payoff applications and to justify investments in new technology. Particularly in the beginning stages of OA, top management typically requires a clear statement of returns on investments. After a project is completed, understanding the payoff is necessary to evaluating the results. Thus, skill in measuring payoff is critical to all aspects of implementing OA. Here too we must define our terms.

OA can improve the efficiency or the effectiveness of office work. Derived from these two different dimensions are two very different

Figure 1.2. Two Types of Benefits

* "Cost-displacement" refers to improved efficiency or productivity. Cost-displacement applications save either money or time by delegating tasks to the tool.	VS.	* "Value-added" applications focus on effectiveness rather than on efficiency. In these cases, OA allows people to do a better job, or to do things they could not do before.

types of benefits resulting from OA: cost-displacement and value-added, as defined in Figure 1.2.

Applications are considered to be cost-displacement when the computer helps the user perform tasks more efficiently. The effects are direct: the user is made more productive. Value-added applications make the user more effective, although they do not necessarily save time. The effectiveness has leverage on a greater portion of the organization — it in turn produces profits, making many others more productive by directly contributing to the organization's profits or mission. Its focus is on business results rather than on the costs of office work, and the value of the benefits often far exceeds potential time savings.

Each of these two types of benefits is appropriate in different situations. Let's explore the applicability of these two concepts to measuring office work. First, we will analyze the more conventional concept of cost-displacement.

Productivity and Cost-Displacement

Cost-displacement applications save money or time by making people more productive. Most people equate productivity with efficiency. Productivity is measured in terms of outputs divided by inputs. For example, a word processor can help a secretary type more pages in less time.

In some cases, it is possible to actually identify the money that is saved ("hard dollar" savings). Efficiency gains may reduce the costs, for example, of temporary secretaries or outside services. Hard-dollar savings do not always imply cutbacks, however. "Cost-avoidance" benefits occur when the efficiency gains allow you to do more with the same resources. For example, a word processor may allow a business to grow without hiring more secretaries.

There are cases in which the money associated with efficiency gains is not easily measured. For example, when we save a manager's time, we rarely think about reducing the number of managers or not hiring future managers. Instead, we assume that the manager puts the extra time to good use. When we can measure time savings but not money savings, the benefits are termed "soft-dollar." So long as we assume that the time is put to good use, the savings can be evaluated based on the cost of the time. If, for example, we help a manager save one day a month, then the benefits of that application will be the cost of the manager's salary for one day each month.

Cost-displacement applications are particularly important when financial conditions are bad and a firm is forced to cut back its scope of activities, or when the firm is in a mature, no-growth market and its primary competitive advantage is its operating margins.

The cost-displacement approach is the traditional means of evaluating the benefits of technology. Cost savings are a direct (if not leveraged) contribution to profits because they reduce expenses. There is no leverage; an hour saved is worth only what the organization paid for it.

The Problem with Measuring Management Productivity

To measure productivity — that is, outputs divided by inputs — we must be able to measure the users' outputs and inputs. We can measure the outputs if the users' jobs are such that they produce a well-defined product. We can measure the inputs if their work is well structured — that is, if we know what goes into producing their outputs.

Can we measure managerial productivity? Unfortunately, the work of managers is rarely simple. Managers and professionals, for the most part, perform relatively unstructured work, and the well-structured work that they do perform (such as administrative tasks) may be the least relevant to their business success.

Consider an important decision made by a manager or an executive. It is very unlikely that we can measure the outputs of that decision — the amount of money made by the company because of the decision. Often we don't know the inputs — the information, judgment, and experience that went into making that decision. One thing about managerial work is clear: we do not pay these high-priced people to have meetings, write memos, and talk on the phone; we pay them to do business. Managers contribute judgment as well as effort;

they may well earn their salary in five minutes out of the week by attaining a single insight or making a difficult decision.

Even if we could measure managerial outputs and inputs, productivity gains tend to be relatively small—typically, 30 to 100 per cent. Thus, to have a significant impact on the business, tasks must be repetitive. It is of little value to make someone twice as efficient at a task that he performs only once a year. Most executives, managers, and professionals do not produce measurable outputs, their inputs are unclear, and their jobs are not routine. Therefore, productivity measures do not apply.

Indeed, equating productivity and efficiency at office tasks with success is dangerous. It may lead to projects that make an insignificant task very efficient, while disrupting other steps in the total process and perhaps damaging the creative environment. For example, many early word-processing centers forced managers to stand in line at copiers because their personal secretaries had been moved into the centers and away from their bosses.

From the organizational perspective, flexibility and effectiveness grow increasingly important as our organizational, economic, political and social environments become more volatile and complex. Optimizing individual managerial tasks may lock them in with detailed procedures and investments just when organizational flexibility is most needed. Thus, a focus on managerial efficiency alone is likely to create only minor productivity gains. Meanwhile, implementors may miss the real payoff of office automation, or, even worse, actually damage an organization's effectiveness for the sake of minor cost savings. Imagine a sailor who contemplates ways to conserve rope while the ship is sinking!

Where do we find jobs that are measurable and routine? Cost-displacement benefits are generally found only in applications that help clerks and secretaries with administrative support. Historically, data processing has primarily focused on clerical tasks such as accounting, payroll, order entry, and inventory tracking. Word processing has focused primarily on secretarial efficiency. Thus, cost-displacement, or productivity, has been the traditional measure of computer applications.

The Value-Added Benefits

As we enter the era of end-user computing, we face a new justification challenge. Managers and professionals cannot be measured in terms of productivity, but this does not mean that they cannot be measured.

It means that we need different terms and new approaches to measurement.

The term "value-added" refers to those applications that focus on organizational effectiveness. Value-added applications do not save money or time, but are aimed at achieving the users' business mission. The payoff is leveraged in the same way that management time produces more in profits than it costs.

Specifically, OA tools build effectiveness by granting three types of freedom. First, they free *time*, by relieving managers of administrative tasks and by permitting them to leave and then easily pick up work at any time, in or out of the office. Second, they free *thinking*, by allowing managers to quickly capture and work with information and ideas, and to consider many alternatives. Third, they free *collaboration*, by expanding communications circles and permitting worldwide project teams to work together on a daily basis. Value-added measurements recognize these impacts on business effectiveness.

In the early stages of new technologies — such as office automation in most organizations — it is possible to identify applications with dramatic impacts.

Returns on investment of 1,000 to 100,000 per cent are described in this book. Examples of the significant payoff resulting from a focus on value-added include getting a new product to market sooner, reducing business risk in major decisions, building greater international collaboration and cooperation, developing proactive strategic plans that account for many contingencies, improving the ability of the organization to respond quickly to competitive moves, and delivering entirely new services via the technology.

Not only is the potential payoff greater, but the need for management effectiveness is increasingly pressing. We must now live with worldwide competition, with complex interdependent economies, with a fast rate of technological change, and with larger and more complex organizations. Executives are more concerned with their organization's survival and (we hope) its growth than with administrative efficiency, and they are more dependent than ever on the effectiveness of managers and professionals.

Value-added applications address issues that managers are worried about — what they are there to do rather than the administrative processes that support them. It is unlikely that line managers are critically concerned about administrative cost savings, a relatively small part of their budget. Saving expenses may be required by one's boss or the corporate controller, but it is rarely central to a user's mission. In fact, executives generally don't have time to save time!

In practice, while cost-saving applications are relatively easy to identify and measure, they may be more difficult to implement for lack of management interest and support. Computers are relevant to top management when they are applied to the organizations's primary business mission. In most organizations, a value-added focus is more practical in that it maintains top management interest and rallies their support by delivering significant long- and short-term payoffs on central business issues.

OA is opening new horizons for computers, creating an opportunity to make them an important part of corporate strategy. We can do so by focusing our implementation efforts on the critical business success factors, not just on productivity gains that are easy to measure.

Measuring Value-Added Benefits

Like cost-displacement, value-added applications can sometimes be measured in hard dollars, that is, in clear monetary terms. There are cases in which sales volume has been increased because of OA. There are cases in which OA can improve margins, for example, by optimizing product mix or making better inventory decisions. There are cases in which OA can get new products to market sooner, and in which the benefits are extra months of profitable operations as well as a competitive edge. There are even cases in which, because of OA, entirely new products or market opportunities were identified. When OA brings in additional revenues, the benefits are measurable.

There are other cases in which value-added benefits must be measured in soft dollars. OA may improve your competitive edge and help gain market share by making you more responsive to customers and the marketplace. OA may reduce business risks through better-informed decisions and more effective analysis. It may make an organization more adaptable in times of change by assisting in bringing two groups together during a merger or acquisition, or by helping project teams collaborate. OA may build a more highly motivated, creative, and collaborative working environment by improving the quality of work life. In these cases, measuring the benefits requires a greater degree of estimation and judgment.

Value-added is generally more difficult to measure than productivity. Traditional approaches such as industrial engineering (productivity studies) and systems analysis (paper-flow studies) invariably fail. By analyzing the tasks people do (such as answering the phone and writing memoranda), these methodologies measure productivity but miss value-added opportunities.

Another common measurement technique, organization-wide surveys, also fails to find value-added opportunities. Standard metrics that apply to an entire organization can capture only efficiency gains in standard tasks that everyone does, such as administering an office. These are rarely critical to the success of the organization.

Effectiveness can be defined only in the context of the *purpose* of the tasks — that is, the users' business mission. Just as for most of us there is no one right way to know what our efforts yesterday were worth to our company, there is no one right way to measure value-added gains. To help people with their business missions, our methodologies must be derived from their unique roles and responsibilities. In other words, value-added metrics must be context-specific and must involve a detailed understanding of the user's business. A great deal of creativity on the part of both implementors and users is required to identify value-added opportunities. The case examples in this book may help to unleash people's imaginations with respect to uses for OA tools.

Perhaps there are applications whose payoff has been low. Certainly, not every user is in a position to contribute to the bottom line in dramatic ways. But after all, it takes only one million-dollar success to pay for hundreds of office work stations. This book is intended to help people find that one success.

Notes

1. Portions of this chapter were previously published in N.D. Meyer, "The Relationship of Office Automation to Productivity," *National Productivity Review* 2, no. 1 (Winter 1983). Used by permission.

The Emerging Understanding of Value-Added

Although high-payoff OA applications are not rare, understanding of the value-added perspective is just emerging.[1] For the most part, the measurement of the benefits of OA has been based on task efficiency rather than on the value-added approach to measuring organizational effectiveness. Understanding the difference between efficiency and effectiveness is critical to the pursuit of value-added measurements of OA.

Chester Barnard first made the distinction in 1938 in his seminal work, *The Functions of the Executive*.[2] Efficiency (productivity) and effectiveness (mission or profits) evolved into two different bodies of science as applied to management, and they represent entirely different approaches to applying and measuring the benefits of technology.

In this chapter, we trace both approaches from their origins in early twentieth-century management philosophy to current practices. We begin by examining the historic development of interest in efficiency and productivity from "scientific management" to recent attempts to measure managerial productivity. Taking stock of what we have discovered, we note where it falls short of useful approaches to measuring management applications of technology. We then consider the concept of effectiveness and various scientific approaches to understanding the role of management. In this vein, we trace the emerging understanding of the strategic importance of information and information tools. This leads us to consider applications of MIS with strategic value as precursors to OA applications, and early experiments with OA to enhance managerial thinking.

Given this perspective on the state of practice in applying information technologies to organizational effectiveness, we describe the evolution of measurement techniques. Many attempts at measurement have failed, either for lack of rigor or because their theoretical bases were unsound. Some held promise, and can be considered the forerunners of the methodology developed in this book.

By considering this historic perspective, we can learn from the mistakes and successes of the past. This context helps us to understand justification and evaluation issues, and what needs to be done to develop measures of the benefits of OA.

Improving Business Efficiency

The idea of applying the scientific method to management is not new. A milestone in the literature was the work of Frederick Taylor, embodied in the term "scientific management." Taylor studied the movements of blue-collar workers and attempted to program their activities so as to improve their efficiency. He showed that work planning can have dramatic impacts on the productivity of manual labor.

After the development of scientific management came the profession of industrial engineering, which spawned the wealth of efficiency and time-and-motion studies so popular at the turn of the century. The notion of an empirical, task-level approach to improving productivity was alive and healthy in the factory, and established a tradition for applying computers and measuring the results.

Data Processing and Productivity

The use of computers began to spread through industry in the 1950s and 1960s. The early computers were difficult to program and were limited in speed and memory. They were most applicable to tasks that required little analysis and a great deal of sorting, calculating, and filing. Except for research laboratories and government experiments, early computer applications improved the efficiency of clerical activities such as accounting, payroll, order processing, inventory maintenance, and customer recordkeeping.

The payoff from early data-processing applications was gained by delegating—that is, by automating tasks formerly performed by clerks who required salaries, benefits, management, and job security. Computers were significantly faster, more accurate, and less expensive in spite of their limited capabilities, high purchase price, and high cost of maintenance. Given the nature of these early applications, a precedent was set for measuring computers in terms of the costs they reduce—especially personnel costs.

The focus of these early applications was on clerical productivity. Concerns that computers might replace people were well-founded, since this was what they were primarily intended to do. Union and worker fear and resistance were entirely natural. There is no evidence, however, that technology reduces total employment levels in the economy. But even though many other jobs were created to support the technologies, this was little consolation to the clerks who found themselves unemployed. Whatever the net effect may have been, it is clear that technology has caused massive structural changes in the work force.

The value-added perspective documented in this book demonstrates that OA is *not* designed to replace people or to make them work faster, but rather to help them become more effective; we hope it counters fears by encouraging the use of computers as tools for people rather than the other way around.

Unfortunately, following the precedent for "reducing headcount" set by early computer applications, management began to view information technology almost exclusively as a way of reducing salary costs and as a tool for administrative staff rather than managers. This perspective was carried directly into the field of OA.

Efficiency in the Office

Although there were numerous experiments with the use of computers in the office (some of which are described below), the first OA tool to have significant impacts on industry was word processing (WP). In 1964, IBM introduced the Magnetic-Tape Selectric Typewriter, and in the following year a Magnetic-Card Selectric Typewriter.

Originally, WP was intended for volume typing applications where large typing pools existed—for example, in insurance companies. IBM was surprised to see the enthusiastic reception of the MCSTs by their customers, who used the machines in a variety of applications, including general secretarial typing. Users often reorganized their administrative staff into typing pools to ensure the most efficient use of the equipment.

Like early DP applications, these WP applications focused on productivity in routine tasks. In innumerable studies, users demonstrated the significant impact of WP on secretarial efficiency. One of the most thorough of these studies was conducted by the British civil service. In 1977 and 1978, the Central Computing and Telecommunications Agency conducted detailed studies of clerical productivity gains by replacing electric typewriters with word processors.[3] The agency found little advantage in using word processing for the initial entry of text or for editing documents of a page or less. Word processors were 12 per cent more productive for amendments to medium-sized documents (one to five pages), and 23 per cent more productive when used for editing documents longer than five pages. Where standard ("boilerplate") text was used, the word processor increased productivity by 32 per cent.

When complete jobs were examined, these task-efficiency gains accumulated dramatic results. The more proficient operators were about 50 per cent more productive across their mix of jobs. On reports of four pages or more, light revisions (no more than 23 per cent of the lines on each page) were an average of 102 per cent more productive. Where a medium level of revision was required (no more than 34 per cent of the lines on a page), average productivity gains were 36 per cent. Retyping was more productive when over half the lines on each page had to be changed. Clearly, significant productivity could be gained on longer typing tasks.

Managerial Efficiency

Following the pattern of secretarial studies, early studies attempted to measure managers and analysts in terms of time-and-task efficiency. Studies of managerial behavior patterns at the task level developed the groundwork for those attempting to determine the effects of OA on higher-level white-collar workers.

Henry Mintzberg is well known for his study of the patterns of executive use of time. Through a methodology labeled "structured observation," Mintzberg examined the activity patterns of senior managers.[4] By categorizing managerial activities and noting the amount or percentage of time spent in each category, Mintzberg's study provided an early exploration of the tasks managers actually perform in the office.

Mintzberg opened executive offices to scrutiny; while not originally intended as such, his work was a milestone in the development of productivity-oriented office studies. Following in the tradition of a focus on task efficiency, many OA needs-assessment methodologies and impact studies attempted to show that OA can help a manager reduce the time it takes to perform tasks such as writing memoranda, filing notes, talking on the telephone, or holding meetings. Carrying the tradition of systems analysis from DP into the office, many consultants, vendors, and practitioners spawned a plethora of needs-assessment methodologies that measure paper flows, communications patterns, and office transactions.

One of the best known of these managerial time-by-task studies was conducted by the consulting firm of Booz, Allen and Hamilton.[5] The primary shortcoming of the managerial productivity studies is their failure to tell us anything about the *effectiveness* of the managers who were studied. The astute observer will see the absence of any linkage between task efficiency and job effectiveness. For example, one of the categories in the Booz, Allen study was "totally unproductive time." Activities that fell into this category were defined as follows: "Mainly the time spent traveling outside or within a building or waiting for meetings to start or a machine to become available. On average, each hour spent at an external site requires an additional 40 minutes of idle travel time."

Whether or not Mintzberg would have approved of such follow-on studies is questionable. Mintzberg did not make value judgments about the categories he examined; he did not label categories as "productive" or "unproductive." Who is to say that the time spent talking to a colleague at the copying machine is "unproductive?" A manager might come up with an idea during "unproductive" time that eventually makes or saves millions of dollars for a company.

Task-level productivity studies such as Booz, Allen and Hamilton's were not only unconvincing; in many ways they were also misleading. They promised that OA would reduce the size of the management work force, creating user fear of job loss and executive disillusionment when the promises were not met. In fact, saving a few minutes of a manager's time may simply allow him to get to the golf course a bit earlier. (Many executives questioned this very point.) On the other hand, a manager may earn his salary in five minutes out of the week with a single critical insight or decision. To say that Booz, Allen and Hamilton missed the mark with their study is an understatement. Basic to their approach was the assumption that managers are paid to push papers, talk on the telephone, and hold meetings.

At best, this focus on the efficiency of managerial administrative tasks released some time for other mission-oriented work. (The studies, of course, never captured the value of this other work, but rather claimed the cost of the time saved as the benefit.) At worst, these studies directed implementors away from focusing on the users' business missions and kept them concerned with peripheral administrative support functions, thus encouraging executives to view OA as related solely to secretaries and non-strategic issues such as routine administration. When management systems are implemented based on such studies, they risk optimizing administrative tasks while perhaps damaging organizational effectiveness, just as word processing forced administrative tasks on managers in order to create efficient typing pools.

The critical component missing from this task-efficiency approach is an understanding of the business goals of the user. Therefore, the focus on efficiency and productivity—task-level time-and-motion studies of managers—met with a dead end. What is the alternative? To identify meaningful impacts on the users' missions and strategies, we must look more closely at how the tools are used to achieve business goals. To provide a perspective, the next section examines the evolution of the recognition of information as a strategic resource.

Applying Science to Business Effectiveness

OA implementors are not alone in facing the dichotomy between efficiency and effectiveness. As industrial engineering began to flourish, there were those who became concerned that its methodologies for optimizing well-structured work did not help managers with their thinking, collaborating, and decision making.

Operations Research and Management Science

According to Herbert Simon, the Nobel Prize-winning decision scientist, operations research and management science (OR/MS) did not emerge directly from scientific management or industrial engineering, although the fields were all integrally related. In *The New Science of Management Decision*[6] Simon describes how operations research began as a sociological movement emerging out of the military requirements of the Second World War. At that time, mathematicians and statisticians became involved with the decision-making problems of management, and, in particular, with decision making by military leaders.

Simon made the distinction between programmed and non-programmed decisions. Programmed decisions are those that are routine and highly repetitive and have specific procedures associated with them; they are amenable to productivity measures. Non-programmed decisions involve a higher level of subjectivity that is more typical of top management; they are the areas in which highly structured approaches to measurement fail. Operations researchers shared ideas with mathematical economists, according to Simon, and the "new" scientific management was born. This new generation of theorists and practitioners viewed the organization as an interrelated system.

The systems approach brought a more holistic perspective to those studying the needs of management. Systems theorists attempted to assess the effects of changes to individual components on the entire system. Thus, individual decisions began to be viewed from the perspective of how they might affect the entire organization. The fundamental text on operations research was written by West Churchman and his colleagues in 1957.[7]

Cybernetics

The science of cybernetics — the study of the control mechanisms in systems — expanded the OR/MS view of the organization as a network of decisions to consider the information channels that serve as feedback loops. A basic principle of cybernetics, as expressed by Ross Ashby, is that a management system can effectively control only as much "variety" (that is, complexity) as the management system itself has.[8] To avoid hiring a manager for every worker, an organizational system places filters (such as summary reports) on the information that flows up from the organization to management, and amplifiers (such as policy statements) on the information that flows down from management to the organization.

A major contributor to the application of cybernetics to management was Stafford Beer. Beer explained how measures of efficiency are unhelpful in determining the structural problems inherent in many organizations and institutions. He implied the need for a value-added perspective (although he did not use that term) when he said, "If a man who wished to go somewhere miles distant suddenly realized he were working a treadmill, would he redouble his efforts? Would he use his command of technology to drive the treadmill at even faster speeds until the bearings failed? He would not. He would step off the treadmill and start walking, however long the journey."[9] Rather than oversimplifying the world, Beer suggested that we should increase the "variety" (or complexity) of the management system to match the variety of the world. Computers, he said, should be used as a tool to increase our understanding of an entire system rather than to optimize those subsystems we have deemed important because they are easy to measure. Beer proposed that institutions begin a course of structural change to establish a healthy basis for organizational evolution.

Operations research represents a bridge between the empirical, reductionist application of scientific methods to task productivity and the more recent attempts to improve the less structured, ill-defined aspects of management decision making. (See Figure 2.1.) Work on decision making in operations research provided a backdrop for the management science movement that followed. In the

Figure 2.1.   Two Views of Scientific Management

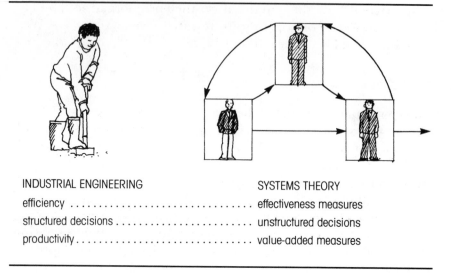

INDUSTRIAL ENGINEERING	SYSTEMS THEORY
efficiency	effectiveness measures
structured decisions	unstructured decisions
productivity.	value-added measures

1960s and 1970s, management scientists applied systems theory and quantitative decision-making techniques to an increasingly wide domain of managerial problems. In professional journals such as *Interfaces,* they documented a series of case studies that traced the effects of their mathematical techniques and computer-based tools to profits.

Measuring the Value of Information

Given the subjective nature of non-programmed decisions, the measurement of their effectiveness becomes difficult but not impossible, according to Simon. "It is dangerous to assume that something is essentially qualitative and not reducible to mathematical form until an applied mathematician has had a try at it ... Many things that seem intangible and inherently qualitative can be reduced, for management decision-making purposes, to dollars and cents ... Operations Research techniques are now applied in a vast number of practical management situations. In many of these situations, when mathematical techniques were first proposed there was much head-shaking and muttering about judgement."[10] In essence, Simon proposed that we use mathematics to clarify decisions as much as possible, recognizing that improving management decision making requires better, not perfect, information.

Beer agreed. He suggested that we stop trying to explain the world simply in terms of those variables we can understand and measure easily. He presented operations research and cybernetics as accessible and practical: "OR is empirical science: it is about observation, measurement and experiment. It is concerned with finding ways to make the worse somewhat better. It narrows the area of risk. It studies the vulnerability of alternative policies to a range of possible futures. It looks at the real world where the action is, where real people live under real constraints. Does this offend mathematical purists? My answer is: let us first get the sign right. Does this offend those charged with government? My answer is: let us manage the real world, and not a theoretical conception of what ought to count as reality."[11]

The Statistical Value of Information

The science of statistics provides a useful starting point for quantifying the value of information to decision making. The classical statistical approach assumes that we know the value and odds of each potential outcome, being concerned only with extracting objective evidence from research samples. In practice, as statistician Samuel Schmitt explained, "information may come only now and then and in small driblets; or the cost of acquiring information may not be so small that we can immediately ask for the maximum amount. Then we want to analyze our information as it comes in, and make our decisions when we have acquired the proper amount of information — no sooner, no later."[12]

Bayes contributed a statistical approach. Inferential statistics can be used to measure the value of information in terms of reducing the risk associated with decision making in conditions of uncertainty. When we lack any information about the potential outcomes of a decision, we must assume that each possible outcome has an equal chance of occurring. As we perform research and gather more data, Bayesian statistics can be used to bring those new data into the decision tree and to revise the expected values. The information has value to the extent that it causes us to change the decision we would have made without the information; that value is the difference between the value of the selected alternative and the one we otherwise would have chosen.

While mathematicians still debate the validity of subjective probabilities, the use of statistics to quantify management judgments is common practice among decision scientists. Statistical techniques provide a clear way to incorporate new information into our subjective assessment and measure its value in quantitative terms. Thus, statistics form the basis for the expected value calculations we make in presenting the cases in this book. The industry has generally been unsuccessful in applying statistical measurement to specific bits of information, however.[13]

The Value of Information Systems

The availability of information plays a key role in reducing risk and uncertainty in decision making. This perception evolved through the 1970s into a discipline called information resource management (IRM). IRM was developed on the premise that information should be treated as a resource of strategic value to organizations. One of the leading figures in the IRM field is Robert Holland, who explains, "Organizations must come to terms with the fact that data is a resource — as indispensable to success as raw materials, facilities, cash reserves, or employees. IRM is (1) the management philosophy, (2) the analytical methods, and (3) the implementation guidelines which enable an organization to integrate and share its information resource."[14]

This does not automatically mean that more information is better. A landmark essay on understanding the importance of information systems to management was written by Russell Ackoff of the University of Pennsylvania.[15] He pointed out five basic misconceptions about management's need for information:

- Managers lack relevant information.
- The manager needs the information that he wants.
- If a manager has the information he needs, his decision making will improve.
- More communication means better performance.
- A manager does not have to understand how an information system works, only how to use it.

In contrast, Ackoff suggests that:

- Managers suffer from an overabundance of irrelevant information.
- One cannot specify what information is required for decision making until an explanatory model of the decision process and the system involved has been constructed and tested.
- It is necessary to determine how well managers can use needed information. When, because of the complexity of the decision

process, they can't use it well, they should be provided either with decision rules or with performance feedback so that they can identify and learn from their mistakes.

- When organizational units use inappropriate measures of performance that put them in conflict with each other, as is often the case, communication between the units may hurt organizational performance, not help it.
- In failing to evaluate their MIS, managers delegate much of the control of the organization to the system's designers and operators, who seldom possess managerial competence.

John Rockart of MIT was another pioneer in the movement toward a realistic view of the value of information. Rockart developed the "critical success factors" methodology to help executives learn how to focus their attention on relevant information.[16] Rockart cites D. Ronald Daniel as the original source of the "success factors" approach,[17] which he then applies as a means of dealing with information overload and eliminating the "irrelevant information" problem elucidated by Ackoff. Rockart defines critical success factors as "the limited number of areas in which results, if they are satisfactory, will ensure successful competitive performance for the organization. Critical success factors are the few key areas where 'things must go right' for the business to flourish. If results in these areas are not adequate, the organization's efforts for the period will be less than desired."[18]

More recent articles by Rockart indicate further development of the association between information technology and business strategy. He cites companies that are benefiting from "judicial use of technology," and urges executives to get off the sidelines. "Recognizing that information is a strategic resource implies a clear need to link information systems to business strategy, and especially to ensure that business strategy is developed in the context of the new IT (information technology) environment. In short, senior executives are increasingly feeling the need to become informed, energized and engaged in information systems."[19] Rockart's notion of critical success factors is highly relevant to our method of measuring value-added benefits of information technology. The "critical success" areas of the organization are the most fruitful source of value-added applications.

F. Warren McFarlan also develops the linkage between systems and corporate strategy.[20] In searching for opportunities to increase competitive advantage through the use of information technology, McFarlan suggests that executives ask, "Can information systems technology build barriers to entry?" In describing the issues this question raises, he mentions value-added benefits. "The payoff from value-added features that increase both sales and market share is particularly noteworthy for industries in which there are great economies of scale and price is important to the customer. By moving first down the learning curve, a company can gain a cost advantage that enables it to put great pressure on its competitors."

Michael Porter elaborates on the three ways in which information technology is changing the rules of competition. "First, advances in information technology are changing the industry structure. Second, information technology is an increasingly important lever that companies can use to create competitive advantage. A company's search for competitive advantage through information technology often also spreads to affect industry structure as competitors imitate the leader's strategic innovations. Finally, the information revolution is spawning completely new businesses."[21]

Data Processing and Organizational Effectiveness

Several visionary companies understood the strategic value of information and information tools long before industry observers developed the theoretical foundations. These companies established a successful track record early by applying their data-processing systems to key business goals.

American Hospital Supply

One of the early and often-cited applications was accomplished by American Hospital Supply Corporation (AHSC). Their systems staff focused on the corporation's relationship to customers rather than on internal administration. They developed an order entry and distribution system that directly links the majority of customers in large hospitals to AHSC computers. This system is attractive to customers: it simplifies the ordering process by providing current data on availability and price; it presents customers with a single source of information rather than a sales representative from each AHSC division; and it saves time and money by automatically generating a purchase order.

This system has benefited AHSC in a number of strategic ways. AHSC is able to present a unified image to customers across their many divisions; for example, this consolidation lets AHSC create and manage price incentives across product lines. Furthermore, the system reduces transaction costs for both the supplier and the customer. Most important, it allows AHSC to gain market share by making it relatively more difficult for the customer to order from rival distributors. In addition, customers can use the AHSC computer to perform for themselves functions such as inventory control, resulting in a new source of revenues to AHSC. AHSC now uses the data it has accumulated to do sophisticated market research, identifying trends in ordering and enabling the company to anticipate customer needs.[22]

McKesson

Another familiar success story comes from McKesson, the largest drug distributor in the United States. McKesson provides its drug-store customers with terminals for ordering products, which makes it easier to ask for and receive those products. As an added incentive to customers, users of the system get McKesson's help collecting payments from Medicare and insurance companies. Furthermore, a shelf-space management program helps McKesson track inventories and improve its profitability. If a customer orders from a competitor, the inventory management program loses its validity and requires extra work by the customer; further, the shelf-space profitability model no longer reflects the actual configuration of the store, and can no longer be used. Thus, the system builds customer loyalty and locks out competitors. The system also makes order processing easier for McKesson. The computer is an aid in forecasting demand and in matching invoices to items actually received. The technology allows the company to make three strategic moves: increased control of inventory, McKesson's most vital asset; improved cash flow; and higher productivity of its employees in handling more items.[23]

Other Pacesetters

A number of other companies are using systems to serve customers better while ensuring their loyalty. For example, a Scandinavian manufacturer and distributor of farm-animal feed is providing farmers with an order-entry system that includes a model that optimizes the feed mix. Farmers gain better return on their livestock by remaining loyal to this supplier. Essentially, the information service adds value to a commodity product, and in doing so makes it costly for the customer to switch to a competitor.

DAKA Inc., a hotel management and food service company in Massachusetts, has provided one of its university customers with a food service accounting system that links the university's accounting system directly to a machine that reads student cafeteria-entry cards. The university sees better accounting data with less administrative cost, and has reduced student cheating on food plans. The flexibility the system provides allows the university to offer new food plans in order to tailor services to student needs. Now, in addition to the full 21-meal-per-week plan, 15-meal and 10-meal plans are offered. This has resulted in an additional 130 students participating in the program, and $250,000 per year in additional revenue to the school.

Customer order-entry systems are the most common approach to gaining a competitive advantage through data processing. By adding value to the product with information services, they make the customer's market somewhat less efficient and increase customer loyalty.

Another strategic application of data processing applies to the other major external interface: suppliers. Here, systems such as the inventory management system being developed by General Motors make the market more efficient, so that the buying firm can more easily shop the marketplace and move back and forth among suppliers. Standardizing product codes and specifications through procurement systems will gain the buyer an advantage, generally at the expense of the seller.

A third area of strategic opportunity for data processing is, as Porter suggested, in information-based products and services. Data processing can be a profit center in itself, or it can lead to entirely new lines of business. Merrill Lynch Pierce Fenner and Smith, a large retail financial services company, provides an example of a business made possible by data processing. Their Cash Management Account was created on the basis of computing power. The CMA allows for a single computerized monthly statement listing credit card, checking, saving, and securities accounts. Their computers automatically transfer customer's idle funds into interest-bearing accounts in a registered bank. The system permits Merrill Lynch to provide banking services as a part of their product line, although they are not a bank. Merrill Lynch hopes to draw customers (and money) away from other brokers by their broad, easy-to-use portfolio of financial services.[24]

American Airlines illustrates the use of data processing as a business in itself. Their Sabre system led the airline industry in computerized reservation systems. Sabre serves approximately 48 per cent of the automated travel agents in the United States. The system is expected to earn $170 million before taxes in 1985 on $338 million in revenues.[25] It is unlikely that the airline industry could rent hotel rooms and cars along with selling airline tickets without the aid of the online reservation systems.

Similarly, International Stamp Exchange Corp., a small company in Miami, Florida, differentiated its market niche through data processing. An online market for collectors' stamps is made on the computer, and the company collects a 3 per cent commission from the buyer and a 6 per cent fee from the seller on successful trades.[26] In each of these cases, the data-processing system opened new business opportunities while enhancing competitive position and market share.

OA and Organizational Effectiveness

The precedents set by operations research and management science led to a new way of thinking about managerial effectiveness. This, combined with the evidence presented by strategic applications of data-processing systems, encouraged many companies to explore the use of OA to gain a competitive edge.

The use of information technology to support individuals in their mission-related office tasks actually began with experiments designed to aid scientists and engineers in their calculations. More highly focused research on developing tools for thinking began in the 1960s.

The Augmented Knowledge Workshop

In the 1960s, as operations-research professionals were developing numeric tools for decision makers, experiments in writing online began. One of the earliest research groups was created by Dr. Douglas C. Engelbart at Stanford Research Institute.[27] Engelbart hoped to increase people's ability to work with complex thought processes by providing computer-based tools for manipulating language and symbols. The systems created by this research group became commercially available in the late 1970s and served as a design model for a number of today's management systems.

One of the first "paperless office" experiments was conducted by Dr. Harold Bamford at the National Science Foundation from July 1976 through March 1978.[28] A manager, four professionals, and a secretary used Engelbart's Augment system as comprehensively as possible in conducting their normal business. Only three types of paper were handled: printouts for those outside the group, paper received from outside, and legally required paper files. Paper received from people outside the group was filed by serial number after being catalogued online.

The Foundation carefully measured the productivity impacts of working online, and compared the results to those gained before the tools were introduced. The professionals experienced productivity gains of 32 per cent in their correspondence and other writing tasks. The secretary experienced productivity gains of 73 per cent in typing, 45 per cent in filing and retrieval, and 29 per cent in other professional support activities. (The Foundation works with a high proportion of long reports, which are well suited to online editing.) Engelbart's intended use for the system was not office productivity, however. He envisioned tools that would "augment human intellect." Throughout the life of his research group, Engelbart and his staff performed all of their information work online, in hopes of improving thinking rather than reducing paper.

In 1970, the U.S. Department of Defense linked many of its research contractors (in consulting and engineering companies and universities) with the first packet-switched computer network. Sponsored by the Department of Defense Advanced Research Projects Agency (ARPA), the network put leading information-systems researchers in contact with each other through electronic mail. Thus, in the early 1970s, tools for thinking were flourishing among computer scientists.

Outside of this elite world of research, there was little managerial use of OA tools until the later 1970s. Early corporate experiments, often centering on electronic mail, began around 1978 in a number of leading-edge organizations. In 1978, the personal computer also became a practicality with the introduction of the Apple II. Within two years, progressive managers were experimenting with personal tools to aid them in their thinking work. By 1981, when IBM introduced its personal computer, the majority of North American companies had formed OA groups, and Europe's leading edge began its first OA pilot projects.

Now, in the latter half of the 1980s, we see work stations on the desks of 15 to 25 per cent of the white-collar workers in large North American companies. OA trials have begun in most large European companies. We have a rich base of experience from which to study the relationship between OA and organizational success. This pragmatic implementation experience has contributed little to our ability to measure value-added benefits, however. The development of measurement techniques has lagged behind the implementation of creative applications.

Measuring the Value of OA

The Term "Value-Added"

Throughout this book, we use the term "value-added" to describe the strategic, mission-oriented benefits of OA. The term first appears in economic theory. Economists consider value-added to be the incremental worth added to a product at each step in the production chain. In the strictest sense, value-added is the selling price of a product minus the cost of the raw materials used to produce the product. A value-added tax (which is widely used in the Common Market countries of Europe) is one that is levied on the incremental worth added at each stage of production.

The term "value-added" has been used to mean a number of different things in the field of information technologies. For example, a company that provides specialized services delivered through standard telecommunications networks is a "value-added carrier." Similarly, those who buy general-purpose computers and customize them for specific applications are called "value-added resellers."

The term "value-added" can also be applied within an organization to refer to the various steps in the production of goods and services. For example, Michael Porter analyzes each step in the "value-added chain" within an organization to identify the key strategic issues. Tracing the term's economic origins, Porter says that "economists have characterized the firm as having a production function that defines how inputs are converted into outputs ... The value chain formulation focuses on how these activities create value and what determines their cost, giving the firm considerable latitude in determining how activities are configured and combined ... Comparing the value chains of competitors exposes differences that determine competitive advantage."[29]

Porter goes on to explain that information technology is one of the major support activities for the value chain. "Information systems technology is particularly pervasive in the value chain, since every value activity creates and uses information ... The recent, rapid technological change in information systems is having a profound impact on competition and competitive advantages because of the pervasive role of information in the value chain ... Change in the way office functions can be performed is one of the most important types of technological trends occurring today for many firms, though few are devoting substantial resources to it ... A firm that can discover a better technology for performing an activity than its competitors thus gains competitive advantage."[30]

Like many inventions, good ideas often arise simultaneously in different places. It is likely that the term "value-added benefits of OA" came into use in a number of arenas in the late 1970s. The first use of which we are aware began in 1978, when Larry Day of the Diebold Automated Office Program began using the term "value-added" to refer to OA systems that resulted in effectiveness rather than efficiency gains. Since then, the term has come into widespread use in this context.

Measuring Organization-Wide Value-Added

Because the term originated in the field of economics, it is natural to turn to economic theory as a way to measure the effects of OA on profits. In a much-quoted study, Alan Purchase of Stanford Research Institute (now SRI International) estimates that the average capital investment in white-collar workers was only $3,000, as compared with $10,000 per factory worker and $15,000 per farm worker. These statistics are frequently used to argue that greater investment in OA is justifiable. Of course, the analogy breaks down in this context, as it is not necessarily true that the same level of capitalization is appropriate for managers and farmers.

Paul Strassmann has attempted to measure value-added benefits on a macroeconomic level.[31] Strassmann used the PIMS database of historic financial results of a range of corporations to compare investments in information technology with profitability. He concludes, "There does not seem to be any direct causal relationship between information technology costs and management productivity."[32]

In all likelihood, Strassmann's econometric analyses of management labor-factor productivity were unable to control the many extraneous and intervening variables. For example, his comparisons across time cannot control for structural changes in industry. Comparisons across companies do not account for the size of the organization or for the quality of management. There are cases recounted in this book where a single application returned as much benefit as the entire data-processing department in other companies. This wide variance in the quality of management will disrupt statistical correlations of profits to investments in computers.

While he did not find a correlation at the organizational level,

Strassman got close to measures of value-added at the departmental level. The 1981 National Retail Merchants Association financial data book allowed him to look at labor-factor productivity by department. He suggested that investment opportunities occur when one's labor-factor costs are higher than the industry average.

This approach may indicate areas of opportunity with favorable returns on technology investments, but it is likely to miss opportunities for strategic advantage from OA. There is no guarantee that increasing people's productivity in an under-capitalized department will indeed affect the competitive position of the firm in significant ways. If the product is not defined in qualitative as well as quantitative terms, it may even hurt the firm's ability to compete. For example, if a user's mission is customer relations in a market that is highly sensitive to service, increasing labor-factor productivity may damage the firm's relationship with customers as representatives try to process more calls per hour.

Statistical analyses may not help managers measure the benefits that they intuitively know exist. Measuring the relationship between OA tools and business success requires a deep understanding of the mission of each user group. There is no single correct way to measure value-added benefits, and simple economic or financial statistics will never reflect the unique contribution of tools in each user organization. We have found that a financial and decision analysis assessment of case experiences is the fruitful way to estimate value-added benefits.

The closer one gets to a specific application within a specific user group, the better the measures will be. Indeed, in spite of his economic research approach, Strassmann notes that productivity is best understood by examining "rare cases of excellence rather than by gathering data about averages or failures."[33]

A Case-Study Approach to Measurement

A few authors have taken a context-specific approach to measuring benefits from office systems. Fred McFadden and James Suver use value-added measurements to determine the potential benefits to be derived from a database system.[34] They develop a "benefit forecast" by directly asking line managers to estimate expected increases in sales and profits and expected savings in production. For example, in one study they asked for conservative estimates from managers, who felt that their sales growth rate could be increased from its current 5 per cent to 10 per cent over a three-year period with the assistance of a database. They also consulted the financial manager, who "estimated that he could reduce his annual operating budget by 10 per cent if these [database] aids were available."

By asking managers who were involved in daily operations to estimate the worth of the system, McFadden and Suver collected more relevant information than if they had done the estimates themselves. "The analysis of benefits and cost can provide a firm foundation for companies to move into the database era ... One major advantage of such a study is the involvement of key managers. The benefits can be estimated by the managers themselves rather than the study team ... Another major advantage of this kind of analysis is the development of a preliminary set of priorities for database development."

Encouraging progress has also been made by Peter G. Sassone and A. Perry Schwartz at the Georgia Institute of Technology. In several recent publications, they present viable methods for determining the value of information centers (and the office technologies those centers employ). In one paper, they used a cash flow acceleration model to measure the value of the information center to a company.[35] In another paper, they outlined an objectively anchored rating technique for measuring the benefits of the information center when those benefits cannot be converted directly to their dollar equivalents.[36] They categorized benefits as being commensurable (measurable in monetary terms) or incommensurable (intangible). When the benefits are ranked, the incommensurable benefits can be compared in value to the commensurable benefits of approximately equal rank.

Seeking tangible measures, Sassone and Schwartz propose a "hedonic model" which measures a shift in managers' use of their time from "lower-value" tasks such as administration to "higher-value" tasks such as analysis and planning.[37] While this approach identifies valuable behavioral impacts of information tools, it still does not measure the impact of OA on profits. The hedonic model tends to focus on making managers better administrators in order to free time for other work, and leads to images of a decision maker "deciding" eight hours a day. However, more time spent on decision making may or may not generate better decisions. In fact, creative insight and good judgment don't take time; they do take clear thinking and creative insights. In many cases, "unproductive" time may be creative time. In any case, the more powerful and relevant benefits of OA accrue from applications that contribute to an organization's mission directly rather than indirectly through administrative time savings.

The hedonic model may be useful in a different context — to estimate the organization-wide potential of OA. Since value-added benefits cannot be measured without understanding each user's mission, it is virtually impossible to measure organization-wide value-added contributions or to determine an average contribution to profits per employee. However, average salaries and shifts in the task mix by type of employee are more easily calculated. The hedonic model may help demonstrate the importance of OA programs at the organizational level, although this approach is inappropriate for justifying and evaluating specific projects.

Reasons for a New Measurement Approach

Schwartz and Sassone report that they have found many firms "which have tried up to a dozen different measurement schemes to demonstrate the value of a pilot office system project. Yet, many firms appear to be no closer to proving the value of their systems than when they started."[38] Many information systems managers share their frustration. Rex Hartgraves, the manager of information systems at the U.S. Forest Service, is responsible for one of the largest government procurements of office systems. In his words, "If I keep promising Congress productivity, they have every right to come back in a year and ask for headcount [reductions]. It's a never-ending downward spiral."

Schwartz and Sassone go further to describe the problem. "Faced with the failure to prove a compelling business case, some conclude that the measurements used to determine the value of management technology have been largely off the mark. They argue for more accuracy. Others suggest that the value of management technology cannot or should not be measured. They ask firms to accept the value on faith. Skeptics judge the lack of conclusive measurements to mean that management technology falls far short of its promised value. They suggest that firms delay their commitment to the technology. We reject all of these views ... We suggest that the whole question of the value of management technology needs to be reformulated."

We agree, as do the many information systems managers with whom we have spoken in the course of this study. Traditional productivity measures of information tasks do not capture the mission of user organizations. Strassmann's attempt to measure value-added impacts on an organization-wide and department-wide level yielded no valid correlations. The most encouraging work has taken a financial approach to understanding the benefits of office tools in the context of specific applications.

Although many commentators cite the importance of information technologies in gaining a competitive edge, they do not offer clear measures of that competitive advantage.[39] Consultants and vendors worldwide claim that information is of strategic value, and offer taxonomies of benefits and theories of the value of information. But the literature is sorely lacking an empirical base, and evidence is limited to a few well-worn stories primarily based on data-processing systems. In the face of all of these claims, senior managers are increasingly demanding proof of the return on their already substantial investments in OA. This book is designed to fill that credibility gap.

In this book, we examine value-added benefits on a case-by-case basis, attempting to capture the unique business goals of each application. We consider successful uses of the range of OA tools in each of the major functional areas of business in a variety of industries. Based on this extensive research, we attempt to provide evidence that supports or qualifies the many claims made on behalf of OA, using the best financial techniques that capture the user's mission (rather than more accurate measures of less relevant benefits).

Measuring the benefits of OA in terms of business goals brings a host of opportunities and problems. Clearly, it addresses the important business issues; yet we find that quantification is a difficult and dangerous task. Our approach attempts to tackle that task head-on and to bring believable systems evaluations to decision makers. In addition, based on our experience, we offer pragmatic guidelines for finding and measuring value-added applications in the context of unique business goals and challenges.

To our knowledge, this is the first serious attempt to evaluate quantitatively the benefits that are often called the "intangibles." We hope this research directs future implementation efforts and research studies away from industrial engineering and toward the bottom line of business.

Notes

1. The authors thank Larry Day of BRS Information Technologies for his assistance with the on-line literature search, which greatly aided in the development of this chapter.
2. C. Barnard, *The Functions of the Executive* (Cambridge: Harvard University Press, 1938)

3. Central Computer and Telecommunications Agency, "A Report of Trials of Stand-alone Word Processors in U.K. Government Typing Pools" (London: British Civil Service Department, November 1980)

4. H. Mintzberg, *The Nature of Managerial Work* (New York: Harper & Row, 1973); see also H. Mintzberg, "The Manager's Job: Folklore and Fact," *Harvard Business Review* 53, no. 4 (July-August 1975), and H. Mintzberg, "Managerial Work: Analysis from Observation," *Management Science* 18, no. 2 (October 1971) B97-B110.

5. Harvey Poppel, "Who Needs the Office of the Future?" *Harvard Business Review* 60, no. 6 (November-December 1982), 146

6. H. Simon, *The New Science of Management Decision* (Englewood Cliffs, N.J.: Prentice-Hall, 1977)

7. C. West Churchman, Russel L. Ackoff, and E. Leonard Arnoff, *Introduction to Operations Research* (New York: John Wiley & Sons, 1957)

8. W. Ross Ashby, *An Introduction to Cybernetics* (London: Chapman and Hall, 1956)

9. S. Beer, *Platform for Change* (Chichester, U.K.: John Wiley and Sons, 1975), at 26

10. Ibid., at 59-60

11. Ibid., at 66

12. S.A. Schmitt, *Measuring Uncertainty: An Elementary Introduction to Bayesian Statistics* (Reading, Mass.: Addison-Wesley, 1969), at 260

13. Jack P.C. Kleijnen, *Computers and Profits* (Reading, Mass.: Addison-Wesley, 1980), at 127

14. R. Holland, "Understanding Information Resource Management," in *Resource* (Ann Arbor: Holland Systems Corp., 1985), at 3

15. R. Ackoff, "Management Misinformation Systems," *Management Science* 14, no. 4 (December 1967)

16. J. Rockart, "Chief Executives Define Their Own Data Needs," *Harvard Business Review* 57, no. 2 (March-April 1979) 81

17. D.R. Daniel, "Management Information Crisis" *Harvard Business Review* 39, no. 5 (September-October 1961) 111

18. Ibid., at 85

19. John F. Rockart, and Adam D. Crescenzi, "Engaging Top Management in Information Technology," *Sloan Management Review* 25, no 4 (Summer 1984) 3-16

20. F.W. McFarlan, "Information Technology Changes the Way You Compete," *Harvard Business Review* 62, no. 3 (May-June 1984) 98

21. M. Porter, "How Information Gives You Competitive Advantage," *Harvard Business Review* 63, no. 4 (July-August 1985), 149

22. R.I. Benjamin, J.F. Rockart, Michael S. Scott Morton, and John Wyman, "Information Technology: A Strategic Opportunity," *Sloan Management Review* 25, no. 3 (Spring 1984), 3-10. See also C. Harris, "Information Power," *Business Week*, October 14, 1985.

23. M. Porter, "How Information Gives You Competitive Advantage,"

supra note 21; J.F. Rockart and M.S. Scott Morton, "Implications of Changes in Information Technology for Corporate Strategy," *Interfaces* 14, no. 1 (January-February 1984), 84-95; and "Foremost-McKesson: The Computer Moves Distribution to Center Stage," *Business Week*, December 7, 1981

24. "Information Power," *Business Week*, October 14, 1985
25. Ibid.
26. "Business Notes" *Time*, October 7, 1985
27. Douglas C. Englebart, "Augmenting Human Intellect: A Conceptual Framework," final report to the Air Force Office of Scientific Research, ASOSR-3223, Contract AF 49(638)-1024 (Menlo Park, Calif.: Stanford Research Institute, October 1962)
28. Harold E. Bamford Jr., "Assessing the Impact of Computer Augmentation on the Productivity of a Program staff," unpublished working paper (Washington: National Science Foundation, August 1978)
29. M. Porter, *Competitive Advantage* (New York: Free Press, 1985), at 39
30. Ibid., at 168-70.
31. P. Strassmann, *Information Payoff: The Transformation of Work in the Electronic Age* (New York: Free Press, 1985)
32. Ibid., at 244
33. Ibid., at 108
34. F.R. McFadden and James D. Suver, "Costs and Benefits of a Database System," *Harvard Business Review* 56, no. 1 (January-February 1978), 131
35. P.G. Sassone and A. Perry Schwartz, "Corporate Strategy for End-User Computing," *AFIPS Office Automation Conference*, 1985, at 157-64
36. A. Perry Schwartz and Peter G. Sassone, "The Value of Incommensurable Information Center Benefits: An Objectively Anchored Rating Technique" (Atlanta: Georgia Institute of Technology, June 1984)
37. Peter G. Sassone and A. Perry Schwartz, "Cost-Justifying OA," *Datamation* 32, no. 4 (February 15, 1986) 83
38. A. Perry Schwartz and Peter G. Sassone, "Is Management Technology Living Up to Its Promise?" *Business Forum*, Fall 1984
39. "Information Power: How Companies Are Using New Technologies to Gain a Competitive Edge," *Business Week*, October 14, 1985

EVIDENCE (AND IDEAS)

It is important that readers understand this introduction to Part 2 before reading the cases in chapters 3 through 9. Here we describe our research methodology and how it meets the objectives of this book. This introduction also presents our analytic approach and notes limitations on the interpretation of the case results.

Measuring value-added benefits is more difficult than using traditional productivity approaches, but it is not impossible. In this book, we report the results of intensive research on OA applications that resulted in profits.

We began our research by mailing letters to over 2,000 people we knew to be interested in OA. Vendors assisted in generating leads by telling us about their most successful customers. Of course, we talked about the book to all our friends and colleagues (and even to a seatmate on an airplane), and many responded with examples and cases drawn from their own experience.

Hundreds of people were interviewed in nearly 100 different organizations in North America and Europe. Over 60 cases illustrating the measurable impacts of OA on the bottom line have been selected for presentation. Numerous other cases that produced identifiable impacts on organizational objectives are mentioned to demonstrate the variety of ways of addressing common business objectives. Together, these case studies demonstrate the varied and rich potential of new office information tools.

Results are analyzed in business terms. We do not depend on industrial engineering for measuring time savings. Rather, we examine the direct impacts of OA on profits. Unfortunately, most business results are not easily measured, and the impact of OA tools can be measured no more accurately than the job-related performance of the users. Rather than shying away from the challenge, we have measured each case as accurately as its circumstances and the ability of decision makers permit. Just as with most business decisions, this measurement typically involved subjective judgments. In each case, we interviewed the executive who was in the best position to make such judgments. We asked the interviewees to make conservative estimates, and then verified their judgments by tracing the logic and checking the implications of their statements with them. Afterwards, each interviewee reviewed the written case, corrected errors, and signed a release verifying the authenticity of the facts and his or her belief in the estimates and assumptions. In each case, we were satisfied that the judgments we received were informed and conservative.

As Benjamin Disraeli said, "There are lies, damned lies, and statistics." Our analyses often were complex, since business results are not always easy to define. This natural complexity will lead many to challenge these case analyses on a number of issues. There are those who will question the use of judgment in analyzing benefits, preferring to stick to results that can be measured with a high degree of accuracy. This attitude may result from a lack of trust in the degree to which executives understand their businesses or are able to make judgments, or from an unfamiliarity with techniques for making decisions in conditions of uncertainty.

When readers don't believe an executive's judgments, we suggest that the problem lies outside the domain of OA. Our methodology captured the best estimates of those in the best position to know. The results, while not highly accurate, are reasonable assessments of the business impacts of the tools. In most cases, the conclusions — specifically, the strategic value of office information tools — would not be significantly affected even if these executives' estimates were off by 50 per cent. An unwillingness to make decisions based on the informed judgments of senior managers is a serious problem that will petrify an organization, with or without OA.

Throughout the book, we use accepted analytic techniques for assessing decisions in uncertain conditions. The most common calculation involves expected values of probability distributions to convert chances to common values. While we recognize that risk-averse individuals may place utilities on chances below the expected value, we consistently use this analytic technique as the best approximation of rational decision making.

We compare like dollars through the use of discounted present values, and assume an interest rate of 10 per cent throughout the book. For those who find quantitative decision-making techniques unfamiliar, we have included descriptions of the quantitative methods in chapter 13. Here too an unwillngness to make decisions in the face of uncertainty is a serious organizational problem that extends far beyond OA.

The end result is a chain of logic that identifies what difference the OA tool made and that traces the impact of that difference to profits. This train of logic is developed by asking the users to describe the impact of the tools on their work; we are simply providing a yardstick for the benefits they have experienced and understand intuitively. Each step in the logic train is considered rational and conservative by the decision makers who were involved.

If the resulting profits seem outlandishly high, some readers will discredit the entire case. A more reasoned response would be to consider each step in the logic train and rework the assumptions along the way to render them even more conservative than those stated. It is likely that the result will be a case that remains impressively profitable.

Finally, some readers may be concerned that we are presenting the few rare successful cases and ignoring the many failures where payoff was low. The chosen interviews do not represent a statistical sample of the user marketplace; our purpose is not projecting the size of value-added benefits in the world or in the typical organization (if there is such a thing).

For good reason, our research examined successes, not failures. Our purpose is to understand the measurable benefits of OA—not how to implement new systems. Issues of organizational change are already well-treated in the literature, and there is no further need to study failures and report on the mistakes of the past. Our research focused on the most successful, creative, and high-payoff applications of common OA tools, where the users' experiences show us the benefits of the tools and suggest ways to measure results.

Furthermore, we do not attempt to project the size of the potential benefits to an entire organization or industry. It is important to remember this point, because without it the cases may be used to oversell the potential of OA. Attempts at gauging the overall impact of technology have typically failed because of the difficulty of controlling for the many other factors that determine organizational success. Some trends can be observed among the cases; however, we do not attempt to generalize patterns. Since we are not interested in projections and patterns, we do not need to know the proportion of successes to failures, nor do we need to choose a representative sample.

This research was designed to help us understand how successful implementors and users have made money for their companies by using OA, and how to measure these results. Doing so requires an understanding of each user's business mission and the way it contributes to profits. Value-added, by its nature, must be measured at the application-specific level. Thus, we look at a series of successes in the context of their unique business missions.

One might reasonably ask, then, whether these results can be replicated in other organizations. We have noted that value-added applications are not uncommon. In almost every organization that we have studied, examples were found. Half of these proved to be measurable in monetary terms. Our intent is not to sell office automation by overstating its benefits. In fact, we disagree strongly with those who are technology-driven and sell computers as an end rather than a means. Nonetheless, we believe that a business-driven implementation process can produce similar results in most organizations. Chapters 12 through 14 discuss techniques for doing exactly that — finding high-payoff, value-added opportunities.

To be practical, we must help implementors justify investments in value-added OA applications. The cases in this book were of necessity analyzed after the fact. One might question whether, as part of a project or budget justification, value-added benefits can be anticipated. Some can; others cannot. For those that can be seen in advance, the cases and methodologies in this book can help implementors see, define, and forecast benefits. For those that can be discovered only by experience, the preponderance of evidence that a very high payoff is really possible should tip the risk-return balance in favor of greater investments in OA experimentation.

Selling

Selling is critical to the success of virtually every organization, including governments. Because of the direct relationship between sales and profits, the success of the sales force is of concern to every senior manager in most firms. We begin our series of value-added case studies with applications of OA that directly support the sales force.

In this chapter, we consider four key aspects to selling. First, we look at the sales representative's ability to convince customers to buy. Second, we consider the ability of the sales force to respond quickly to customer requests when time is critical to closing the sale. Third, we examine the role of communications in building the organization's relationship with its customers. Finally, we look at professionalism in selling, which helps improve the chances of closing each sale.

Showing the Customer the Benefits

OA has a direct impact on profits when it helps to close a sale. We offer two examples of this, one from a large manufacturing company and the other from a small service firm. These cases both come from industries in which significant sales time is invested in each customer. In each case, OA was used to help customers understand the benefits of the proposed product or service. As you read these two cases, consider what factors customers use to make purchasing decisions in your marketplace. In the light of these decision factors, OA may be able to help clarify and demonstrate your competitive advantage.

Selling Complex Manufacturing Equipment

Dorr-Oliver, of Stamford, Connecticut, manufactures equipment for process manufacturing that separates solids suspended in liquids. In

1984, the company introduced a new technology that utilizes membranes. The membrane systems provide an attractive alternative to competitive products; furthermore, they may be so cost-effective as to warrant replacing existing equipment.[1]

The sales process on these large capital investments is long and involved. First, the customer must be convinced that the membrane system can do the required job in a cost-effective way. Then, months of testing validate expected results. Finally, the investment proposal must gain the approval of the customer's board of directors. The sales cycle may take as long as three years.

The first step, projecting costs and the potential return on investments in membrane systems, is critical. If the cost projections are too high, the customer will not be interested and the opportunity will be lost. If they are too low, the customer will be disappointed in test results and will have wasted its resources performing the tests; in the process, Dorr-Oliver's credibility as well as the sale may be lost. Furthermore, poor projections would cause Dorr-Oliver to spend significant amounts of sales time and testing resources on unlikely prospects while perhaps ignoring better opportunities. With enough staff to work on only about a dozen opportunities a year, the ability to focus efforts on high-payoff opportunities is critical to profitability.

Projecting capital and operating costs and system performance is an extremely complex process. Many details describing the customer's manufacturing process are required. There are many possible combinations of membrane equipment, and the sales engineer may have to analyze trade-offs such as the efficiency of the membrane versus how much energy is required to force liquids through it. The proposed system must then be compared to a wide variety of existing or competitive equipment. Finally, results are presented to a range of customer representatives, from engineers to executives.

This analysis is necessary not only to attract attention to the new membrane technology, but also to assist customers in planning their manufacturing plants. In a recent customer preference study, Dorr-Oliver's customers said that their number-one criterion for their supplier is the technical competence of the sales force.

Fred Leonard, marketing manager for biological systems, responded to this challenge by developing on a personal computer a projection model using a spreadsheet. Analyses that used to take four hours on a calculator can now be done in five minutes, with improved accuracy and portrayal. The model is used by sales representatives in North America, Europe, and Japan.

Ivars Bemberis, the marketing manager for membranes, cites numerous benefits resulting from the model. The model portrays more clearly the customer's options, and allows them to do "what if" analyses to explore more options. The model also brings consistency to projections worldwide. Benefits of the new technology are more clearly documented, and the selling process is far more professional.

The model allows the company to capture the customer's interest early in the process, and in the longer term builds a collaborative relationship as the company assists the customer in its planning. Furthermore, by allowing testing of many parameter changes on paper rather than by experimentation, the model can help to focus the testing and cut the test period in half. The associated cost savings can add 10 per cent to the profitability of the project. Bemberis points out that the model can also be used to explore new applications of the technology and to open new marketing areas.

We asked him to estimate conservatively the combined effect of better customer relations, less time spent on unlikely prospects, and the ability to look at new business opportunities. He is 95 per cent sure that the model will result in at least one extra sale per year, and 50 per cent sure that it will result in at least two extra sales per year. He hopes that it will result in an incremental three or four sales each year. Taking the expected value, Bemberis feels that the model will gain the company an average of 1.45 sales per year.

The typical project contributes $200,000 to profits. Thus, Bemberis expects the profit contribution of the model to be about $290,000. The software development and the 14 personal computers (which are used for many other tasks) cost about $100,000. This one application contributes to profits each year an amount equal to three times Dorr-Oliver's entire investment in microcomputers for its sales offices (see Table 3.1).

Each sale is critical since each represents a large capital investment, and a great deal of sales time is devoted each prospect. OA addressed the essential function of explaining the advantages of a new, and initially more expensive, technology. OA gave the prospect a better understanding of alternatives, and helped to balance initial capital and operating costs — two key customer decision factors. The spreadsheet was not intended to save sales representatives' time (cost-displacement), but rather to improve their chances of closing each deal (value-added).

Table 3.1.   Selling Complex Manufacturing Equipment

ODDS	MINIMUM NUMBER OF INCREMENTAL SALES PER YEAR
95%	1
50%	2
Expected value, sales per year	1.45
Profit contribution per (small) sale	$200,000
Net benefit per year	$290,000
Present value, five years, 10%	$1,099,000
Development cost	$100,000
One-year return on investment	190%
Five-year return on investment	999%

Selling Insurance

Applications like the one described above need not be limited to large capital investments or high-technology products. Similar opportunities arise whenever direct customer contact gives the sales force a chance to explain the advantages of their product or service in the context of the customer's unique needs. The next case deals with a retail sale and a small insurance agency.

Two associates in a very successful insurance agency in Stamford, Connecticut, are successful in part because they are hard-driving and personable, and in part because they are innovative. They point out that selling life insurance has never been easy—the competition is fierce and the buyer will never see many of the benefits.

In the past, life insurance companies sold either term life insurance (a death benefit, with no equity, for an annual cost that increases each year), or permanent life insurance (for a fixed annual cost, and which builds equity). To meet the clients' needs and goals, and to compete with other forms of long-term investments, the agents attempted to mix the two types of policies. To merge these policies into a portfolio that appeared to the client as a single entity, the agent would have to borrow cash against the equity in one policy to pay another, and use the dividends to pay interest on the loans while allocating premium payments between the two policies. This required extensive record-keeping and financial analysis, and placed a significant workload on agents.

The industry responded with a flexible instrument called "universal life." Essentially, payments are invested, and both payments and investment income are used to purchase a death benefit (straight term insurance). The age through which the term insurance continues depends on the payment stream, the administrative death benefit costs, and the success of the investment portfolio.

Universal life insurance allows policyholders to vary the amount they invest each year so that they can tailor the payment streams. For example, the payments could be reduced during those years when the customer is buying a new home or supporting children in college.

When its flexibility is combined with the favorable tax treatment of equity growth, universal life competes well with many alternative forms of savings and investments. The insurance industry has attempted to shift customers' investments away from stocks and bonds and into life insurance, increasing the size of the market. For brokers, however, this development creates a new level of complexity. Each insurance company offers a different interest rate and a minimum rate guarantee, uses different mortality tables, and applies different expense loads. Combine these variables with the different payment streams of each client, and the complexity makes it virtually impossible to sell universal life insurance without a computer. Like many agents, the Stamford associates use a spreadsheet with templates supplied by the various insurance companies that they represent.

Is it worth it? These associates estimate that in the first seven months of 1985 universal life policies generated $150,000 in commissions that without the computer would have been lost. For example, by playing with the stream of payments using the computer, they found that by making a large payment in the first year and then payments equal to a simple term premium, they were able to return the client's initial large premium after 20 years with a projected tax-free return of over 15 per cent. They estimate that this, along with other techniques discovered online, has helped them close at least two extra sales per week, each of which is worth about $1,000 in commissions.

The associates also credit their computer with allowing them to make sales they would not have attempted without it. In early 1983, using only a hand calculator, one of them tried to consolidate into one proposal the 12 policies held by a corporation through a competitive broker. The analysis took over 100 hours, and the associate lost the deal because he couldn't adjust the numbers in response to the customer's questions. In 1984, he reworked the proposal using his spreadsheet and won the sale. In 1985, the associates successfully consolidated 187 policies into a single proposal that took one week to prepare, representing commissions of over $110,000. "If we didn't have the computer, the computations would have taken a year. We would have had to walk away from the opportunity," one says.

These two entrepreneurs know the value of money. Based on a single successful account, the payback period on their first computer was less than two weeks (see Table 3.2).

Table 3.2.   Selling Insurance

Net benefit per year (seven months' results)	$150,000
Present value, five years, 10%	$569,000
Development cost	$10,000
One-year return on investment	1,400%
Five-year return on investment	5,600%

The time of the two principals is a precious resource, but they do not use OA tools simply to save time (cost-displacement). They have creatively applied the tools to tailor insurance packages to customer needs, thus increasing their chances of closing each sale. They also use the tools to attack opportunities that otherwise might be prohibitively difficult. Here, too, value-added leverage is gained by increasing the success rate of their selling efforts and opening prospects that otherwise might not have been within their scope. We have noted similar applications in a variety of industries. For example, a national bakery company uses a custom model to show chains of grocery stores that they can increase their profits by giving the company's brands more shelf space. (In the next section, we describe a case where a spreadsheet was used to design a large service contract to the customer's liking.)

Whenever convincing the customer is a critical success factor in selling, OA has great potential. In presenting a more compelling sales case, OA improves the chances of closing a sale. The value-added leverage in these applications is very high, and benefits accrue year after year. This is a lucrative application area for any firm with direct sales activities.

Responding Quickly to Customer Needs

In the case described in the last section, OA helped sell a product by better demonstrating the advantages to customers. There are many instances when the customer is convinced, but the sale rests on the organization's ability to respond quickly to customer requests. These situations are particularly prevalent in commodity markets, where the firm differentiates itself as much on customer service as on product quality.

Responsiveness may take the form of answering customer questions, as our first case, that of a large manufacturing company, demonstrates. In the second case, that of a medium-sized service firm, responsiveness means accepting last-minute changes in the order, giving the customer greater flexibility. The third case demonstrates that government agencies also sell; fast response was needed because of the timing of the budgeting cycle. In each case, the organization's ability to get back to the customer quickly with answers helped close the sale.

This Sale Is Now or Never

A large food manufacturing company has a field sales force serving grocery stores and chain accounts. In the past, after visiting with the customer, the sales representative spent over a week gathering cost data from headquarters before preparing a proposal. This is a highly competitive industry, and the products from various suppliers are relatively interchangeable, particularly in the institutional food market. In the week that the company spent preparing a proposal, competitors had an opportunity to win the customer away.[2]

The company installed a central online database that allowed the sales representatives to calculate the cost of proposed shipments themselves. Although it was run on mainframe computers, it is still considered part of OA since it provided interactive query of the data, similar to local database management systems.

The online database cut the time it took to deliver proposals from seven to 10 days down to one or two days. This gave the sales force an information edge that was critical in certain selling situations. In this $100 million business, about 20 per cent of sales are time sensitive, particularly those to chain accounts. The director of sales estimates that in the past 40 per cent of sales were at risk owing to delays in generating proposals. Of these, the company typically lost about 40

Table 3.3.   This Sale Is Now or Never

Size of business	$100,000,000
Time-sensitive portion	20%
Time-sensitive business	$20,000,000
At risk to competition	40%
Business at risk	$8,000,000
Lost due to untimely response	40%
Losses prevented by system	$3,200,000
Profit margin	20%
Net benefit per year	$640,000
Present value, five years, 10%	$2,426,000

per cent. Now, with immediate access to cost data from field work stations, the company need no longer lose this $3 million in revenue or $600,000 in profits (see Table 3.3).

Here, the ability to return with a proposal quickly was of great interest to the customer. With fierce competitive pressure and only marginal differences between competing products, servicing the account became a key factor in the customers' decision process.

In a similar case, a leasing company in the midwest attained an information edge from its use of electronic mail. After the terms of a lease are negotiated, the contract must be sent to the home office for approval. This approval process used to require two days, during which the customer might play one competitor against the other to seek a better deal. The electronic mail system allows the salesperson to negotiate the deal in the morning and send a message to home office from the customer's site before lunch. An answer from home office awaits her when she returns from lunch. The salesperson never leaves the prospect alone, thus reducing significantly the risk of losing a deal.[3]

In both cases, OA saved time, but its value was not counted in terms of minutes of sales force time saved (cost-displacement). Rather, the time savings were used to be more timely — that is, to service the customer better. The value-added leverage was in reducing the risk of losing a sale to the competition.

Last-Minute Changes

The need for timeliness may arise from causes other than simple competitive pressure. In some cases, the customer is under time pressure, which may result from its competitive marketplace or from other factors that set a deadline on its purchase decision.

For example, in one case, the vice-president of a large communications consulting firm had prepared a business plan for a client that included a large budget (200 line items over five years) developed using a spreadsheet. This business plan was the basis for a proposed project that would generate over $1 million in revenue.

The vice-president presented the final report from this business-planning assignment to his client on a Friday afternoon. Together, they modified some of the assumptions based on recent client data and recomputed the entire plan. A company representative accompanied the client on the plane ride home, and during the trip they identified six additional changes that had to be made before the client's Monday presentation to his board of directors. From a pay telephone in the airport at 10 P.M., they called the vice-president at home and dictated the changes. In less than a minute, the vice-president gave them revised profit figures for five years, and then sent a copy of the new spreadsheet by courier for delivery on Sunday.

The client was impressed with the firm's responsiveness. More important, he made the presentation on Monday morning with greater assurance, since he personally had selected all of the cost and revenue assumptions in the business plan. The project was approved by the client's board.

From his discussions with the client, the vice-president of the consulting firm believes that their responsiveness, made possible by the spreadsheet, increased the chances of winning that approval from 75 per cent to 90 per cent. This difference of 15 per cent in the odds of winning a $1 million contract is worth $150,000 in expected revenue. Using an industry-average 20 per cent profit margin, the spreadsheet is worth $30,000.

The vice-president of the consulting group estimates that time-pressure situations such as this one occur at least once a year, and that this is typical of the size of such contracts. Thus, over a five-year period, the present value of the spreadsheet (discounted at 10 per cent) is at least $114,000. The cost of the two computers (in the office and at home) combined was less than $4,000, for a return on investment from this application alone of over 2,700 per cent (see Table 3.4).

Table 3.4.   Last-Minute Changes

Odds of sale without OA	75%
Odds of sale with OA	90%
Improvement in odds	15%
Size of sale	$1,000,000
Expected value of improvement in odds	$150,000
Industry-average profit margin	20%
Net benefit, this sale	$30,000
Frequency of time-pressured situations per year	1
Net benefit per year	$30,000
Present value, 5 years, 10%	$114,000
Development cost	$4,000
One-year return on investment	650%
Five-year return on investment	2,700%

The customer's internal time pressure made timeliness and responsiveness a key decision factor in the sale. OA improved the chance of winning the sale by improving the customer's ability to sell the entire project internally. Cost-displacement was of little interest in this case; additional hours or staff could not have had the same effect. The immediate response to the customer's telephone call ensured a supportive and effective internal advocate. The time between that 10 P.M. telephone call on Friday night and the courier pick-up on Saturday was fixed; to expect the vice-president to spend Saturday retyping a presentable proposal would be unrealistic.

A similar situation arises frequently in marketing discount coupon services. There usually is frenetic activity around the time of order closing.[4] Clients may place coupons in newspapers and other media or may drop out at the last minute, creating the need to make a great number of changes in several versions. At Marketing Corporation of America, a database is used to tell a salesperson calling into headquarters from a client's office what space is available. "I'd say that our capability to respond immediately to a salesperson's request probably helps us close at least one more sale per issue," explains Larry Schneider, an MCA vice-president.

In both of these cases, the value-added leverage produced by OA took the form of increasing the customer's ability to do the entire project, and hence the company's ability to close the sale.

Winning Budget from Congress

The concept of "selling" also applies to government agencies. All government organizations compete for a limited national budget each year, and must convince the legislative decision makers of the importance of their budgeted activities.

An example is provided by an inventory control point (ICP) of the U.S. armed forces. The ICP developed its $100 million budget for fiscal year 1984 on a spreadsheet. The budget was combined with those from other parts of the military worldwide before it was submitted to a congressional committee. In the "roll up" process, a line item worth $10 million was accidentally left out. When the military budget was approved, the ICP budget was less than expected.

Normally, the cause of this error would not have been identified until months later, when the department would have sought supplemental funding, an unpredictable and difficult process. The odds of winning such mid-year funding are typically no better than 40 per cent. In this case, the ICP representative at the committee hearings called a supply systems analyst at the ICP, who examined the original spreadsheet and identified the missing item overnight. Because they were able to respond before committee hearings closed, the $10 million was again included in the budget. They credit the personal computer (which cost less than $10,000) with improving their odds from 40 to 100 per cent on the missing $10 million, which was worth $6 million in budget (see Table 3.5).

Table 3.5. Winning Budget from Congress

Odds of regaining budget with OA	100%
Odds of regaining budget without OA	40%
Difference in odds due to OA	60%
Size of budget at stake	$10,000,000
Expected value of OA in this case	$6,000,000
Development cost	$10,000
One-year return on investment	59,900%

In this rather unusual case, the organization had unique insights into the "customer's" decision process. The responsiveness made possible by OA avoided an error that otherwise would have significantly reduced revenue. The value of saving time in budget preparation and analysis (cost-displacement) was dwarfed by the value-added benefit of responsiveness.

Whenever accuracy is a critical issue in the sale, OA can make a similar contribution. In this case, there was no way to anticipate these benefits when the spreadsheet was installed, although similar errors had occurred in the past. Rather, the users recognized the importance of fast and accurate analysis in the budget selling process, and intuitively applied the tools to an area of critical concern.

In essence, responsiveness increased the value of the service to the customer. In the food manufacturer's case, shortening the sales cycle is of value to the customer; it can mean lower inventory carrying costs and lessened risk of running out of stock. In other industries, such as the coupon business, the responsiveness of the supplier is of immense value when it in turn gives the customer a competitive edge. Of course, the enhanced relationship with the customer is an added benefit that can be left in the domain of the "intangibles," since the tangible sales impact so clearly justifies these value-added applications.

Close to the Customer Through Communications

This section shows the potential of OA to improve timely communications between a sales representative and an individual customer. The contribution of information tools to customer communications can be analyzed at a higher level—that is, communicating with all customers. In this section, the cases demonstrate the value of improved communications between headquarters and the field.

Two cases show a general improvement in customer communications and the impact on sales. The first, from a relatively small computer systems vendor, shows how OA solved a bottleneck to growth: communications between headquarters and a decentralized sales force. The second case describes the use of OA in permitting headquarters to communicate directly with a group of customers.

Selling Computer Systems

In some firms, lack of communication with the sales force can be a constraint to growth. Particularly in smaller companies, where a decentralized sales management structure may be absent, the link between the sales force and headquarters can be crucial to both internal and customer communication.

Coin Financial is a company that designs, manufactures, and sells computer systems to automate the processing of loans. The company headquarters is located in Norcross, Georgia. Because there are no regional offices, the national sales force uses the headquarters as a remote "home base."[5]

A year ago, the telephone was the primary means of linking this widely dispersed group. Unfortunately, the telephone alone was not adequate. The switchboard in Norcross was overwhelmed with the traffic, averaging 20,000 calls per month. The telephone had other limitations: time zone problems and unending stacks of telephone messages.

Limited channels of communication can have indirect detrimental effects on sales. Mark Singleton, president of Coin, comments, "When salespeople are on their own, there can be motivation problems, especially if you don't have an effective, quick way of communicating." Coin Financial's solution to this communications problem was to install a voice message system to motivate and maintain close contact with the sales force. Singleton believes the voice messaging system has helped in a number of ways. "With the voice messaging system, we can stay in touch with our sales force and we can respond more quickly to our customers," he says. "The salespeople send their itineraries to a special mailbox in the system. This way a receptionist can locate salespeople and respond to customer questions quickly."

Paul Shanahan, marketing director for Coin, gives an example that illustrates the system's ability to motivate the sales force. "We have a 'Victory' mailbox where sales reps call in when they have closed a sale. They report sales tips and the closing techniques used. One sales rep had a client who had agreed to pay $30,000 for a product that cost $35,000. He broke the $5,000 difference down into a cost per day over five years, and the client agreed to pay the full price. Then the rep got on the voice messaging system and told the story of how he made the sale. It just so happened that another sales rep was in a similar situation and heard the message. He was able to use the same tactic and subsequently close his sale. This kind of thing happens at least a couple of times a month. We can also broadcast special incentives so that salespeople get information about two to three weeks sooner than they used to with written memos. These incentives or special deals on equipment often help salespeople close sales—

when the information went out by memo, there were a lot of missed opportunities because the information got there too late."

As president of the company, Mark Singleton is in a position to estimate the total value of the voice message system to his business: "All things have remained relatively equal in the company since last year. We have approximately the same number of salespeople with approximately the same level of training, and competition has remained the same. One important figure has changed, however, and that is our sales. Last year we received $7.4 million in revenues; this year we received $15.1 million. Because all of the other factors remained so steady, and because I have firsthand experience of how effective the system is, I feel very comfortable in saying I believe that the voice message system is responsible for half of that increase in revenues." Singleton believes that the system, which cost approximately $80,000, contributed an additional $3.85 million of revenue. With their average margin of 10 per cent, this represents an incremental $385,000 of profits in one year (see Table 3.6).

OA helped the company through a difficult growth period. Without OA, a network of regional sales offices might have been required to support the sales representatives. This large expenditure may still be required at some point, but the president is convinced that sales growth would have been slowed had the company not overcome this constraint quickly by using OA technology.

Table 3.6. Selling Computer Systems

1985 revenues	$15,100,000
1984 revenues	$7,400,000
One-year revenue growth	$7,700,000
Credit given to OA	50%
Incremental revenue per year	$3,850,000
Average profit margin	10%
Net benefit per year	$385,000
Present value, five years, 10%	$1,460,000
Development cost	$80,000
One-year return on investment	380%
Five-year return on investment	1,700%

OA was essentially the medium through which sales support services were delivered. Thus, the value-added leverage is in the better utilization of headquarters resources, providing the needed support sooner and at far less cost than a regional network of offices could. The result was growth that otherwise may well have been delayed or lost altogether.

Selling Investments While Interest Rates Fall

In other situations, sales support can be delivered through direct communications between headquarters and a group of customers. Merrill Lynch Pierce Fenner and Smith, the largest financial services firm in the world, used teleconferencing to encourage sales when a change in the economy threatened its customer base.

In the fall of 1981, interest rates dropped sharply to single-digit percentages after a long period of time in the low teens. Money-market customers were naturally concerned about their rate of return, and as their financial adviser Merrill Lynch shared their concern. Furthermore, Merrill Lynch faced the danger of losing accounts. Merrill Lynch could offer many alternatives because it was a full-service financial services institution; the challenge was to inform customers of other investment opportunities within Merrill Lynch's broad range of products.

To build customer awareness, the company hosted a one-way video teleconference. During this conference, advisers suggested five ways to get a high yield in times of falling interest rates. Owing to space limitations, only customers with at least $10,000 in money-market funds or maturing "All Savers" certificates were invited. Serendipitously, on the day of the teleconference the stock market jumped 30 points, and demand for the teleconference far exceeded the available seats. Over 30,000 people attended from conference rooms in 27 cities.

According to Jeanette Lerman, then manager of the Merrill Lynch video network, the results of this teleconference were dramatic. Based on a survey of branch managers, one-third of the audience—over 10,000 people—bought something from Merrill Lynch based on the timely information they received that night. In addition, the teleconference contributed to customer loyalty by showing Merrill Lynch's concern for the profitable management of its customers' assets. It also further established Merrill Lynch's image as a company that utilizes the latest technologies on behalf of its customers.

While some new investment dollars were also attracted, even the shifting of money to higher-yield products generated significant commissions. According to Edwin H. Hall Jr., then director of the investment product marketing division, the average transaction among these large customers involved at least $17,000. Commission rates varied from 2.0 to 2.5 per cent for equities to between 6 and 8 per cent for mutual funds and annuities. Hall believes the average commission rate was at least 2.5 per cent across these transactions. Thus, the $170 million in transactions generated by the teleconference represented at least $4.25 million of commission revenue.

Merrill Lynch operates with a majority of its costs fixed; using the published figures from the 1984 annual report, we calculate that these incremental commissions, less brokerage, clearing, and exchange fees, represent about $3.75 million in contribution to profits. The cost of this 27-city video teleconference was about $300,000. Merrill Lynch's return on investment was over 1,100 per cent (see Table 3.7).

Table 3.7. Selling Investments While Interest Rates Fall

Attendees	30,000
Portion who acted based on information	33%
Transactions	10,000
Average size of transaction	$17,000
Total volume of transactions	$170,000,000
Average commission rate	2.5%
Commission revenue	$4,250,000
Brokerage, clearing, and exchange fees	12%
Estimated contribution to profits	$3,740,000
Development cost	$300,000
One-year return on investment	1,100%

In this case, the communications from headquarters to customers reacted in a timely way to a potential threat to Merrill Lynch's market base. OA made possible a fast response and a high-quality program that was of significant value to customers. This sales support program, complemented by the efforts of the sales force, generated significant incremental revenues that otherwise would not have occurred.

More important, it maintained a customer relationship and a business goal equal in importance to profits: "customer assets managed."

Both of the cases in this section portray OA as a medium of communication from headquarters outward. The value-added leverage in both arises from better delivery of sales support to the field, whether to sales representatives or directly to customers. Any headquarters sales support program can offer similar opportunities for increased delivery efficiency and sales effectiveness.

Professionalism in Selling

Our final section in this chapter describes cases in which OA improved the professionalism of the sales force. In the first case, better information improved the quality of a proposal developed by a large government contractor. In the second case, OA allowed more and better proposals to be produced under time pressure. Other related cases describe tools that improved the chance of closing more sales by helping with various selling tasks and enhancing the professional development of the sales force.

Jumping to the Leading Edge

The quality of sales proposals is critical to sales force effectiveness. A firm is judged not only on the basis of its past products and services, but on the customer's trust in its ability to deliver what it promises. The facts and analyses that go into a proposal are an important indicator of the seller's understanding of the task at hand and its ability to deliver quality results.

Dr. Jack J. Grossman and Dr. Walter H. Kroy Jr., members of the technical staff of a large government contracting organization, completed an independent research project with the conclusion that the specifications of a major government project could be relaxed, resulting in reduced government costs. Further research would be required to verify this hunch, but no funds were then available. Grossman decided to submit an unsolicited proposal to the government.[6] The proposed research involved the use of leading-edge statistical concepts involving "multi-dimensional temporal-spatial correlations." To write a convincing proposal, Grossman and Kroy had to demonstrate that they were fully aware of the state of the art in this field of statistics, and that they would make the best possible use of research funds by taking advantage of the work that others had done. Kroy was assigned the task of reviewing the relevant literature.

In the past, Kroy might have spent six to nine months doing a literature search in libraries. In this case, he used the services of an external database search group. The literature review was completed in a few days. Kroy's report took only three months to complete. Kroy feels that even if he had had the time, he could not have done as thorough a job without the online tools. He estimates that at least one-third of his references might not have been found without the tools. As an example of relevant work of which he otherwise might not have been aware, Kroy cites a recent paper from a professor who mathematically modeled gravitational fields in limited areas.

Grossman and Kroy point out numerous benefits from the comprehensive search. The references helped to justify the belief that the proposed procedure was a valid way to begin their investigation, and that the results would extend to a range of applications. It made them aware of the work others had completed so that they would not reinvent techniques, and of the work in process by others that might be useful later in the investigation. The references introduced them to other experts who could provide consulting assistance when needed. The search allowed them to demonstrate that they were aware of the state of the art by including recent references and terminology.

The result of the online search was a more attractive proposal, and Grossman felt better able to field questions from its reviewers. He is confident that if funds are available the proposal will be approved, and gives it a 50 per cent chance. Without the external database search, Grossman feels, the increased technical risk would reduce his odds to 20 per cent. The tools increased the odds of winning the research grant by 30 per cent.

This research, in turn, may affect the specifications of a related large government project. Grossman says there is a 60 per cent chance that their findings will have no effect, for either technical or non-technical reasons; there is a 35 per cent chance they will be able to relax the specifications of the large project; and there is a 5 per cent chance that they will discover that the specifications must be more stringent. Thus, there is a 40 per cent chance that the research will have an impact on the large project's specifications one way or the other.

Relaxing or tightening the specifications is easier and less expensive early in the project than doing so at the end during testing. The difference, according to Grossman, could be over $100 million over the program life cycle; even those skeptical about the project estimate a difference of at least $10 million. A 40 per cent chance of $10 million

Table 3.8.   Jumping to the Leading Edge

Odds of winning research grant with OA	50%
Odds of winning research grant without OA	20%
Improvement in odds of winning research grant	30%
Odds that research will affect larger project	40%
Size of potential impact on larger project	$10,000,000
Expected value of research	$4,000,000
Cost of research	$3,000,000
Expected net gain from research	$1,000,000
Improvement in odds of winning research grant	30%
Expected value of benefit of OA	$300,000
Development cost	$1,000
One-year return on investment	29,900%

is worth $4 million. The research will cost no more than $3 million, for an expected net gain of $1 million.

The external database search, costing less than $1,000, improved the odds of gaining this million-dollar opportunity by 30 per cent, for an expected value of $300,000 to the taxpayer (see Table 3.8).

In this case, OA helped the scientists develop a more convincing research proposal. The better information provided by external databases improved their chances of winning the grant. The leverage could simply be the profits resulting from that small research project. In this case, however, even greater leverage resulted. The small research project affected a very large program, part of which is likely to be fulfilled by this company. Thus, the research itself has high-leverage benefits. When OA is traced all the way through to the larger program, the benefit to taxpayers is tremendous.

Of course, the firm itself may or may not benefit from that secondary leverage. We note, however, that it is likely to benefit from a better relationship with the government funding agency and from a better understanding of the requirements of the larger program. At the time of writing, we must leave these profit-oriented benefits to the firm in the realm of intangibles.

One can find numerous examples of better-quality information improving the effectiveness of a sales proposal. One case shows the importance of internal databases. Harris Broadcast Products sells radio and television broadcasting equipment. Don Anderson, then director of information systems, placed small word processors in the homes of each member of the sales staff nationwide. Headquarters staff transmit price and technical data directly to the remote word processors, and have written a program that prompts the salesperson with questions and automatically drafts a proposal.[7] The benefits of this system are numerous. Pricing is more accurate, and the company can avoid mistakes that in the past have each cost it thousands of dollars. The system also allows quick price changes to correct errors or to respond to competition.

The technical configuration data transmitted to the word processors is an essential part of a proposal. Sales staff spend less time questioning home office engineers by telephone. Their proposals carry precise specifications, and component compatibility problems have been reduced. Harris is losing less time and money in field engineering of newly installed systems, and is able to announce engineering changes quickly. In addition to presenting a neat and professional appearance, the standard text written by expert marketing staff (rather than sales staff) produces more effective proposals.

Harris's management is firmly committed to the word-processing system for sales support. They believe it produces more revenue per salesperson, thus increasing market share. It also reduces future problems with better-configured systems, and allows the company to respond to market changes more quickly. These are value-added benefits that go far beyond simply saving sales representatives time; leverage is gained as the better proposals contribute directly to market share and profits.

Typing Proposals

The next case illustrates direct impact of OA on profits, again through increasing the firm's ability to generate quality proposals. DAKA Inc. is a hotel management and food service company located near Boston.[8] To gain new cafeteria management contracts, DAKA produces extensive proposals that describe menu and cost options and contract relationships. Much of the proposal is boilerplate text—for example, paragraphs relating to compliance with equal employment opportunity laws. In other sections, standard text is modified only slightly—for example, paragraphs relating to menus. Since DAKA deals with many universities, its business is cyclical. A disproportionate number of proposals are written in just four months of the year. During these periods, all of the 85 people in headquarters help wherever possible, since new business opportunities are their highest priority.

In fiscal year 1982, DAKA produced 60 proposals. The company was constrained not by a lack of opportunities, but rather by its ability to respond to requests for proposals in a high-quality manner. DAKA did not rent typewriters and hire temporary secretaries; in many cases, this does little to increase the production of proposals, since full-time staff still have to write the proposals and proofread the results, and are diverted from producing the work to managing the temporary staff.

Early in 1983, Ralph DeAngelis, manager of data processing, installed a word processor for the secretaries to the vice-president of marketing and the vice-president of sales. With the help of all of the executive secretaries, they made a concerted effort to enter and update their boilerplate text, and soon after its installation began using the word processor for all proposals.

As a result of the improved administrative efficiency, the number of proposals they were able to write rose dramatically. In 1983, 1984, and 1985, DAKA issued 102, 108, and 112 proposals respectively. Their success rate remained at one-third, as it had been in 1982. Thus, they closed an additional 14 to 17 sales per year.

Contracts contribute an average of $7,000 per year to profits. Their average duration is three years, although some clients cancel after the first year. (The industry standard is approximately 11 per cent. If they survive the first year, they rarely cancel for the duration of the contract.) Thus, the average present value of each contract (discounted at 10 per cent) is $16,200.

The word processor is credited with at least 42 incremental proposals and 14 incremental sales per year, with a present value of $226,800 per year. Over five years (discounted at 10 per cent), the incremental proposals made possible by the word processor have a present value of nearly $860,000. In addition, new business and renewal proposals enhance the company's image of high quality, and set a tough standard for competitors to match.

The equipment that DeAngelis put into use for word processing was a fully depreciated, excess data-processing system with little or no market value (to replace the two-terminal system would cost about

Table 3.9.   Typing Proposals

Proposals per year with OA	102
Proposals per year without OA	60
Incremental proposals	42
Close ratio	33%
Incremental sales	14
Average profit contribution per year	$7,000
Percentage that drop after first year	11%
Present value of profit per proposal, three years, 10%	$16,200
Present value of profit generated by incremental sales	$226,800
Net benefit per year	$226,800
Present value, five years, 10%	$859,750
Development cost	$10,000
One-year return on investment	2,200%
Five-year return on investment	8,500%

$10,000). Thus, the one-year return on investment was 2,200 per cent, and the present value over a five-year period equates to a return on investment of more than 8,500 per cent (see Table 3.9).

Word processing for typing efficiency often results simply in secretarial cost savings. There are cases such as this one, however, where typing efficiency is of strategic value to an organization. The cyclical nature of the business made it expensive to add permanent staff to solve the problem. Instead, management took a course of controlled growth. By removing a key constraint, the growth rate was increased.

The benefits were counted not in terms of secretarial time savings (cost-displacement), but in terms of the additional sales enabled by the increase in quantity and quality of proposals. The value-added leverage was gained by eliminating a bottleneck and increasing the capability of the entire sales organization.

Sales Force Coordination

OA need not be limited to generating proposals to improve professionalism. We found a number of cases in which sales force effectiveness was improved by the use of electronic mail or voice message
systems for better coordination.

Digital Equipment Corporation (DEC) provides a comprehensive
example of the use of electronic mail in the field.[9] Sales of computer
and digital telecommunications systems are complex, and require
significant technical support. Sales representatives work via electronic mail with the relevant technical support staff and product
managers to develop proposals. Electronic mail permits faster and
more accurate response to prospects' requests for proposals. DEC uses
electronic mail between headquarters and the field to coordinate
prospective customers' visits to headquarters.[10]

Sales staff talk to each other as well as to headquarters. DEC sales
staff broadcast electronic mail messages to one another when they
need to locate existing customers who can serve as references. (Similarly, in one large pharmaceutical firm, a highly valued prospect
was on the verge of selecting a competitor's product. The salesman
sent a voice message describing the situation to sales managers
nationwide. Within three days, over one hundred suggestions were
received, leading to a successful sale.)

Electronic mail can also play a role in the sales management
process. Messages from DEC sales managers to their staff give direction, schedule meetings, announce product or price changes, and
distribute information such as analyses of competitors' announcements. By facilitating outward communications, electronic mail
helps to implement policy and objectives, coordinate sales support
activities, and free sales managers' time for involvement in actual
selling.

In the other direction, messages from sales representatives to their
sales managers report results and compliance with directives, and
provide feedback on market conditions. DEC reports cases in which
electronic mail allowed it to respond more quickly to changes in the
marketplace because of timely feedback on customer responses and
competitive tactics.

Throughout all of these cases runs a common theme: better information and communication can improve the quality of selling activities. In turn, added revenue is generated. By focusing on quality
rather than on saving sales force time, value-added leverage is gained.

OA and Selling

The cases in this chapter demonstrate a variety of ways in which OA can help to generate revenue. OA helps persuade the customer to buy. One common application focuses on communications between headquarters and the field. When they bid for contracts, sales representatives can respond more quickly because they can get approval on pricing from the executives in home office. Similarly, sales representatives can respond to rush orders in a timely way, thus gaining a competitive edge.

In other cases, OA allows headquarters to deliver sales support programs more effectively. By increasing the quality of a range of selling activities, OA contributes to sales force effectiveness.

These applications span a number of industries, including capital goods manufacturing, consumer products wholesaling and retailing, financial and food services, research, and government. The users range from vice-presidents to scientists, in jobs throughout the organization that either sell or directly support sales.

To find such opportunities, organizations might analyze the customer decision factors that are most critical, and the internal barriers to "delivering" those factors. In some industries, the key to successful selling is product differentiation and competitive advantage. In others, it is building an effective long-term relationship with the customer through responsiveness and services. Applications may be suggested by analyzing how information and communication can enhance key decision factors.

Another area of opportunity lies in improving the internal sales management process. Here a company might see the need for improving sales administrative support, account problem solving, or coordination. Applications of OA might be suggested by looking at ways in which to improve the professionalism of the sales force.

Because selling is critical to the success of most organizations, it is likely to be among the success factors cited by top managers. And because it is relatively easy to measure the contribution of the sales force to profits, applications of OA in this area are among the easiest to measure. OA applications that support the sales force are among the most lucrative value-added opportunities.

Notes

1. The authors thank Denise Donohue of Dorr-Oliver for the introduction to this case.
2. The authors thank James Herget of Lamalie Associates for the introduction to this case.
3. N. Dean Meyer, "The Productivity Impacts of Electronic Mail," *National Productivity Review* 2, no. 2 (Spring 1983)
4. The authors thank Nancy Cox of Wang Laboratories for the introduction to this case.
5. The authors thank Dave Torrey of Octel Communications for the introduction to this case.
6. The authors thank Mary MacKintosh and Mary Gillespie for the introduction to this case.
7. N. Dean Meyer, "The Productivity Impacts of Word Processing," *National Productivity Review* 2, no. 3 (Summer 1983)
8. The authors thank the International Society of Wang Users for the introduction to this case.
9. See Albert B. Crawford, "Corporate Electronic Mail — A Communication-Intensive Application of Information Technology," *MIS Quarterly* 6, no. 3 (September 1982).
10. Dr. Kenneth E. Mayers, "EMS Business-Use Short Stories," DEC memorandum dated December 13, 1982

Marketing

Marketing encompasses the range of activities that find marketplace opportunities and position the organization's products and services. It is a critical undertaking in virtually every growth market, particularly if competition can threaten market share. In addition to designated marketing staff, top executives tend to be personally involved in marketing, and particularly in strategy formulation.

We found numerous cases in which OA has assisted the marketing function. In the first section, we look at the process of formulating strategy and making key decisions such as pricing. The second section focuses on the tactical rather than the strategic level of identifying marketplace opportunities — prospecting. Third, we look at the way marketing services can enhance sales by calibrating the timing of sales efforts. Finally, we look at the impact of OA on publicity and management of the corporate image.

Formulating Strategy

At the highest level, marketing involves setting strategic directions for the organization within its current or new marketplaces. Inherent within this key marketing responsibility is the challenge of ensuring a match between customer needs and the organization's products or services. All too often, company product offerings are driven by their abilities rather than by the needs of the consumer: "find a fill and need it." Successful companies track customer needs carefully and design their services to fit the market.

This section describes two cases in which OA tools helped executives to identify strategic market opportunities and match products and services to needs: one involves a non-profit institution, the other a small-business venture. A third case from a relatively large company demonstrates the impact of OA on pricing. In all three cases, the tools helped decision makers position their firms within competitive marketplaces.

Managing a Credit Union

Our first case demonstrates the leverage that strategic market planning can have on the success of an organization, and the impact OA can have on strategic thinking. When Tom Almus accepted the position of chairman of the board of the General Foods Federal Credit Union, the credit union had $10 million in assets and was ranked by the National Credit Union Association in the 85th percentile nationwide in solvency, reserves, and services. The credit union was already reasonably successful, but Almus intended to make it even more so.[1]

The board of directors, composed of people from a variety of disciplines with differing levels of financial knowledge, used to spend most of its time examining the numbers in financial statements to be sure that the credit union remained sound (as was its fiduciary responsibility). Almus felt that the board did not spend enough time considering and developing strategic directions.

The credit union had been growing at a rate of more than 30 per cent per year over the past five years. As the credit union grew, so did the complexity of the tasks facing the board of directors. In addition to a broader range of services offered by the credit union, its larger size subjected it to increased regulation and competition. Almus was sure that its growth would slow without a strategic focus, and he anticipated a plateau of between $30 and $35 million in assets.

To initiate a discussion of strategic issues, Almus had the credit union staff present the board with color-graphic representations of the financial statements over time, generated by a personal computer. As a result, Almus says, "I saw a change in the dynamics of the meeting ... instead of spending a great deal of time reviewing yesterday's numbers, we started looking at trends [such as] where our money was coming from, its uses, [and] the distribution of loan demand."

Board budget reviews now take 45 minutes instead of four to five hours, partly because of Almus's hard-driving management style and partly because of the tools. The board members no longer try to calculate numbers during the meeting, and they examine opportunities through analysis rather than debate. Most important, the board is able to take a strategic perspective, and in doing so they identify market opportunities that they otherwise would have missed.

The result can be seen in the numbers. In 1984, the credit union managed $47 million in assets, and doubled the number of services offered to their members. Almus points out that they didn't just think

Table 4.1. Managing a Credit Union

1985 assets managed	$47,000,000
Expected plateau	$35,000,000
Growth in assets due to improved strategy	$12,000,000
Portion credited to OA	50%
Growth in assets credited to OA	$6,000,000
Development cost (estimated)	$10,000

about growth; they planned for "quality growth that we can manage." Of the $25 million to $50 million credit unions nationwide, they were ranked in the 95th percentile.

Almus concludes, "The [microcomputer-based] graphics were the catalyst for discussing strategy, goals, and opportunities instead of just numbers." Asked how much of the growth beyond the anticipated plateau he could have obtained without graphics and other support tools, Almus estimates no more than half. Thus, $6 million of growth in the asset base was attributed to graphics-oriented decision support systems (see Table 4.1).

In this case, we see a decision maker using OA as a catalyst to encourage strategic market planning by the board of directors. OA is credited with shifting the focus of attention from monitoring operations to identifying opportunities.

The graphs could have been generated in other, more labor-intensive, ways; but they had not been in the past, perhaps because of the limited staff in this not-for-profit institution. OA was not just saving staff time (cost-displacement), but was the enabling factor that pushed this credit union to the top of its peer group. The value-added leverage is obtained by assisting those who sit on the board of directors; when OA helps them see more clearly the strategic issues, their improved decision making has tremendous influence on the operations of the credit union and its success in meeting its goals.

Finding Market Opportunities

In the case of the credit union, better strategy made possible more participation in a traditional marketplace. In other cases, strategic thinking extends the domain of the firm into entirely new niches and markets. The next case offers such an example.

In December 1979, two hospital administrators and two practicing veterinary-medicine specialists began a new business, Cardiopet, which provided electrocardiogram (ECG) analyses for animals via telephone as a service to veterinary hospitals. Of the approximately 16,000 animal hospitals in the United States, the four-person team estimated that they could sell their service to 300. To their surprise, they had 1,000 clients after the first three months of operation. Clearly, the company had far greater potential than they had anticipated.[2]

The partners determined that the value of the company was not in their original idea of sending ECG analyses over the phone, but rather in their ability to reach so large a portion of the veterinary market. The more profitable potential was in providing a range of products and services for this market. The key issue was which products and services should be offered.

Steve Rabinovici, president of Cardiopet, says, "The problem was that we knew we had a huge market, but didn't know what they needed. We were a classical small company with many more needs than we had resources. Our biggest fear was a loss of opportunity if we made the wrong choices. We were in the fragile stages of starting a business, and everybody knows that your early mistakes cost you the most. At that time, we were just getting started and we couldn't afford sophisticated market intelligence. We didn't have the resources to hire a market research team or to send out an internal group of researchers. I saw an advertisement for Information on Demand while I was on The Source one day, and I decided that it might be a solution."

The searches gave them information such as the size of the veterinary industry (between $8 billion and $10 billion), along with a breakdown of how the money is spent (for example, $4 billion to $5 billion is spent for clinical services). They learned that there are two major factors affecting the industry: first, large companies that also provide human drugs dominate the drug market (for example, Upjohn); second, the industry is species-oriented. His team also learned that the diagnostic lab business represents about $30 million to $40 million, and that 80 or 90 very small companies provide diagnostic services.

"The search identified our competitors, helped us determine the size of the market in specific, targeted areas, and was essential to the determination of our product line," says Rabinovici. "The external database search led us down the right paths. Our entire long-range plan is based on the information we received from the searches. We talked to our distributors and we made well-informed decisions. We got extremely good market information for a fraction of the cost of traditional methods."

The success of Cardiopet speaks well of the choices the team made. In 1980 the company made $500,000 in sales; in 1981, Cardiopet sales grew to $1.2 million, and continued their upward spiral to $3.5 million in 1984. The business that began in 1979 by providing one service to veterinarians has now grown to serve the community in four ways: (1) assistance in diagnosis; (2) recommendation of therapy; (3) therapeutic services and devices; and (4) overall management of veterinary practices. Cardiopet conducted a successful public stock offering in 1984. Nine million dollars' worth of sales are anticipated for fiscal 1985, with profit margins that are at least industry-average. Revenue is projected to be between $20 million and $25 million by 1987, and profit margins will grow.

"I believe one of the key ingredients to the growth of our company was our access to market information through [external] database searches. We simply didn't know what to sell. Information was critical to our development and this was the only way we could afford to get it," says Rabinovici. While the public offering was essential to continued growth, according to Rabinovici, "without the market research we would not have had the growth that led to the successful public offering. I simply do not believe that we would have had the resources to go beyond our idea of providing the ECG service without the database searches," although the ECG business would itself have grown somewhat over the five-year history of the firm. Rabinovici estimates that 80 per cent of the growth from $500,000 to the current $10 million in annual revenue was based on the new businesses made possible by the market information.

Rabinovici estimates that in 1980, before undertaking the search, Cardiopet was worth between $4 million and $5 million. In 1985, the stock market evaluated the worth of the firm at about $90 million. Rabinovici credits the use of external databases with 80 per cent of this growth, or $68 million. Discounting (at 10 per cent) to 1980 when they performed the search, the president of this successful growth company credits the external databases with creating an additional $42 million of value to the owners. All of the searches cost less than $5,000 (see Table 4.2).

In this case, the users were the principal executives in a small firm. OA was used throughout their strategic planning to find new market opportunities that allowed their dramatic growth. Without the tools, they might have missed opportunities, made mistakes that could

Table 4.2. Finding Market Opportunities

1985 value of firm	$90,000,000
1980 value of firm	$5,000,000
Growth in value of firm	$85,000,000
Portion credited to OA	80%
Expected value of OA, 1985 dollars	$68,000,000
Expected value of OA, 1980 dollars	$42,000,000
Development cost	$5,000
One-year return on investment	830,000%

destroy a small firm, or wasted significant time and resources on less profitable options. The key was obtaining information on the market that was both accurate and comprehensive to support their creative thinking.

Information is relatively inexpensive, yet its potential impact is vast. The return on investment is far above normal expectations. The value-added leverage comes from influencing key decisions in which a great deal of money is at stake, and improving the quality of decision making.

Pricing Analysis

There are numerous decisions to be made within the realm of marketing that do not identify market opportunities but do affect the firm's position vis-à-vis its competitors. A common example is pricing. Modern managers do not set prices strictly based on their costs; rather, they carefully analyze market forces such as competitive pricing and customer price sensitivity. Pricing is more important to some industries than to others. Retail products and services are especially sensitive to pricing decisions.

Hardee's Food Systems, Inc., a subsidiary of Canadian-based IMASCO Limited, is the fourth largest hamburger-oriented fast-food company in the United States, with approximately 2,500 restaurants primarily located east of the Rocky Mountains. They are vertically integrated, handling all of their own manufacturing and distribution.[3]

Several years ago, Hardee's acquired another hamburger-oriented fast-food chain called Burger Chef. When the acquisition was made, their traditional data-processing group was completely tied up with routine conversions of financial and operating data. "Because DP was so tied up, we were virtually forced into end-user computing," explains John C. Wilson, Hardee's vice-president and chief financial officer. "We put a decision support system (DSS) into the hands of our upper-middle management and our senior financial analysts."

The system includes an interactive database that is fed from a mainframe data-processing system, which in turn is connected to point-of-sale terminals. In addition to interactive access to the data, the system allows users to build models to analyze data and develop forecasts. Some common models were developed for everyone's use; users also develop their own models as needed for particular analyses. The entire system is integrated with electronic mail and mainframe graphics tools. "The system was not cheap," Wilson admits. "Including the hardware, we spent about half a million dollars. But the paybacks were tremendous."

One of the most lucrative examples was the system's use in a periodic pricing study. Based on competitive analysis, Hardee's periodically identifies opportunities to raise prices on more than 50 items in 850 stores. Because both Hardee's and its competitors are franchise operations that set prices differently among regions (or even stores), it was difficult to track their own prices and even more difficult to track competitors' prices. Nonetheless, prices were revised twice per year.

In the spring of 1982, Hardee's increased its prices by an average of 3.5 cents per item, for a total impact of $10 million annually. "We were able to implement a pricing project and reduce the 'time float' from three to four months down to a week and a half. The program was implemented by one analyst in that week and a half," Wilson says. Hardee's received the increased revenue three months earlier, representing an incremental $2.5 million increase in revenue and contribution to profits. Wilson concludes, "We had some real skeptics at first, but after we had that first application for the pricing structure, they got very interested."

Eliminating the "time float" was a one-time effect, but the system also produced ongoing benefits. Hardee's is now able to analyze its pricing quarterly rather than semi-annually. By doing so, it takes half of the semi-annual price increase three months sooner than it otherwise would. A price increase of $5 million per year is considered relatively small. Hardee's is raising prices $1.25 million (annualized) on a quarterly basis rather than $2.5 million (annualized) semi-annually. Therefore, thanks to the system, Hardee's is receiving an

Table 4.3.   Pricing Analysis

One-time effect: moved forward date of price increase	
Revenue impact per year of price increase	$10,000,000
Time saved by OA, months	3
Revenue impact over three months of price increase	$2,500,000
Ongoing effect: quarterly rather than semi-annual adjustments	
Average (small) annual price increase	$5,000,000
Semi-annual price increase, annualized	$2,500,000
Incremental revenue/quarter of semi-annual increase	$625,000
Quarterly price increase, annualized	$1,250,000
Incremental revenue/quarter of quarterly increase	$312,500

Incremental revenues over beginning of year rates

	WITH OA	WITHOUT OA
Quarter 1	$0	$0
Quarter 2	$312,500	$0
Quarter 3	$625,000	$625,000
Quarter 4	$937,500	$625,000
	$1,875,000	$1,250,000
Difference in incremental revenues per year		$625,000
Present value, five years, 10%		$2,369,000
Total benefits, one-time and ongoing		$4,869,000
Development cost		$500,000
One-year return on investment, one-time only		400%
Five-year return on investment		870%

incremental $1.25 million annualized price increase—or an additional $312,500 over three months—twice per year. This incremental $625,000 per year in revenue, almost entirely a contribution to profits, has a present value (discounted at 10 per cent) over five years of $2.5 million. Just this one use pays for the entire decision support system (see Table 4.3).

At Hardee's, pricing is a critical marketing decision. Better information has helped in qualitative ways, so that the company maintains market share while increasing prices. More tangibly, it has allowed Hardee's to make pricing decisions on a more timely basis. The benefit was not considered to be the time saved by marketing staff (cost-displacement), but rather the incremental revenues from earlier and more frequent pricing adjustments.

In all three of the cases in this section, better information improved the quality and timeliness of strategic decision making. The cost of the time saved was insignificant when compared to the stakes of the decisions, providing tremendous value-added leverage to the strategic market planning applications of OA.

Identifying Prospects

At the tactical level, identifying market opportunities is a matter of generating leads for the sales force, termed "prospecting." OA helps not only in working with the lists that are readily available in computer-readable form, but also in finding unexpected sources of business, approaching and qualifying prospects, and tracking them through the sales cycle. In this section, we will examine the prospecting process in large and small organizations. Each demonstrates a different aspect of working with prospect data.

Finding Those Most Likely to Buy

Many firms market by direct mail. This can be costly, particularly when the target list is counted in tens of millions. A huge consumer marketing company provides an example of the use of OA in the form of interactive statistical tools to get the most out of marketing dollars.[4]

To maximize their profitability, direct-mail operations must select the subset of their master list that consists of those who are most likely to be interested in each particular promotion. In the past, this was done using relatively simple filters based on geography, demographic and psychographic data, and previous buying patterns. An innovative large direct-mail operation found a better way. By applying statistical tools such as multiple regression analysis to past buying behaviors and other selection criteria, this firm was able to improve significantly the return on their mailings.

The statistical group was able to gain much of the potential benefits of this technique using batch computing tools. But with the limited lead time before each mailing, they were not able to fine-tune their selection formulae as much as they would have liked. Recognizing the importance of interactive access to mainframe data, their MIS vice-president provided online query and statistical tools to the group. (These interactive tools are within the domain of OA, although they often are run on mainframes and may predate the internal OA group. OA does not depend on personal computers in every case.)

As a result of these interactive decision support tools, the company was able to apply more analysis to each mailing. A company executive was certain that this additional fine-tuning improved the return rate by at least 10 per cent, and was 75 per cent sure that it improved it by 20 per cent, for an expected increase of 17.5 per cent. On a base of at least 800,000 orders per year resulting from mailings that had been statistically screened, this additional fine-tuning resulted in 140,000 additional sales.

The online statistical tools also gave the group time to analyze mailings that they otherwise would not have analyzed. The vice-president estimates that they analyzed additional mailings that produced at least 200,000 orders. As compared with no statistical analysis at all, these online analyses improved response rates by at least 20 per cent, for an additional 40,000 orders.

In total, the vice-president conservatively credits the interactive decision support systems with 180,000 orders per year. The average price of the company's products is $25. Thus, the tools brought in incremental revenues of $4.5 million, or over $1.1 million in incremental profits. The $500,000 worth of systems offered a 125 per cent return on investment in the first year alone, and a return on investment of over 750 per cent over a five-year period (see Table 4.4).

In this company, the response rate on direct mail was critical to the success of the entire firm. A statistical analysis group in marketing had a great deal of impact on response rate, and proved to be a lucrative opportunity for OA. The interactive numeric tools saved them time, but this was not taken as cost-displacement; that is, it did not reduce the staff size. Rather, the time was used to put more analysis into many of the large mailings, and to analyze mailings that formerly did not get the advantage of their services. Time savings were converted to value-added benefits, with leverage inherent in the tremendous profits that resulted from this group doing a slightly better job.

Table 4.4.   Finding Those Most Likely to Buy

Fine-tuning of mailings that used to be statistically filtered:	
ODDS	IMPROVEMENT IN RETURN RATE
100%	10%
75%	20%
Expected value of improvement in return rate	17.5%
Prior orders per year	800,000
Expected incremental orders per year, more fine-tuning	140,000
Analysis of mailings that formerly were not analyzed:	
Improvement in return rate	20%
Prior orders per year	200,000
Expected incremental orders per year, new analysis	40,000
Total expected incremental orders per year	180,000
Average price of products	$25
Incremental revenue per year	$4,500,000
Approximate profit margin	25%
Expected incremental profits per year	$1,125,000
Present value, five years, 10%	$4,265,000
Development cost	$500,000
One-year return on investment	125%
Five-year return on investment	750%

Online Prospecting

The leverage of OA on prospecting activity need not be limited to large firms. OA in the form of external databases can be an excellent source of sales leads, as evidenced by EIC/Intelligence's use of their own information service. EIC provides a database on the telecommunications industry, called Tele/Scope, that covers corporate activities, new products, research and development, and regulatory actions and issues. Susan Babcock, Tele/Scope product manager, regularly uses the system to find leads.

For example, in February 1985, Babcock learned that a large European telecommunications equipment vendor had just opened a U.S. office. The database gave her the name of the manager, who was impressed with her speedy action. Within two weeks, she had a sale worth $6,500 per year. Although she would have eventually approached them without the online database search, Babcock estimates that it would have taken her at least another four months to find them. This four-month information edge was worth over $1,500 in profit contribution. The search cost less than $20.

Another example occurred in August 1985, when a sales representative scheduled a trip to visit a telephone company in upstate New York. Before leaving, he scanned the database for the city and discovered that a large manufacturing company, also located there, was active in telecommunications. The database gave him the name of the telecommunications manager, and he made an appointment. The visit won him a sale. According to Babcock, the marketing strategy had focused on large telecommunications vendors, and the sales rep was not likely to have called on more diversified companies such as this one for another year. One year's profit contribution, worth $1,575, can be credited to the system. Again, only a few minutes of search time were used, at a cost of less than $20.

Babcock is certain that at least 15 per cent of the company's revenue is generated by leads from the database, and is 75 per cent sure that at least 20 per cent of sales come from online leads, for an expected value of 18.75 per cent of total sales. Furthermore, Babcock expects that, as the obvious large prospects are exhausted, the database will supply an increasing proportion of business.

Using Tele/Scope's total revenue of nearly $1 million, we calculate that the database-generated leads brought in over $180,000 in sales in 1985. Using industry-standard profit rates (between 12 and 15 per cent), we estimate that these incremental sales are worth at least $21,000 in profits to EIC/Intelligence.

The sales department uses the system specifically for sales leads an average of two times per week, incurring a total cost (at commercial rates) of about $5,000 per year, for a net benefit of over $16,000 annually and a present value over five years (discounted at 10 per cent) of more than $60,000. The only initial investment required was a terminal and user training, for a return on investment of over 1,000 per cent (see Table 4.5).

A number of Tele/Scope clients also use the system for prospecting. Better information generates leads that otherwise might not have

Table 4.5. Online Prospecting

ODDS	PORTION OF REVENUE
100%	15%
75%	20%
Expected value, portion of revenue from online leads	18.75%
Approximate revenue	$1,000,000
Incremental revenue credited to online information	$180,000
Industry-standard profit margin	12%
Incremental profit per year credited to online leads	$21,600
Operating costs per year	$5,000
Net benefit per year	$16,600
Present value, five years, 10%	$62,900
Development cost	$5,000
One-year return on investment	230%
Five-year return on investment	1,200%

been pursued. Again, saving time is not the issue. Simply hiring a clipping service or purchasing lists of prospects would not work; either alternative would generate leads only within a predefined market niche. It takes creativity and industry knowledge to recognize additional opportunities. The creative exploration of current events generated prospects that would not otherwise have been seen, and value-added leverage was gained by feeding the sales organization a greater number of high-probability leads.

No Longer Singing the Blues

The previous two cases demonstrated two aspects to prospecting: generating leads and qualifying them so as to focus selling efforts. A third activity is approaching those leads in a timely, professional manner, and tracking the customer relationship over time. The third case on handling prospects emphasizes these follow-through activities.

The case also demonstrates that OA opportunities are not limited to large organizations. This delightful example of the marketing power of OA comes from the other end of the spectrum, a very small business. Rob Nathanson is a classical guitarist living in Wilmington, North Carolina. He is an excellent musician, but he knows that talent alone is not enough. Like any other small businessman, he is dependent on marketing for his success.[5]

Nathanson's market is a nine-state area in which he performs at concerts, university recitals, and festivals, and with orchestras. In 1984, to establish himself in the area, he made an average of six contacts per week offering his services. After each call, he typed a personal letter and then followed it up by telephone sometime later. "It was exhausting—a real mental energy drain," says Nathanson. By year-end, his name was known to about 20 per cent of the major concert sponsors in his home state.

In December 1984, Nathanson acquired a word processor with a database management system. He developed about 30 different cover letters, tailored for each of the types of events in which he plays. He now makes an average of 23 calls per week, and follows up with a tailored letter in a matter of minutes after each call. "Because of my fast response, now they always remember who I am when I call to follow up," says Nathanson. In the past, he estimates, no more than half would remember him. He keeps notes online about his conversations with prospects, so that he has an easy conversation starter. He also notes the materials he sent and the follow-up dates in the database. Nathanson estimates that as of the end of 1985, virtually every significant concert promoter in the state knew his name.

In addition, Nathanson has begun to issue press releases using the system. He also updates his biography more frequently, so that it reflects his latest appearances (which often are the most prestigious). Furthermore, with the graphic output abilities of his word processor, he now gives his clients camera-ready programs and saves them the cost of typesetting.

Nathanson still does between 15 and 20 performances per year, but since he began to use the PC-based word processor and database management system, the fees that he commands have gone up by a factor of four. In the fiscal year ending in June 1986, his income from concerts was about $8,000, as compared to $2,500 in the prior year.

Nathanson says that regional musicians might expect their income to plateau at about $20,000 per year (unless they gain national fame). He expects to earn $15,000 in fiscal 1987, and to reach the plateau of $20,000 in 1988. Discounting (at 10 per cent) back to Decembr 1984 when he bought the PC, the present value of his earnings over a five-year period is expected to be $60,000.

Table 4.6.   No Longer Singing the Blues

INCOME FORECAST	WITH OA	WITHOUT OA
1985	$8,000	$3,500
1986	$15,000	$7,500
1987	$20,000	$11,500
1988	$20,000	$15,000
1989	$20,000	$20,000
Present value, 1984 dollars, 10%	$60,774	$32,546
		(after 20% agent commission)
Net benefit		$28,228
Development cost		$5,000
One-year return on investment		–10%
Five-year return on investment		465%

Without the OA tools, Nathanson would have had to use a "minor" agent. Doing so would cost 15 per cent of his fees plus expenses, or an average of 20 per cent. Furthermore, he feels that using an agent would mean taking an additional two years to reach the $20,000 plateau. In that scenario, the present value of five years of income would be $32,500 (see Table 4.6).

Nathanson credits this $28,000 difference in career success to his $5,000 personal computer with word-processing and database management tools. His return on investment (over five years of use) will be 460 per cent. In fact, this figure may underestimate the contribution of the computer. Nathanson hopes to break the $20,000 plateau with interstate exposure; he has been accepted into the Southern Arts Federation Touring Program and will be performing in nine states. Nathanson says, "I became a fairly hot item and subsequently have picked up strong management. All of this came about largely, I feel, because of the dramatic amount of exposure I have generated since I purchased the computer."

Nathanson's income depends on two things: his talent and his market image. His challenge was not to identify prospects, but rather to market. His marketing efforts take the form of telephone conversations and follow-through by mail. OA helps him with both of these marketing tasks.

The time saved by OA was not taken as cost-displacement; in fact, cost-displacement in this context has little meaning. The tools were used to improve the quality of his marketing. OA helped him tailor materials and remember conversations that impressed his customer base and that helped him achieve name-recognition. The value-added leverage is evidenced in the bigger fees that he now commands.

Value-added benefits are gained when marketing staff can feed the sales pipeline with more and better prospects, and help sales staff turn prospects into sales through better marketing-support materials.

The Right Place at the Right Time

Timing is essential to successful sales. It does little good to approach a prospect who is not ready to buy. Conversely, a sale is lost when the firm does not satisfy customer needs in time. OA tools can help to provide marketing services that enhance the timing of selling efforts.

In the following example, OA is the medium through which a marketing service is offered that helps match buyers to products. In the second case in this section, OA tools coordinate multiple sales forces so that each can approach a prospect at just the right time. These applications are of critical importance whenever there is a limited time in which a sale is possible.

Making a Market Electronically

Timing issues occur when there is a chance of a mismatch between market demand and production schedules. There are two solutions that work in tandem to correct such timing problems: the first is the seller's inventory, and the second is the buyer's. When buyers' inventories play a significant role in smoothing supply and demand, the seller may be able to gain a marketing advantage by helping customers manage their inventories.

A clever example of the use of OA in this context was provided by Black & Decker's power tools division, which sells a wide range of construction and home maintenance products. The primary customers are hardware distributors and retailers. At times, a customer might have an excess of a certain product and would return it to Black & Decker for credit. Meanwhile, in another part of the country, another customer might require that product. If buyer and seller could be matched, the goods could be shipped directly rather than processed through Black & Decker's inventories.[6]

In the past, when a customer asked to return goods, the local district sales manager sent a letter to other sales representatives in his or her district. If they didn't know of a buyer, the area manager might send a similar letter to area personnel. If a swap was arranged, it would typically take two to three weeks. In fact, only 10 per cent of the requests were satisfied by swaps, and the remaining 90 per cent of the excess goods were returned.

Black & Decker installed an electronic mail system to serve its headquarters and its field sales staff of 210 sales representatives and 50 sales managers. The system is used for a variety of communications, including order entry, product-line shortage reports, and managerial communications. One of the more innovative applications is the online "swap shop." When a customer wishes to return goods, a message is sent to the swap shop coordinator. If it cannot be matched with a buyer, a notice is sent to the entire sales force. Using electronic mail, requests are resolved in less than 48 hours, and the success rate has risen from 10 to 80 per cent. Since the customer pays a restocking fee that covers Black & Decker's direct expenses, a return simply cancels the original sale from a financial perspective. A swap is equivalent to a return of goods that are subsequently resold.

Generally, encouraging swaps does nothing to enhance profits. There is an exception that makes this application worthwhile, however. Some portion of Black & Decker's product line is likely to be out of stock temporarily, until production schedules replenish inventories. When a particular item is unavailable, the customer is likely to buy a similar product from a competitor. Thus, a two-week delay in restocking and reshipping could lose a sale. And, by the time the excess goods are restocked, the shortage is likely to disappear as the product is again scheduled for production. Therefore, Black & Decker lost one sale with the return of goods but did not gain a compensating sale that they wouldn't have otherwise gotten. In such cases, the returned goods represented a net loss of revenue for Black & Decker.

Electronic mail increased swaps of returned goods by 70 per cent. Ten per cent of those swaps might have been in short supply, and would have constituted returns with no compensating sales. Thus, 7 per cent of the total excess goods would represent reduced revenues were it not for electronic mail. On an annual basis, this would mean lost profits of $70,000 per year.

The swap shop consumes about 5 per cent of the total electronic mail traffic, at an annual cost of about $7,200 (including computer

Table 4.7.   Making a Market Electronically

Increase in swaps due to OA, as portion of returned goods	70%
Portion of returns not resold (no indirect swap)	10%
Portion of return goods as incremental sales	7%
Profits represented by returned goods	$1,000,000
Profits per year which would have been lost without OA	$70,000
Operating cost of system	$7,200
Net benefit per year	$62,800
Present value, five years, 10%	$238,000
Development cost (assumed, not disclosed)	$10,000
One-year return on investment	530%
Five-year return on investment	2,300%

time and amortization of terminal equipment). Even if other applications had not warranted the installation of portable terminals, the swap shop alone returns enough to pay for its variable costs plus all of the terminal equipment in the field (see Table 4.7).

This marketing service addressed a particular timing issue: excess inventories in one customer's warehouse may be in temporary short supply and needed elsewhere. By enabling an effective swap shop, OA prevented goods being returned in one location while a customer went to a competitor for similar goods in another location. In this highly competitive market with large batch-manufacturing schedules, such situations represented a significant loss of profits, and a significant value-added opportunity for OA.

Saving users time (cost-displacement) was unimportant in this case; the benefits depended on timeliness, and the matchmaking was just one step in the process. Most of the time was taken up in communications throughout the field organization. Value-added leverage was gained by speeding up communications and making the market for swaps more efficient.

Coordinating Customer Relocation Needs

Another example of the importance of timing is provided by a relocation service firm. William M. Raveis Inc., an independent real estate and financial service firm, uses a database management system to track properties and families who are relocating. In Connecticut, the public multiple listing service lists available properties by township. Each township lists a slightly different set of data on properties, and their formats vary. Raveis's staff enters the MLS data for over 90 towns in Connecticut in a standard format. These data are stored centrally and may be accessed from any location.

The Raveis system, which the company has developed and patented under the name "Homelink," is the first of its type. The 450 real estate agents have small portable terminals that they carry with them on remote visits. When she is with a prospective buyer or seller, the agent has access to the entire Homelink database on all Connecticut towns covered by the firm. She can give the customer "a printout of everything listed in his price range, what has sold and for how much, and suggest the best listing price for his home," says Raveis. This competitive edge helped the firm become, in just 11 years, the largest independent real estate broker in the state, handling over $540 million in properties in 1984.

Another use of the database is tracking the competition. The database shows Raveis the market penetration of the competition by geographic area and the overall strength or weakness of competitors. This assists Raveis in making management decisions such as selecting markets on which to concentrate. Raveis says, "This would be almost impossible to keep up-to-date by hand." The database also tracks sales. Using an average number of days from sale to closing, Raveis can forecast his cash flow more accurately. This reduces the company's working capital requirements.

The database organizes information on customers as well as properties. Raveis also operates a finance company that issues mortgages. Using an associated system called "Mortgage-Link," Raveis loan officers can quickly process loans based on data already stored in the system. The buyer can then sign all of the paperwork at once. Since it is more convenient to the buyer, the mortgage company can attract a significant share of the financing business. And because mortgages are issued more quickly, closing can take place sooner. This is an advantage for sellers and buyers, and a competitive edge for Raveis. Furthermore, by speeding up the closing process, the system accelerates Raveis's cash flow.

Raveis says that "one of the greatest advantages of the system is that it ties together all of our companies—real estate, relocation, mortgage and insurance." For example, the relocation service represents about 400 corporations, many of them *Fortune* 500 companies. When a transfer is initiated, the relocation department enters information on the person and switches it to one of 17 local real estate branch offices via electronic mail. The local agent works with the transferee to find a home to buy. Then, once the agent submits the binder as a down payment, the mortgage company picks up the transaction, ensuring that a loan officer gets in touch with the buyer quickly.

When the binder is submitted on a property, the information is also sent to the insurance company so that it can reach the buyer before its competitors do. "Most people don't think about insurance for 30 to 60 days, until they close. We get to them in five days," says Raveis.

It is difficult to trace any single sale to the system, since the database has changed the way the entire Raveis organization works. To evaluate the worth of the $950,000 computer system, we must turn to management judgment. "Basically, we couldn't live without this computer," says Raveis. "I had a million dollars to invest in either expanding my offices or purchasing a computer system. I made the right choice with the computer system. Because we can quote faster, I would say that we have increased our insurance business by about 400 policies which would total approximately $80,000 in commissions. The system also probably accounted for 15 per cent of our real estate business, and that is worth about $40 million in sales. It is even more crucial to our mortgage company; I'd say it's worth 25 to 40 per cent

Table 4.8.   Coordinating Customer Relocation Needs

INCREMENTAL REVENUES:	
Insurance	$80,000
Real estate	$40,000,000
Mortgage	$30,000,000
Total incremental revenues	$70,000,000
Conservative profitability assumption (not disclosed)	2%
Net benefit per year	$1,400,000
Present value, five years, 10%	$5,300,000
Development cost	$950,000
One-year return on investment	47%
Five-year return on investment	460%

of the business of $30 to $40 million in sales." The $950,000 system generated over $70 million in incremental revenues for Raveis, and helped make it the largest independent broker in Connecticut (see Table 4.8).

In this case, customer readiness to buy the services of one division was well known to another division. The database was used to tie together all of the divisions' services as a customer moved from one house to another. This marketing system ensured perfect timing of sales calls.

The system was not used to save staff time in handling customer records (cost-displacement), although it undoubtedly had such a favorable side effect. Rather, value-added leverage was gained by encouraging better use of field sales representatives' time, and beating the competition to the prospect.

In both of the cases in this section, OA allowed the organization to satisfy a customer's need at precisely the right time. Both were of strategic concern because of the limited duration of the customer's readiness to buy. In both cases, a marketing service based on OA ensured that the sales forces appeared in the right place at the right time.

Publicity and Corporate Image

Marketing is responsible for building an organization's public image through advertising, media relations, community-oriented communications, and customer education. These activities are particularly crucial to organizations that deal directly with the public. Corporate communications is an information-intensive activity, and is highly suitable for OA.

We begin by looking at a number of ideas for using OA to gain media coverage. One interesting case describes how OA helped to get coverage in magazine articles. Another case, drawn from the public sector, illustrates a unique application of OA in supporting community-oriented communications. Finally, an example of direct customer communications is offered.

Getting Press Coverage

Information tools can help a company gain advantageous press coverage in a variety of ways. Sometimes just staying well-informed is essential to successful media relations. The most direct effects of OA on media relations are gained when OA assists in a news conference. A number of organizations have held new conferences via teleconferencing, using both video and audio technologies. Teleconferences can extend coverage beyond those who can attend a face-to-face meeting in one of the major cities.

In addition to news coverage, organizations seeking public exposure value mentions in editorials and articles. Here too OA can provide significant help. Ron Coulson, section manager of corporate relations at Saskatchewan Telecommunications (SaskTel), is responsible for press relations as well as for internal awareness of relevant news. For most of his 30-year career, he wrote and proofread in the conventional way—on paper.

When Coulson joined SaskTel in 1984, he found his small staff very busy issuing press releases to more than 60 community newspapers spread throughout this large Canadian province. Their purpose was to keep the mostly rural population of about one million people informed of the investments SaskTel was making on their behalf, improvements that are hard to see (such as central office switching equipment). This major responsibility left little time for Coulson's staff to do anything else. Coulson felt that they could do much more. His solution was to install a word processor for use by his writers and himself.

Using the "merge list" capability, Coulson found that he could tailor press releases to each small-town newspaper. He began to include information such as the telephone number of the SaskTel office and the name of a local manager who was available for quotation. Coulson feels this noticeable improvement in the quality of news releases has had a significant impact on the quantity and quality of coverage. He recalls one editor calling him to say, "I never knew you people were investing so much in my community!"

The value of improved press coverage is extremely difficult to measure. Another benefit was relatively easier. In North America (unlike Europe) there are numerous trade magazines that carry stories written by practitioners rather than journalists. (We ask our European readers to note that these journals are oriented toward case studies and concepts, and do not substitute for newspapers or threaten the objectivity of the press.) In addition to serving the news-oriented press with news releases, Coulson also places feature stories and articles in various trade and business journals. Coulson hoped to place at least one article every quarter, but felt that with SaskTel's prior productivity he had only a 25 per cent chance of meeting each quarter's goal. Thus, the odds were that SaskTel would place only one article per year.

The word processor, according to Coulson, at least tripled Sask-Tel's writing and editing capabilities. As a result, his group had sufficient time to work on articles in addition to their normal work-load. In the first quarter of 1985, SaskTel placed three feature articles (one of which included a cover photograph) totalling 11 pages. Now, Coulson is sure that he will place at least six per year and feels there is a good chance of his producing two articles per quarter. Coulson credits the word processor with enabling him to place at least an additional five articles per year.

While advertisements and articles serve entirely different purposes, and while one cannot substitute for the other, it is commonly felt in the corporate communications industry that a page of editorial coverage is far more valuable to a corporation than a page of advertising, since articles carry more credibility and generally have a higher readership. Articles average three pages in length. The cost of an advertising page averages $5,000. On this scale, ignoring the extra value of articles over advertising and the appeal of cover photographs, each article is worth $15,000 in publicity value.

Thus, a word-processing system that cost $55,000 produced an advertising-equivalent value of $75,000 per year. Over five years (discounted at 10 per cent), the advertising-equivalent value has a present value of $284,000. Note that the equipment costs were nearly recouped in the first quarter of 1985 alone, and the five-year return on investment is 417 per cent (see Table 4.9).

Coulson's group is one key interface to the public in an organization that must be sensitive to public opinion. As the telecommunications business becomes increasingly deregulated and competitive, telephone companies such as SaskTel are placing growing emphasis on their marketing departments. In this case, OA helped a key group in a critical function to expand its activities and to better meet its objectives. The word processor saved Coulson and his group significant amounts of time in writing and editing. The increased productivity was not taken as expense reduction (cost-displacement), but was reinvested in an entirely new activity of significant value to the company. Since hiring more people was not an option in this case, OA was the factor that made possible these value-added benefits.

Presidential Campaign

Publicity programs benefit from enhanced quality as well as quantity. One way OA can help is to support the creative thinking that goes into designing promotional campaigns. In other cases, OA can help to

Table 4.9.   Gaining Free Advertising

Goal in articles per year without OA	4
Odds of achieving goal	25%
Expected value, articles per year without OA	1
Articles per year with OA	6
Incremental article per year	5
Average article length, pages	3
Incremental pages per year of media exposure	15
Advertising cost per page	$5,000
Advertising-equivalent cost of incremental media exposure	$75,000
Present value, five years, 10%	$284,000
Development cost	$55,000
One-year return on investment	36%
Five-year return on investment	420%

coordinate the execution of such campaigns. Political campaigns are among the most complex of publicity programs, and effective execution of marketing plans is essential to their success.

Presidential elections are very sensitive to the candidate's ability to coordinate his or her messages with the vice-presidential candidate, and both candidates must carefully coordinate their nationwide campaigning activities with their headquarters staff. In 1976, the Carter-Mondale campaign gained a competitive edge through the use of electronic mail.[7] During the campaign, the U.S. presidential and vice-presidential candidates rarely had time to talk with each other, and their interactions with their campaign headquarters were limited. While one was making a speech, the other was likely to be traveling to another city. This made it difficult for them to coordinate their statements and to keep up with current events.

Through electronic mail terminals in each of the leased airplanes, the candidates were able to maintain dialogue with each other and with their campaign headquarters. Political commentators noticed how well-informed and well-coordinated both candidates were— evidence of the success of the application. This added credibility to the campaign and gave the team a competitive edge.

While corporations rarely face such a dramatic need for coordination, numerous examples occur in the normal course of business. Speeches, media events, advertising campaigns, and sales efforts must all be synchronized to get the best effect from any announcement. OA can help by linking all of the participants inside and outside the organization throughout the marketing project. The value-added leverage is gained by making the entire promotional budget slightly more effective.

Talking Directly to Customers

Corporate communications can speak directly to customers, and OA can improve the quality and timeliness of these channels of communication. For example, for many years a pharmaceutical firm has educated its customers through a regular series of audio teleconferences on medical topics. Each course is made up of one or more sessions led by an independent expert in a medical specialty. The courses are not product-oriented, but are accredited continuing medical education. The benefits to the firm are increased name recognition and brand loyalty.[8] Similarly, the United Steelworkers of America believe they made a strong impact by presenting a news teleconference on the needs of the jobless and the retired just before a presidential election. In addition to gaining greater coverage, they feel, the teleconference encouraged timely grass-roots political action by their members.[9]

That corporate communications functions benefit from telecommunications technologies should come as no surprise. OA tools may help develop a message, coordinate its delivery, or improve the channels of communication. In any case, the value-added leverage comes not from more efficient use of people's time, but from the more efficient and effective use of the promotional budget.

OA and Marketing

This chapter has described a range of marketing services that enhance selling efforts. OA assists senior managers in finding market opportunities, formulating strategy, and making key decisions. Executives credit OA with helping them position their organizations for success in competitive markets. At the tactical level, marketing provides a range of sales support services. OA has improved the effectiveness of the prospecting process, and brought in more and better leads. OA has coordinated selling efforts to ensure that customers are approached at the time they are most ready to buy. In all of these cases, the value-added benefits appeared in the form of more successful selling efforts. Finally, this chapter has described a number of ways in which OA can build a favorable corporate image through media relations and direct communication with customers. These cases are difficult to evaluate in terms of revenue enhancement, but other measures can be found.

These OA opportunities in marketing have spanned a variety of organizations, from an individual to huge service and product-marketing companies. The users of OA tools ranged from marketing analysts to top executives.

Marketing opportunities might be discovered by a top-down analysis of marketing goals. In some organizations, the key marketing issues will be in the domain of strategy formulation. This is likely to be particularly important in growth-oriented businesses. The tactical issues are crucial when a business attempts to penetrate further a known market. Tactical issues focus on sales support when direct selling is involved; corporate image is important when distribution channels are less direct.

There are numerous ways in which OA can leverage a marketing budget. Generally, only a small incremental return on marketing resources will have a large impact on profits, making marketing another high-leverage opportunity area for OA.

Notes

1. The authors thank James Herget of Lamalie Associates for the introduction to this case.
2. The authors thank Riva Basch of Information on Demand for the introduction to this case.
3. The authors thank Pilot Information Systems and Lorie Robak of Raymond, Kowal & Wicks for the introduction to this case.
4. The authors thank Robert Holland of Holland Systems Corporation for the introduction to this case.
5. The authors thank John Shulman for the introduction to this case.
6. The authors thank Robert Holland of Holland Systems Corporation for the introduction to this case.
7. S. Slade, "The Carter Presidential Campaign (1976)," presentation to the Diebold Automated Office Program, working session 78-2, November 1, 1978.
8. T.W. Hoff, "Case Study: Audio Teleconferencing in Marketing," presentation to the Diebold Automated Office Program, working session 80-4, December 3, 1980.
9. *TeleSpan* September 15, 1982, at 10

Operations

This chapter examines the impact of OA on the operational functions that deliver an organization's primary product or service. The automation of factories and material handling have direct impacts on operational effectiveness; they are beyond the scope of this book, however. OA also has an indirect impact on operations by making operational managers and professionals more effective. These indirect but tangible benefits are the subject of the cases in this chapter.

Operational effectiveness is built on the two pillars of quality and productivity. In some ways these two essential pillars are antithetical; increases in one can damage the other. Effective production management attempts to maximize each without sacrificing the other. The first section of this chapter shows the contribution of OA to quality control, while holding productivity at least constant. The second section considers operational efficiency. Although these cases involve cost savings, they are still value-added cases. An application would be considered "cost-displacement" if the tools directly replaced people or processes, or made them more efficient. These cases describe ways in which OA improves the effectiveness of managers, who in turn make the many people and processes that they manage more efficient. Value-added leverage is gained by improving the management of operations rather than the operations themselves.

The final section of the chapter considers cases in which information is part of the organization's product. In those industries, OA directly applies to the operational processes, analogous to factory automation. Here too we focus on the value-added benefits with value beyond productivity and cost-savings in the production of information-based products and services.

Quality Control

Quality control in manufacturing and distribution is essential to the success of most firms. Companies compete on the basis of quality, and quality control can have a significant impact on manufacturing and distribution costs. The first case describes a situation in which quality affects competitive position; the remaining cases trace quality control to operational costs.

Manufacturing Quality Control

This case is one of the most dramatic in the book. It shows that improving the quality of the product can gain a significant competitive edge, particularly when quality in turn affects the customer's manufacturing costs.

A medium-sized chemical company manufactures a dispersant that is used to spread other chemicals over fibers in the manufacturing of yarn. In its five years of producing the dispersant virtually all of the production fell within acceptable tolerances, but none was within 15 per cent of the ideal specification. The company had been tracking 25 parameters in the manufacture of the dispersant, but had not been able to improve the reliability of the production process.

When the company supplied the chemical engineer with a personal computer and a spreadsheet, he began tracking 128 parameters rather than the original 25. Two relatively obscure parameters correlated with the production variance. In one case, he found that a time-related chemical reaction was not linear, as he had originally assumed. In the other case, he found that a digital scale was required to measure quantities more accurately. In all, modifications to the production process cost the company $25,000.

As a result of these two changes, virtually all of the production now falls within 15 per cent of ideal. The company, whose marketing strategies are based on quality rather than cost, mounted a campaign to advertise this meticulous quality control. As a direct result of the improvements to quality control, the company increased its share of the market; it has gone from meeting half the needs of two major yarn manufacturers to meeting all of the requirements of four manufacturers. This represents a growth in revenue from $5 million to $50 million per year. The spreadsheet was instrumental in bringing the company approximately $20 million per year in additional profits (see Table 5.1).

Table 5.1.   Manufacturing Quality Control

Revenue before introduction of OA	$5,000,000
Revenue after introduction of OA	$50,000,000
Revenue growth credited to OA	$45,000,000
Profit margin	45%
Incremental profits per year	$20,000,000
Present value, five years, 10%	$76,000,000
Development cost (estimated with marketing program)	$1,000,000
One-year return on investment	1,900%
Five-year return on investment	7,500%

Obviously, OA is not the only way to solve this type of problem. Although it could have been dealt with by using conventional tools of analysis and engineering time, for five years it remained unsolved, perhaps because it was just one of many difficulties facing the production managers and engineers. OA was, in this case, the catalyst that brought a solution to light. The tremendous value-added leverage shown here results from supplying just the right tool to an individual who is essential to quality control, and hence to the success of the firm.

There's a Limit to Quality

Quality control is a two-way street; its purpose is to keep product specifications within a target range, avoiding variances in either direction. In some cases, excess quality has little benefit to the manufacturer or the customer, but costs the manufacturer dearly.

A large food manufacturing company maintains excellent quality control. Its quality control department is primarily concerned with defending the interests of the customer. For example, it is quick to catch situations where product quality is insufficient, but is less likely to detect an excess of one of the ingredients.[1]

In the past, excess contents were detected in the monthly inventory analysis, usually five to 15 days after the close of each month's production. With a high-volume production line, a significant amount of money could be wasted before excess usage problems were identified.

Table 5.2.   There's a Limit to Quality

Time to identify excess usage without OA	5 weeks
Time to identify excess usage with OA	1 week
Time during which excess usage was avoided	4 weeks
Cost of materials for excess usage for one month	$40,000
Frequency per year of excess usage problems	3
Cost avoided per year of materials for excess usage	$120,000
Present value, five years, 10%	$455,000

The company provided interactive access to the inventory database at the local plant level. The query system was built on MIS databases, but is also considered within the domain of OA since it provides interactive tools to individual managers. The managers had been receiving MIS reports for years prior to the installation of the interactive query system; it was the extension of information tools to the managers' desks that made the difference in this case.

The immediate availability of data at the local level permitted plants to examine inventory at any time rather than only through lengthy audits after the receipt of monthly MIS reports. In one instance, excess usage was identified in one week rather than in the month that it otherwise would have taken. The production line was using an excess of a very expensive ingredient; had it not been caught for a month, it would have cost the company $40,000 unnecessarily. Similar problems occurred on an average of three times per year. Local access to the inventory database saved at least $120,000 per year in wasted materials (see Table 5.2).

The information tools delivered data to the level of the organization that had direct responsibility for production. Local management was able to control costs more tightly. The system did little to save plant managers' time (a cost-displacement effect). Its primary advantage was better management. The value-added leverage is inherent in the value of the goods, and far exceeds the salary costs of those who produce them.

Proposing the Right Products

The issue of quality control is not limited to the factory; it applies to distribution channels as well. For example, selling computer systems requires that all parts be specified correctly on an order, and that they be compatible with existing customer equipment.

Richard A. Gariepy, manager of corporate sales productivity and automation programs for Digital Equipment Corporation, explained the magnitude of the distribution system's quality-control problem. Gariepy estimates that "there are over 64,000 different potential configurations of boards, backplanes, etc., for [DEC's] VAX-11/780 processors alone. The ability to mix and match products from such a broad spectrum sometimes leads to inadvertent errors in the selection of all necessary components." To make matters worse, complexity is growing as the industry moves toward a greater number of smaller computers, integrated networks, a greater variety of software and peripherals, and customer installation of the smaller systems. And as DEC's product line grows, the number of possible combinations grows exponentially.

In the past, DEC technical specialists inspected each order for technical completeness, compatibility, and appropriateness. "If problems occurred during the installation of the system," Gariepy says, "the customer was not burdened; but both the sales representatives and field engineering staff specified priority orders to obtain the correct parts—at DEC's expense."

DEC found that its technical specialists were overloaded, and became concerned about the spiraling expense of hiring enough specialists in the right locations to handle the demand. Using its own artificial-intelligence development tools, they built an interactive "rule-structured" database (called XCON) to check and validate all VAX orders for correctness and completeness. In parallel, a "sales language" inquiry system (XSEL) was provided as the equivalent of the best technical experts readily available at the time of the initial customer-needs assessment.

XSEL and XCON can configure ten families of processors, specify all necessary parts for new systems, aid in the selection of upgrading requirements, and help plan for future expansion. They provide guidelines on backplane and board arrangement, cabling, and physical room arrangement, accounting for floor loading, power, and air-conditioning requirements.

During fiscal year 1985, XSEL and XCON assisted in the development of over 6,500 proposals, conservatively estimated at more than 10 per cent of DEC's total number of proposals. Gariepy believes the system could grow to handle 75 per cent of the proposals.

The system is used both before and after the receipt of a customer's purchase order. It virtually eliminates the need for DEC to give away parts that were inadvertently omitted from the original order — called the "allowance for technical inaccuracy." At the current level of usage, Gariepy believes this could save DEC in excess of $10 million per year.

The system also reduces the effort necessary to complete a proposal. Sales staff can configure systems in 20 minutes instead of three to four hours, and can spend less time dealing with problems after the order has been placed. "If this time were used for selling at an average rate of return," says Gariepy, "it could generate additional revenues in excess of $40 million." If only 25 per cent of this were actually captured, the increased revenue would be over $10 million. Based on DEC's annual report, this would represent profits of over $2 million.

These two value-added effects together contributed over $12 million to DEC's bottom line in fiscal 1985. The cost of ongoing development and operation of the software, rule database, and computer systems, at DEC's customers' cost levels, is between $4 million and $5 million per year. Thus, the net benefit is at least $7 million per year. Gariepy believes that "as usage grows over the next five years, the benefits could grow by a factor of five" (see Table 5.3).

The productivity gains from this tool apply to technical experts, field engineers, and sales staff. In this case, there were a few hundred thousand dollars of cost-displacement benefits, which were dwarfed by the value-added benefits. The value-added leverage comes from identifying a step in the distribution process that affects large quantities of materials.

Table 5.3. Proposing the Right Products

Avoid giving away parts	$10,000,000
Sales time in expected revenue production	$40,000,000
Portion of freed time applied to selling	25%
Incremental revenues generated	$10,000,000
Profit contribution margin (from annual report)	20%
Incremental profits from sales generated	$2,000,000
Total benefit of system per year	$12,000,000
Operating costs per year (estimated, with enhancements)	$5,000,000
Net benefit per year	$7,000,000
Present value, five years, 10%	$27,000,000

DEC will not disclose the initial development costs of the system, since they are intertwined with their AI product-oriented research and development. Thus, we were unable to calculate their return on investment. With the aid of today's expert system development environments, however, AI projects can generate significant value-added leverage by archiving and making available scarce expertise in strategic areas of the organization.

Operational Efficiency

Production efficiency is the second pillar of operational effectiveness. In this context it is easy to confuse the concepts of cost-displacement and value-added. When tools are applied directly to the factory and its workers to make them more efficient, the benefits are counted in terms of productivity gains, or cost savings. This is an appropriate measure for factory automation.

Value-added leverage is gained from a different type of application. When the tools are used by managers to help run the production process, the effect is far greater than simply saving the manager time; efficiency gains ripple throughout the production process, providing value-added leverage.

In this section we look at three different types of production processes. One case describes the use of tools for scheduling the production facilities; another focuses on a different type of management planning, product design; the final case illustrates the challenge of maintaining plant and equipment.

Scheduling Production Capacity

In any capital-intensive industry, the scheduling of production facilities is critical to profitable operations. The quality of management planning affects the return on resources that cost far more than the manager's salary, offering an opportunity for value-added leverage.

Airlines must schedule aircraft on their routes just as factories schedule their machine tools on jobs. This is an extremely complex problem. For the airline to remain profitable, the size and capability of the equipment must match the demand throughout an intricate network of routes.

This scheduling challenge is more complex than merely matching supply to demand. There are limitations in the number and types of airplane each airport can handle. Crew scheduling must take into consideration the location of crew members trained in each type of aircraft. Every two or three days, each plane must spend a night in a city that has a mechanical shop for maintenance. Customer preferences (for example, for larger airplanes on longer flights) must be considered and accommodated to the extent possible. Related to the scheduling problem is the fact that airlines must constantly decide on which types of aircraft to buy and sell. Each type of aircraft, given its capacity, cost, and operating expense, will be profitable on some routes and not on others.

In the past, scheduling was done by hand. Decisions on changes in the fleet were analyzed on the assumption that new equipment replaced old without changing route assignments. In both cases, decisions were less than ideal and profits suffered.

One large airline company built a decision support model to assist in scheduling and fleet planning. This complex mathematical model helps planners find the most profitable use of current and proposed fleets, given a schedule of routes. The model cost approximately $500,000 to develop, and now costs about $350,000 per year to run. Each run of the model uses the mainframe computer overnight.

Although it uses conventional tools such as models and mainframe computers, this decision support system is an interactive tool rather than a routine data-processing system. OA is not limited to personal computers; in fact, as chapter 2 pointed out, tools that aid thinking have a history virtually as long as that of data processing.

The results of this well-placed decision support system are significant. Operating profit contributions have increased dramatically. Purchase decisions also were affected. For example, the airline had planned to sell its older small planes and buy new medium-sized craft; instead, it bought more small planes and sold some of its larger ones.

The model itself is used to calculate the profit contributions of the old and new schedules. Accounting for all factors, even for the difference in cost of capital for the new fleet plan, the director of strategic planning estimates the increase in after-tax profit contribution to be about $150 million per year, and expects this incremental profit to grow to $200 million as crew domiciles are adjusted. In spite of the cost of this complex system, the first year of use of the model produced a remarkable return on the airline's investment (see Table 5.4).

Since the airline industry is so capital-intensive, the efficient utilization of productive capacity is critical to success. The closely related problem of planning future production facilities is also addressed by the model. This application of decision support produces such high returns because it helps managers carry out planning tasks central

Table 5.4. Scheduling Production Capacity

Profit contribution per year	$150,000,000
Operating costs per year	$350,000
Net benefit per year	$149,650,000
Present value, five years, 10%	$567,000,000
Development cost	$500,000
One-year return on investment	30,000%
Five-year return on investment	110,000%

to the profitability of every aspect of the company. Similar opportunities to aid in production scheduling are likely to arise whenever the value of the productive capacity is large in comparison to the value of each product.

Building Roads Through the Forests

In other industries, production takes the form of large, unique projects. Here, scheduling of capacity may not be the primary issue. Since the value of each project is relatively large, its design may be the most critical determinant of costs.

We turn to the government in this case for an example of a project-oriented production process. The U.S. Department of Agriculture's Forest Service is responsible for managing the nation's forests to provide a variety of resources, including timber harvesting. Logging of national forest timber helps to meet a national resource need, and provides revenue to the U.S. treasury.[2]

When timber is harvested, several different types of transportation are needed to move logs from the forest to the mills. First, the logs must be moved from where they are felled to central locations for loading onto trucks. This step is called "yarding" and is accomplished by tractors or a system of long cables. Next, the logs must be hauled by truck to the mills. This requires an extensive system of roads that vary all the way from low-speed, single-track roads to higher-speed, double-lane facilities similar to local highways. Using fewer roads means that the logs must be dragged farther to get them to the trucks; conversely, increasing the expenditures on roads will reduce yarding costs. The integration of these different types of transportation, their cost, and the efficiency with which they operate have a significant effect on the revenues received from the sale of timber.

In the past, roads were planned by Forest Service engineers using a batch computer system to process field data and analyze costs. Although the batch system had significantly improved the engineers' ability to analyze and optimize the various components of the transportation system, its slow turnaround time severely limited the number of alternatives that could be considered, and the laborious process kept engineering staff fully occupied planning basic construction of the high-volume roads.

Rex Hartgraves, associate deputy chief for administration, reports that in 1978 the Forest Service installed intelligent terminals and personal computers. These decision support systems include a geographic database and specific topographic contour studies, equations on the placing of yarding cables and support towers and road landings, the value of timber, the costs of various road networks, and the impacts on the visual quality of the landscape. Outputs are both numeric and graphic, and alternatives can be considered in a matter of minutes.

By using this distributed decision support system, the engineers were able to correct errors locally, thereby saving at least one day-long iteration through the batch system. This, combined with many other productivity gains, allowed the shrinking staff of engineers to build an increasing number of miles of roads. The Forest Service estimates that it gained a 500 per cent increase in engineering design productivity, worth $2.5 million annually in cost savings. These benefits, however, are small when compared to the value-added benefits.

The use of interactive work stations allows the forest engineers to look at more variables and examine more alternatives. In addition to basic road design, the engineers are able to expand their predesign — "transportation" planning — which locates the approximate position and path of a road by considering alternative routes through the terrain. According to Clyde Weller, a Forest Service engineer, they now have the ability to examine many more alternative locations than one or two, and they could not have done so with their level of staffing using the prior batch or manual system.

Experience has shown that greater gains in transportation efficiency can be achieved by better planning at this early stage. By simulating a variety of transportation network configurations, planners are able to determine the most cost-efficient total transportation system. For example, in one area of the southwest United

States that they studied, they found that the density of roads ranged between six and 20 miles of road per square mile of forest, when the optimum (considering yarding and road densities) was between two and four. Had transportation planning on interactive decision support systems been available at the time they were built, the Forest Service could have saved the costs of 60 to 80 per cent of the roads.

More typically, Weller is confident that transportation planning has reduced road mileage by at least 20 per cent; he is 70 per cent sure that it has reduced road mileage by 30 per cent; and he is 50 per cent sure of a 40 per cent impact. His best guess (the expected value of this probability distribution) was a 32 per cent reduction in miles of road built. Transportation planning and road design were applicable to about 60 per cent of the $460 million (8,800-mile) road budget in fiscal 1985, for a net savings of nearly 1,700 miles of road that would have cost $88.3 million.

When road density is reduced, yarding costs may rise, since the loggers will have to drag the logs farther to reach the nearest road. Weller and Charles Fudge of the Forest Service timber staff estimate that yarding costs for the affected logging rose at least 5 per cent; there is a 67 per cent chance that they went up at least 10 per cent; and there is a 25 per cent chance costs went up by 15 per cent. The expected value of his estimate is a 9.6 per cent increase in 60 per cent of the yarding budget of about $385 million, for an increase in costs of roughly $22 million.

Thus, the net benefit of intelligent work stations for road design is about $66 million per year, less operating costs of about $1.25 million per year, for an annual net benefit of nearly $65 million.

The costs of the intelligent work stations were about $1.8 million for hardware, $1.6 million for the network infrastructure, and $500,000 for software, for a total of about $3.9 million. The system is used about 75 per cent of the time for road design; considering only the benefits derived from transportation planning, the return on this investment was over 6,200 per cent (see Table 5.5).

The design of roads affects the cost of logging operations; it is a critical success factor in the timber-harvesting process. In this case, decision support systems reduced the cost of building roads, a significant portion of the cost of making timber available to loggers.

Value-added leverage was gained in two ways. First, the tools made key engineers more effective; their designs were more cost-effective to build. Second, further leverage was gained when better design not only reduced the cost per mile of road, but also reduced the number of miles of road that had to be built. The Forest Service benefited from

Table 5.5.   Building Roads Through the Forest

ODDS	REDUCTION OF ROADS
100%	20%
70%	30%
50%	40%
Expected value of reduction in roads	32%
Portion of roads subject to transportation planning	60%
Budget for roads	$460,000,000
Cost savings for roads	$88,300,000
ODDS	INCREASE IN YARDING
100%	5%
67%	10%
25%	15%
Expected value of increase in yarding costs	9.6%
Portion of yarding subject to transportation planning	60%
Budget for yarding	$385,000,000
Increased cost of yarding	$22,200,000
Net savings in transportation per year	$66,100,000
Operating costs per year	$1,250,000
Net benefit per year	$65,000,000
Present value, five years, 10%	$246,000,000
Development cost	$3,900,000
One-year return on investment	1,600%
Five-year return on investment	6,200%

engineering time savings that resulted from interactive decision support systems; but the value-added benefits far exceed productivity
gains, just as the costs of timber harvesting far exceed the salary costs
of forest engineers.

Maintaining Power Plants

In addition to producing the product or service of the organization,
operational managers are responsible for maintaining plant and

equipment. Downtime can be extremely expensive, since overhead costs continue while profit-making potential is lost forever.

OA can help manage maintenance. A remarkable case was reported by a supplier of large power plants, which stations full-time staff at each of the approximately 30 customer sites worldwide to ensure the smooth operation of equipment. These site managers submitted bimonthly technical reports, which were distributed to managers of similar plants within the region. In addition, the site managers might voluntarily communicate with managers of similar plants. Bimonthly reports were also sent to headquarters, where they might subsequently be investigated and sent to other regions in the form of technical reports.[3]

All site managers now use electronic mail to share daily reports in concise outline format. Technical bulletins are broadcast through the electronic mail system as they are published. In one instance, a problem with a pump that was identified in one plant also affected another plant. Since the other plant was in a different region and was dissimilar except for the pump in question, it would not have gotten the information prior to its shutdown for preventive maintenance.

With the electronic mail system, the other plant was notified and the problem was corrected by preventive maintenance (a $170,000 sale of equipment service). Had the problem gone unidentified, there was a chance that the pump might have failed in the year and a half before the next scheduled maintenance. Unscheduled outages cost the customer about $1 million per day.

Because of the high cost of downtime, maintenance was a crucial success factor in this organization. The company saw that more timely sharing of experiences among plant managers could enhance the effectiveness of each. Preventing a single day of downtime will pay for the entire cost of this electronic mail system.

Information as a Product

So far in this chapter, OA has been seen to have an indirect effect on the production process by improving the effectiveness of operations managers. Direct application of computing and telecommunications technologies have been left to the domain of process automation — the automated factory and warehouse. This distinction blurs when information is a significant part of the product or service.

In this section, we look at a small subset of those industries that produce information-based products. We have selected companies in which information is the primary product. There are many other industries in which information is an important, but not predominant, part of the product. While the value-added leverage in these other markets is reduced, similar opportunities should be available.

We begin with an example from a personnel agency — part of an industry that provides a data-based service. The legal industry is another in which the processing of information is inherent in the service. The remainder of the section describes news services, where information itself is the product.

Matching People to Jobs

Bob Gill Associates, Inc. is an executive recruiting firm in New York City. When companies seek to hire staff, Bob Gill Associates is one of a number of firms that are called upon to supply candidates. It accepts assignments on both a search and a contingency basis. The company's profits depend on its ability to match candidates to jobs before competitors can supply the "right" person. Although successful matching requires experience and intuition, personnel search is essentially a data-based service.

Bob Gill, president of the agency, and his vice-president, Ray Meister, vividly remember a case where they worked late into the night on a search for a management position in Connecticut, only to lose it to a competitor. The accepted candidate had been in their files, but they passed over his resumé. They feel that they lost $8,000 in fees because their manual search through paper files was too time-consuming, tedious, and error-prone.

Recognizing the company's dependence on information, Gill acquired a personal computer as soon as they became available, and he hired a consultant to program a database management system to handle both company and applicant files. Applicants are coded by their professional specialty, their location, and a variety of other traits.

Gill recounts a happier incident that occurred after the computer was installed. He received a request for a similar position, this time in New York City. He spent 10 minutes searching the online database and immediately sent three resumés to the company. One of his candidates was hired only three weeks later, generating about $6,000 in fees.

"We use the computer every 10 to 20 minutes throughout the day," says Gill. He feels it helps him to match applicants to jobs more quickly, a major advantage in this highly competitive market. Furthermore, he feels the quality of his candidates is higher — that is,

they are better matched to the requirements of the client company —
because the computer alows him to consider more resumés. "I don't
feel I've left any stone unturned," says Gill.

Gill felt the beneficial effects of the online database within four
months of its installation. He is sure that the $15,000 computer (with
programming) paid for itself within two months. Although his staff
has not grown, his revenues certainly have. Comparing 1983, when
he was completing about 10 placements per month, with 1982, when
his firm completed only five to six, Gill says, "Conservatively speak-
ing, I think the computer increased our revenue by 75 to 100 per cent"
(see Table 5.6).

Table 5.6.   Matching People to Jobs

Net benefit per year (projecting first 2 months)	$90,000
Present value, five years, 10%	$341,000
Development cost	$15,000
One-year return on investment	500%
Five-year return on investment	2,200%

Since matching profiles to the database was the essence of the
company's work, a personal computer provided an affordable opportunity to apply technology to Gill Associates' operations. Gill's
description of the impacts emphasizes improvements in quality over
productivity. It should be noted that company billings depend
equally on quality (the success rate in finding the right person) and
quantity (the number of searches the company undertakes).

A law firm is another professional information-processing enter-
prise. As is now common in the industry, Shearman and Sterling, one
of the largest law firms in New York, uses communicating word
processors to prepare new documents online, store standard contracts
and paragraphs, file client reports, and telecommunicate documents
worldwide.[4]

The tools in the hands of lawyers as well as of administrative staff
have a variety of benefits. Standard text can be fine-tuned over time,
as experience is gained. New versions of documents can be distributed instantly to all offices by telecommunication. The ability to
share documents avoids time wasted on reinventing wording and
enforces consistency across offices; it may also help large firms with

multiple offices to share workload, so as to better handle peak loads and specialist assignments.

The textual database may actually improve the quality of decision making in some cases. Easy document indexing and search capabilities allow lawyers to find a client's other contracts that may impinge on a decision. Furthermore, a law firm's ability to assemble contracts quickly is of significant value to many clients, particularly in the financial services industry.

In a partnership such as a personnel search or law firm, investments in OA directly reduce profits and personal income. The commitment of the partners to OA in these cases offers evidence that the tools produce an information edge. The database management system gave Gill Associates an information edge that they used to double the size of the firm. When OA is applied to the central operational processes in such information-intensive service industries, its value-added leverage is in its direct impact on profits.

Online Publishing

Direct impacts of OA on operations are also found in the publishing industry. An example is provided by American Hospital Publishing Inc. (AHPI), publishers of journals and newsletters of interest to health care institutions. AHPI supplied all of its writers and editors with word processors. According to Wes Curry, a former manager of publications, reporters use the word processor to take notes quietly during telephone interviews, making subsequent writing easier. They produce copy more quickly, and it is generally better organized.

In addition to time savings, AHPI feels more able to produce special features and inserts. Writers have more time for reading and research and feel less stress, leading to better writing. In the process of their daily operation, AHPI is automatically building a machine-readable database for future ventures in electronic publishing.

The word processors also help speed the production process, not just through productivity-based time savings but by the redesign of the actual process. The editorial staff have eliminated proofreading after typing and typesetting. The editor makes comments directly in the online copy, giving clearer feedback to the writer in half the time that editing took on paper. AHPI found significant cost savings in the smaller number of corrections required of the typesetting department, and has experienced fewer missed deadlines since the word processor was installed.

Ted Isaacman, director of the periodicals editorial division, feels that the word processor is a necessary competitive tool for AHPI. By reducing delays in the production process by at least one week, journals and newsletters carry more timely information, which is of significant perceived value to readers.

By this time, AHPI's competitors also have word processors for their editorial staff. If AHPI's information was even one week less timely, there would be some loss in their controlled circulation. More important, there would be a loss in readership. Isaacman is 90 per cent sure that the loss would be at least 5 per cent, 75 per cent sure it would be at least 10 per cent, and 50 per cent sure it would be at least 15 per cent, for an expected loss in readership of 10.75 per cent. A 10 per cent loss of readership, as shown in market surveys, would mean a loss in advertising revenues, which Isaacman estimates at $80,000 per year (see Table 5.7). This lost advertising revenue directly affects the bottom line, since the variable costs are insignificant. The payback period for the word processors is less than one year. In this case, OA tools for authors have become a competitive necessity as they have become commonplace in the publishing industry.

In the case of newspapers, timeliness is even more important and competition even more fierce. OA has prospered in the hands of

Table 5.7. Online Publishing

ODDS	LOSS IN READERSHIP
90%	5%
75%	10%
50%	15%
Expected lost readership	10.75%

ODDS	IMPACT OF 10% LOSS OF READERSHIP ON ADVERTISING REVENUE
100%	$50,000
60%	$100,000
Expected value of lost advertising revenue	$80,000

Net benefit per year, prevented loss of revenue	$80,000
Present value, five years, 10%	$300,000

Development cost (estimated)	$25,000

One-year return on investment	220%
Five-year return on investment	1,100%

professional writers. A comprehensive example is provided by Ritzau Bureau, a news service agency in Copenhagen that provides news to publications throughout Denmark.[5]

Bent Larsen, their information systems executive, explained how electronic mail helped Ritzau in its coverage of the 1984 summer Olympic games in Los Angeles. The various events were spread all over the metropolitan area, with some events taking place as far away as San Diego and San Francisco (a six-hour drive). Therefore, although Ritzau had a central office in California, in the interests of timeliness the reporters relayed stories directly to Copenhagen from the location of each event using portable terminals and electronic mail.

The 11-hour time difference compounded the problem. In the past, Ritzau would have had a secretary working all night to take calls (with a high risk of inaccuracy in the stories). When stories were sent via telex, they had to be retyped in Denmark. Using electronic mail, Ritzau saved the cost of all-night help, and felt the system improved the accuracy of the reporting.

Ritzau has also provided reporters with word-processing tools. Lars Rasmussen, a diplomatic correspondent, says that writing on the word processor is easier and faster. "I can write more stories and they get to the subscribers faster. The stories are probably more accurate ... Often new developments can cause five or six versions of a story to appear in a single day. It is much easier to update stories during the day [with a word processor]."

Once it is gathered, news must be placed in inventory, and then quickly assembled into a publication. The combination of word processing and electronic mail allows Ritzau to store and catalogue stories online. The company finds this more reliable than telephone and telex. For example, one day all the wires went down for two hours, making it impossible for the agency to receive and publish news. Rasmussen explains, "People just kept feeding their stories into the computer, and when the outage was over there were 110 stories waiting to be transmitted." By setting priorities online, the editor was able to get the most important stories out on time in spite of the two-hour loss of communications.

A case drawn from the television industry further illustrates this later stage in the news production process. The throughput of the news-processing organization was put to the test when, on January 17, 1983, the British Broadcasting Corporation (BBC) initiated its first breakfast-time television program. Such a long program had never been broadcast in Britain during the day, nor had a program been aired so early in the day. Furthermore, breakfast television incorporates more "sequences" — many short film clips — than any other programming.[6]

The BBC's solution was to automate the office. The system takes information from the wire service. It maintains a database that allows easy access to stories in progress, program schedules (called diaries), past news events, and research on people and places to use in future stories.

The cost-displacement effects on the administrative workload justify the system. Tam Fry, the BBC manager responsible for the implementation of the system, states, "The system cost 600,000 British pounds. The 15 people we would have been obliged to add would have cost much more by now. I would estimate that the system paid for itself within three years." Fry speaks with even more enthusiasm about the value-added benefits. "What this means for us," he says, "is that more meaningful information is available to the editor, and that results in a more meaningful program — which is our primary goal." As evidence that the system allows the BBC to produce a better-quality program, consider this example. One morning at 8:58 A.M. a news bulletin came in on the wire service reporting a bombing in Paris. The news program ends at 9 A.M.. In the remaining two minutes and 20 seconds, the editor was able to review the story and send it directly to the teleprompter in the studio, just in time for the news reader to include it in the program. Says Fry, "With the old system, we wouldn't have even come close to being able to include the story." The combined database and direct feed to the teleprompter resulted in a greatly increased ability to report accurate, timely, and varied news.

In the news industry, one of the most critical resources is the reporting staff. At both AHPI and Ritzau, OA tools were applied directly to news gathering and editing. Equally important is an organization's ability to assemble news into a publication issue or broadcast; both Ritzau and the BBC use OA for that. The impacts of writing tools to a publisher extend beyond the cost-displacement benefits of productivity. The quality of work, in terms of timeliness and content, is also at stake. OA helped AHPI, Ritzau, and the BBC to improve both. The value-added leverage was measured in the quality of the news, and ultimately in market share.

OA and Operations

This chapter has shown a number of ways in which OA can aid manufacturing and distribution operations. In the first two sections, the tools were used to improve managerial effectiveness, and the value-added leverage was gained from the impact of the managers on high-value productive resources. Cases included process and product manufacturing. The critical success factors were process efficiency and quality control, product design, project management, distribution, and maintenance. Users included engineers, plant managers, and corporate planners. They utilized decision support systems, corporate databases, and electronic mail.

The last section considered those industries in which information is the primary component of the product. Cases included information-processing professionals such as personnel-search and law firms, a periodicals publisher, a newspaper, and a television news program. The tools were given to the writers and to those who assemble information into its final form. They used word processors, electronic mail, and database management systems.

OA opportunities in operational functions are found in two areas: stages of the production process at which decision making is critical, and products and services that are based on information. In either case, the value-added benefits are likely to dwarf productivity gains, just as the profit resulting from the operation exceeds the salaries of manufacturing personnel.

Notes

1. The authors thank James Herget of Lamalie Associates for the introduction to this case.
2. The authors thank Pat Riemitis of Data General for the introduction to this case.
3. The authors thank Linda M. Richman for this case.
4. N. Dean Meyer, "The Productivity Impacts of Word Processing," *National Productivity Review* 2, no. 3 (Summer 1983)
5. The authors thank Jan Bender of Digital Equipment Corporation (Denmark) for the introduction to this case.
6. The authors thank Matthew Young, formerly of the British Civil Service Central Computer and Communications Agency, for the introduction to this case.

People Management

Virtually every functional area of business is dependent on its managers' ability to supervise people. OA can be used to enhance managerial effectiveness in a variety of ways; this chapter provides examples of the use of tools in people management.

We begin by looking at three types of supervisors: line, staff, and project managers. The first section illustrates the use of OA tools by line managers in the direct supervision of their employees; the value-added benefits result from making better use of people's time. The cases in the second section are less direct; the tools helped staff groups to encourage productivity improvement programs throughout the organization. The third section considers the problems of project management; OA tools were used to build collaboration across organizational boundaries. The final section addresses organization-wide people-management issues. We look first at the role of OA in reorganization projects. The remaining cases are drawn from the staff human-resource management function. The first three sections are relevant to every manager; the final section will be of special interest to human-resource professionals and top executives.

Supervising People

Good management depends to a great extent on interpersonal skills, an area in which OA has little impact. Another important aspect of supervision, however, is the decision making that guides the utilization of people's time. Here OA can make a significant contribution. This section describes the use of three different tools by line managers to allocate people in the most productive ways.

Since we are ultimately measuring productivity, the distinction between cost-displacement and value-added benefits may become confusing. Let's clarify our terms in advance. If the tool is applied to save the user time, the application is termed "cost-displacement," and there is no leverage—that is, the benefits equal the cost of the time saved by the user. If the tool makes a manager smarter, and the manager in turn makes many people more productive, then there is significant leverage. Since the direct benefit is managerial effectiveness rather than a saving of time, the application is termed "value-added."

Allocating Service Staff

The first step in allocating staff resources in the most effective manner is to understand the nature and extent of the workload. OA tools can help a manager gain perspectives on trends and patterns in the demand for the group's services. The following case describes a first-line manager who creatively used a database management system to analyze workloads.

Barry Miller is responsible for maintaining and upgrading 35 telephone switching centers spread throughout the southeast area of a Canadian province. When he was given the responsibilities of supervisor in their network services group, he inherited 13 "craft" workers who responded to trouble calls and installed new equipment. He found them to be busy "fighting fires" throughout a wide geographic area.

It would be easy to assume that "fire-fighting" is the nature of the repair business. Miller is an innovator, however; he sought a more systematic way to manage his hard-working staff.

In the past, "trouble tickets" were received from the field on paper. They were tallied at the end of each month on a report and then filed in boxes. This system made further analysis virtually impossible, particularly when historical data were involved.

Miller began entering all trouble reports, automatic alarms, and customer service records on a database on his personal computer. The database made it possible to maintain a detailed history of problems for analysis. Miller defined four reports that helped him look for patterns and trends in reliability problems, by types of equipment, by causes of trouble, and other key factors. He was able to anticipate problems and correct them before they caused outages. Particularly in the smaller offices, which are difficult to travel to and where the lighter traffic means it takes longer to discover a problem, the database allowed Miller to find the source of problems sooner. For example, in one small office that reported poor performance, he traced the problem to one group of subscribers. The people processing over 100 trouble reports a day were not in a position to notice this pattern.

Miller's database helped him get the problem fixed approximately one year earlier than it otherwise would have been. Furthermore, Miller was able to allocate his people so as to perform preventive maintenance more effectively. Given the substantial travel distances in his territory, this planning created significant productivity gains for field repair workers.

As a result of the better planning, which Miller credits to his database, he reduced his staff of 13 to 12 after one year, and to 11 in the second year. Miller's manager estimates that in the same period the quality of service in his area has improved by at least 30 per cent.

Miller states that he might have been able to reduce his staff by one person without the database, but certainly not by two. Each craft worker requires an average salary of $35,000 and benefits of at least $10,000. It appears that the $5,000 personal computer produced a reduction of expenses of $45,000 per year (a 900 per cent return on investment in the first year alone, or a payback period of about six weeks). The value-added leverage is in helping the manager to manage rather than in saving minutes of the manager's time (see Table 6.1).

Table 6.1.   Allocating Service Staff

Positions released without OA	1
Positions released with OA	2
Cost of position per year	$45,000
Present value, five years, 10%	$171,000
Development cost	$5,000
One-year return on investment	800%
Five-year return on investment	3,300%

Note that the tool was not used to save Miller time — that would be simple cost-displacement. Rather, the database management system was used to help him understand workloads, anticipate and prevent problems, and optimize his staff's schedules. The manager's better scheduling and allocation of work made all 11 members of his staff more productive, and created the value-added leverage.

Allocating Resources

In Miller's case, understanding the changing nature of the workload was critical to his success; he had responsibility for just one type of worker (the telephone repair technicians). In other cases, success in supervision may require the manager to have various kinds of professionals perform a greater variety of tasks. In the next case, a spreadsheet was used to plan staffing at various levels of the organization to match the changing demands placed on the department.

The Export Credits Guarantee Department (ECGD) of the British government encourages trade by insuring companies that export British goods. The claims department in the Cardiff office paid 11,500 claims totalling over £800 million in the year ending March 1985.[1]

Gordon Cochrane, assistant secretary in charge of the claims division, manages 150 people, from clerks to senior managers. Claims range from very small amounts to millions of pounds. The higher the value of the claim, the more senior the examiner to which it is assigned. Cochrane had few data available on the distribution of claims by value. "To get that information [in the past] would have been a monumental clerical task, with prohibitive costs," Cochrane says. He was forced to manage the group using only summary data on the total workload and staff levels. This made it difficult to budget for staff requirements at the various levels; as the workload grew, Cochrane found it difficult to decide whether a larger clerical or senior examiner staff was warranted.

David Baird, manager of the ECGD Information Center, provided Cochrane with a personal computer, but did not have time to set the computer up or to train him. When he returned two weeks later to help set up the PC, he found Cochrane already working with a spreadsheet. With the spreadsheet, Cochrane was able to track his division's workload by the type and value of claim. He was able to compare workloads with staffing by grade level and the cost of staff. This gave him a rough indication of the cost-effectiveness of staffing resources. "We were never able to do that before," says Cochrane. "The PC allowed me to demonstrate more convincingly the costs of processing claims at the different staff levels, and ultimately it will assist in identifying the extent to which I need particular types of staff people."

By analyzing workloads, Cochrane was better able to match staffing levels by grade to workload by value of claims. He was also able to build a database that helped him identify patterns and trends in the workload. This not only facilitates budget planning, but also allows him to utilize slack time during slow periods by planning longer-term tasks that otherwise would not be a priority.

The net effect was to identify how a different mix of staff in certain grades could have reduced staff costs by about £50,000 in 1985 while maintaining or improving service levels. Cochrane estimates with 90 per cent certainty that in 1986 he can achieve at least another £25,000 reduction, for a total of £75,000 per year. Cochrane says, "Without the information from the computer, I'd have no idea how I could go about doing this." Thus, the net benefit from this use of his £5,000 personal computer with spreadsheet software is nearly £245,000 in staff time (see Table 6.2).

Table 6.2. Allocating Resources

1985 savings	£50,000
1986 and beyond annual savings (forecasted)	£75,000
Certainty of £25,000 increase in annual impact	90%
Expected value of 1986 savings	£67,500
Present value, 1986-89, 10%, 1985 pounds	£195,000
Total present value, five years, 10%	£245,000
Development cost	£5,000
One-year return on investment	900%
Five-year return on investment	4,800%

The spreadsheet was not used to save Cochrane time, but to improve his planning skills. Cochrane analyzed the changing workload and simulated the allocation of jobs to levels of staff. The spreadsheet helped Cochrane find the distribution of people to match the workload. This made his department operate with greater efficiency, producing the value-added leverage.

Utilizing Slack Time

The two preceding cases illustrate the role of OA in helping managers plan the use of their staff. But plans are of little value if they cannot be implemented. The next case shows the use of a different kind of tool, a voice message system, that aids a manager in day-to-day supervision to ensure good use of staff time.

Every consulting company seeks to keep its people as busy as possible on paid work, minimizing their "unsold" time. When consultants are not busy on client projects, time should be spent on "business development"--that is, marketing or selling new clients.

A principal in the information systems practice of a Boston consulting company explains the difficulty of getting the most from his staff of 10 consultants: "When I'm visiting a client, one of my consultants may be back in the office with some free time. It's hard for me to break loose from a meeting with the client to call the office and put him to work on a business development project. When I do call, my consultant may be away from his phone. Also, I may have an idea that evening, back in my hotel room; it's even harder to reach people then. We used to waste a lot of time this way."

In 1985, the company installed a voice message system. The consultants check their voice mailboxes at least three times a day, and internal communications have improved significantly. The manager reports that his staff is 83 per cent "sold," leaving 17 per cent of their time for office tasks. In the past, he estimates, he utilized only 10 per cent of that time for business development; with the voice message system, he feels he is now utilizing at least 40 per cent.

The manager tracks his staff's progress on business development projects using a database management system on a microcomputer. Every opportunity is carefully monitored, and the database is analyzed in periodic status review meetings.

Better coordination pays off in other ways as well. For example, the manager was held up with a client and was likely to be late for an afternoon sales call to be conducted with one of his consultants. The manager did not have the necessary materials with him, and would not have time to go back to his office as planned. The materials were critical to the sale; the firm intended to supply a set of written standards and procedures, and hoped to show the prospect the table of contents. The consultant was also meeting with a client that morning, and was impossible to reach.

With the voice message system, the manager was able to tell the consultant to bring the materials with him. The system improved the odds of getting in touch with the consultant from 50 per cent to 100 per cent. The use of the material improved the odds of winning the sale from 10 per cent to 90 per cent, a difference of 80 per cent. Thus, the system contributed an additional 40 per cent chance of winning the $50,000 sale. Since the firm's margins are about 20 per cent, the system produced an expected increase in profits of $4,000.

The average growth rate of this consulting company's information systems practice nationwide has been about 30 per cent. The manager is confident that without the voice message system and the database management system he could match that average, and he feels 80 per cent sure that he could produce a growth in revenues of 35 per cent on a base of $1.3 million in 1984. His expected growth rate would have been 34 per cent, creating incremental revenue of about $442,000.

Table 6.3.   Utilizing Slack Time

Slack time available	17%
Portion used for marketing before OA	10%
Portion used for marketing with OA	40%

Expected growth in practice without OA:	
ODDS	EXPECTED GROWTH
100%	30%
80%	35%
Expected value	34%
Expected value of incremental revenues	$442,000

Expected growth in practice with OA:	
ODDS	EXPECTED GROWTH
100%	45%
90%	50%
80%	57%
Expected value	55.1%
Expected value of incremental revenues	$716,000

Incremental revenue growth credited to OA	$274,000
Average profit margin	20%

Net benefit per year	$55,000
Present value, five years, 10%	$208,000

Development cost	$13,000

One-year return on investment	320%
Five-year return on investment	1,500%

With the tools, the manager is committed to increasing his practice by 57 per cent. He feels 80 per cent sure of attaining this goal, 90 per cent sure of 50 per cent growth, and certain of at least 45 per cent growth. His expected growth rate is 55.1 per cent, with increased revenues of $716,000. The tools produced an incremental expected growth in revenues of $274,000, for additional profits of about $55,000.

The microcomputer and the group's share of the voice message system cost about $13,000, for a return on investment of over 300 per cent in the first year alone. The expected present value of the tools over five years (discounted at 10 per cent) is approximately $200,000, even assuming that they provide no help in successive years of growth (see Table 6.3).

As is often the case, the manager was not able to supervise his people directly each day. Because he and his staff travel a great deal, communication difficulties constrained his supervisory abilities. The voice message system bridged that communication gap, and helped him direct available staff time to the most productive uses.

Once again, these cases can be analyzed in value-added terms. The voice message system may have saved the manager a bit of time; however, he found far greater value in the improved quality of communication. The value-added leverage was in improving the productivity of others, not just of the system's user.

Productivity

Value-added leverage is not limited to direct supervision; the multiplier effect occurs whenever improved effectiveness in one area results in improved productivity in many others. This section presents two cases in which the initiatives of staff groups encouraged productivity throughout the line organization. In the first case, OA helped a central staff group support an organization-wide productivity program. In the second case, a staff group responsible for performance monitoring used OA to isolate problems and motivate decentralized solutions.

Encouraging Productivity Initiatives

Many organizations are now implementing organization-wide productivity programs aimed at encouraging all employees to suggest more efficient ways of operating the business. These programs are typically supported by a staff group that encourages and coordinates decentralized efforts. When OA makes this central staff group more effective, an increase in productivity initiatives throughout the organization can result.

The maintenance division of a branch of the U.S. armed forces is responsible for the repair and maintenance of equipment and weapons systems. In the early 1970s, the division faced severe budgetary constraints. Managers realized that they would have to increase their productivity significantly in order to meet their objectives.

After nearly a decade of productivity-improvement efforts, the department felt a need to track and publicize these initiatives more effectively. In 1983 people known as "productivity principals" were hired in their seven maintenance centers to document productivity initiatives.

Headquarters staff found that the resulting paperwork was difficult to manage and analyze. Each request for ideas or summary reports required time-consuming research. Herman Adams, then manager of the maintenance professional information center, developed a productivity-initiatives database using a personal computer and an off-the-shelf database management package. The system allows headquarters staff to catalogue productivity forms and generate reports on behalf of the centers.

Headquarters staff is using the time that the system saved to work with the centers to develop more productivity reports for initiatives that were known of but not formally reported, and to ensure that the data are accurate. As a result, many more initiatives are being tracked: in fiscal 1985, the database grew to 925 initiatives worth over $500 million in annual productivity gains. In the process, headquarters data are more accessible and accurate. With the computer, answers to queries about what others are doing are comprehensive, rather than consisting of just a few handy examples.

Improvement in headquarters' tracking of productivity initiatives has had a number of beneficial effects. For example, headquarters is better able to cross-fertilize good ideas from one center to the other six. In October 1985, a report of all initiatives at all locations was developed and distributed to the seven centers. Almer Reese, then manager of productivity-improvement programs support, said that such a report would not have been produced without the online database.

Because the centers are constantly looking for productivity opportunities, the report was well received. Reese says it could stimulate as many as 75 new initiatives, and he is certain it prompted at least 10 to 12 productivity initiatives that otherwise would not have occurred.

We might conservatively assume that productivity initiatives worth more than $100,000 were being reported and discussed without the aid of the system. The smaller initiatives had an average value (after implementation costs) of $20,000 per year. Thus, the most conservative estimate of the impact of the report is an additional $200,000 in annual productivity savings. These initiatives will result in savings every year from now on. Taken over five years (discounted at 10 per cent), the initiatives generated by the report have a present value of $758,000.

In addition to explicit cross-feeding of ideas, headquarters staff publicizes the entire productivity program in newsletters and magazines distributed throughout the Pentagon, in trade publications, and in internal reports. Instead of using a few well-known examples over and over, the database allows new ideas and successes of different centers to be reported. According to Adams, this is likely to stimulate additional initiatives.

The personal computer cost about $3,000, and development expenses were less than $1,000. Time spent loading the database might have cost as much as $9,000, for a total cost of no more than $13,000. Thus, the return on the investment in a personal computer (ignoring its many other uses) is over 5,000 per cent (see Table 6.4).

It is conceivable that the same effect could have been gained by significantly enlarging the size of the central staff group. In this case, however, additional headcount was unavailable, in spite of the significant leverage the headquarters function has on department-wide productivity. Furthermore, the database management system gave this small staff group more than a quantitative increase in their

Table 6.4.   Encouraging Productivity Initiatives

Number of initiatives generated by the report	10
Average annual contribution of small initiatives	$20,000
Incremental productivity gains due to cross-feeding	$200,000
Present value, five years, 10%	$758,000
Net contribution of system in first year	$758,000
Present value, five years, 10%, if system stays in use	$2,900,000
Development cost	$13,000
One-year return on investment	5,700%
Five-year return on investment	22,000%

personal productivity; it improved the effectiveness of their work by allowing them to organize and report productivity initiative data.

The success of the staff group depends on its ability to influence decentralized staff. OA allowed the group to be more useful through cross-feeding ideas, and made its publicity more convincing. The tools probably saved some time, but the value-added leverage was in the additional productivity programs that the group stimulated throughout the organization.

Field Service Efficiency

Even when an organization has not developed an explicit productivity program, there is much that staff groups can do to encourage and assist line management in improving productivity. This second case demonstrates the use of OA to move a staff group from passively tracking results to actively solving problems.

General Telephone and Electronics' (GTE) General Telephone Company of the South has a "budgets and results" group charged with tracking the performance of all of the company's various service measures. In the past, the group's efforts were spent on developing reasonable measures of service and producing reports to management. The group had little time for special investigations and problem-correction projects.

With the introduction of online database query tools and personal-computer-based spreadsheets, the activities of the group changed considerably. The increase in analytic productivity provided additional time, which was used to analyze issues and alternative explanations of problems, verify results, and provide in-depth analyses of the potential causes of each problem. Furthermore, the group began to prepare management reports that showed historic trends, including charts and graphs that more clearly communicated the problems and motivated management actions.

H. Bryan Edwards, the budgets and results group manager, believes that these tools, in combination with staff who are well-versed in telephone operations, have allowed GTE to identify and bring to management's attention a larger number of problems. This in turn has led to a significant increase in the number of corrective actions taken. As Edwards's director says, "If you want to improve something, measure it." Furthermore, more in-depth analyses have improved the understanding of causes of changes in service measures, and have made corrective actions somewhat more effective.

The impacts on the performance of the telephone company have been widespread. One service measure demonstrates the significance of the contribution of these new analyses. In 1984, the company experienced a 2.5-hour drop in repair time per 100 lines, resulting in a $10 million cost saving per year. Of this drop, one hour can be credited to a decrease in the number of stations per line, leaving a real improvement in repair productivity of 1.5 hours per 100 lines. Edwards feels that at least half of the corrective actions, accounting for 0.75 of the 2.5 hours of improvement in repair time per 100 lines, would not have occurred without the OA tools (even if the group had been given more staff). Thus, the benefit of this one application of decision support tools can be valued at about $3 million per year.

Edwards describes the tools as a lever for cultural change in his group that brought about an investigative analytic culture: "OA didn't get me $3 million; it gave me the vehicle to enable people to become more proficient and productive with their analytical abilities, which [in turn allowed them to] introduce cost-effective measures."

The company's use of the tools expanded in 1985. As a result of the availability of service measures, they began an internal contest modeled on the U.S. Civil War. The company was divided into two segments; one was responsible for the northern part of the territory, the other for the southern. A spreadsheet is used to calculate 10 service measures for each of the 10 divisions every month. Points are awarded for each monthly "battle," and are accumulated through the year.

The Civil War program has been extremely well received, and is being taken very seriously by all levels of management. The director of the group pointed out, "Now they're trying to change their MBO [goals] to win the war; they didn't do that when just their salary incentives depended on them!" The director estimated that the competition will have at least a 1 per cent impact on service measures; his group managers felt his estimate was conservative. In cost containment alone, a 1 per cent improvement is worth about $1.5 million per year. All concurred that the program would not have been possible without the additional time and analytical capabilities generated by decision support tools (see Table 6.5).

Simple cost-displacement measures would evaluate the time that the tools saved this small group, but time saved was not taken as a reduction in staff. Rather, the group used the time and the increased analytical abilities generated by OA to take on an entirely new role: in addition to reporting, the group now identifies the source of line-productivity problems and shepherds solutions through the organization.

Table 6.5.   Field Service Efficiency

Drop in repair time per 100 lines in 1985	2.5 hours
Portion of drop due to fewer stations per line	1.0 hours
Drop in repair time due to improved field productivity	1.5 hours
Portion credited to OA	50%
Drop in repair time due to OA	0.75 hours
Cost of repair time avoided	$3,000,000
Present value, five years, 10%	$11,372,000
Plus Civil War effects:	
Productivity impact of Civil War games	1%
Total cost of service	$150,000,000
Productivity contribution of OA (one-time effect)	$1,500,000
Net benefit, first year	$4,500,000
Present value, five years, 10%	$12,872,000
Development cost (estimated for 10 PCs and programs)	$100,000
One-year return on investment	4,400%
Five-year return on investment	12,800%

OA was the catalyst that helped to transform the role of this staff group from passive to active. The manager notes that simply increasing the size of his staff alone would have been insufficient to help him bring about this transformation in function. Again, we see a staff group that is in a position to encourage productivity improvements by others. The value-added leverage of OA was inherent in the group's contribution to productivity throughout the organization, affecting costs far greater than their own salaries.

Collaboration

The first two sections dealt with managers and analysts who used OA specifically to encourage productivity improvements. By improving managerial effectiveness, the tools delivered leverage productivity gains. The cases were concerned with the effectiveness of managers in both supervisory and staff-watching roles. The productivity of others was an important part of the users' missions.

In this next section, we consider the use of OA to enhance the effectiveness of project teams. Here, the users' mission is not to improve productivity, but to get a job done. The two situations described represent two factors that complicate project-team collaboration. In the first case, the project team must respond in a crisis. In the second case, the project team must overcome geographic distances. In both cases, OA was used to improve team collaboration.

Supplying the Army

Better collaboration across organizational boundaries is essential to daily operations, but becomes especially important during a crisis. The British army operates a logistics center in the Ministry of Defence (MOD) in London, and other supply centers scattered around the United Kingdom and Germany. Although a comprehensive computer network existed for dealing with urgent requisitions, there was no rapid method (other than telephone and telex) to coordinate supply planning. During a crisis, the telex could become completely clogged, and the supply telephone network was not secure.[2] It was concluded that a new communications method was needed. Under the direction of Brigadier John Spackman, then director of supply computer services, an experimental electronic mail system based on the existing supply network was initiated.

While the experimental system was being installed, the Falkland Islands crisis occurred. This posed some unique logistical problems, for no standard military formation with normal equipment met the requirements of this remote location with its difficult terrain and climate. What balance of armor and artillery, what air defense, and what ammunition and supporting equipment would be needed? What clothing for the coming winter in the southern hemisphere would be needed? What was available in the way of special winter equipment?

The British army immediately converted the electronic mail project from an experimental to an operational system. It linked the logistics planners in the Ministry of Defence in London to the operational logistics centers and supply depots throughout the United Kingdom and Germany. Communications between planners, policy makers, and operations staff helped to determine what stores were needed, where they could be acquired, and how they could be transported to the correct ship.

With electronic mail, requests for information were transmitted from desk to desk within three seconds. In addition to its speed, the system decreased the possibility of error or misunderstanding. The system also provided a record of all requests through which questions and responses could be tracked and accountability recorded. Perhaps most significant in this crisis situation, the data were far more secure than if telephone lines had been used for transmission.

The first ship was loaded only three days after the alert; Spackman estimates that it would have taken one to two weeks without the automated supply system and electronic mail. The system is credited with averting a significant delay in mounting the military operation. Furthermore, it is believed that the mix of supplies and equipment was appropriate to the unique operational requirements and climate of the Falkland Islands as a result of better planning and collaboration.

While we have an estimate of the contribution of the tool to the timeliness of the project, it is extremely difficult to place a monetary value on military readiness; this is a subject for legislative debate rather than science. It is believed that in this case the speed of mounting the operation had some military significance; that is, it reduced the cost of winning. There are no monetary measures of this timing advantage, however.

Spackman cites one tangible benefit. At the time, world press debated whether the U.K. involvement in the Falklands was merely a gesture or a serious commitment to protect British citizens and prevent the settlement of a diplomatic issue by force. The speed and effectiveness with which the British army mounted its Falkland operation demonstrated to the world its resolve in this matter, and helped to maintain the support of the international diplomatic community, the press, and Parliament.

As every military leader knows, political will is essential to withstanding casualities and winning a war. In this case electronic mail played a key role, since the speed and efficiency with which the operation was mounted demonstrated clearly the strength of purpose and resolve of the troops, Parliament, and the people. The importance of the value-added contribution of electronic mail stems from the selection of users who are critical to military readiness, and the importance of worldwide collaboration to their effectiveness.

Managing an International Project Team

Problems with collaboration also arise when the project team is geographically dispersed. The preceding case described a common solution, electronic mail. Shared access to data also can bring a team closer together, as the following case demonstrates.

New Zealand has virtually no oil. The country imports 90 per cent of its fuel, which amounts to about 40,000 barrels a day. Because New Zealand has few exports needed by the countries that supply oil, it is forced to pay about $10 million per day in balance of payments. Also, oil must be purchased in U.S. dollars, so the price to New Zealand has doubled in three to four years owing to currency fluctuations. New Zealand felt it needed to increase its self-sufficiency by building a synthetic fuel plant.[3]

Bechtel Power Corporation was awarded the $1 billion project. The project team, headed by Dan Greenberg and Peter Howard, was located in New Zealand, Tokyo and Ariake (Japan), San Francisco, New York, and London. The people in various locations needed up-to-date cost and budgetary information. "The situation had all the ingredients for monumental problems," says Howard. "It was international, there was government ownership, and we had international financing."

The team was given access to a shared central database that held current information on project budgets and expenditures, as well as to a second database for logistics, shipping, and traffic. The procurement-tracking system was updated by shippers and the project team. Access to a common database helped the team to coordinate its efforts. "Without the electronic databases," Howard says, "we clearly would have made less accurate decisions because of a lack of information from the other locations."

The information systems were an advance over what the client had expected: "The information systems more than justified New Zealand's selection of Bechtel to do the project," according to Howard. The systems provided Bechtel with a competitive edge by building its image as a leading-edge, well-run, responsive managing contractor. Most important, with the help of the system, Bechtel finished the project under budget and ahead of schedule. "There's no question that the system significantly assisted us in this project," Howard says. "It made a tremendous contribution to ensuring that the project stayed within budget and ahead of schedule. If there had been an overrun, it would have cost the New Zealand government several million dollars per month. When you consider the scope of this project—the largest privately financed project ever undertaken—that's an important contribution."

In this case, the success of the team depended on its members' ability to work independently on common data. The emphasis was on an interactive database management system rather than on telecommunications tools. The value-added leverage resulted from the importance of timely project delivery. Each day of delay could have cost the client over $100,000.

Because of their differing success factors, the British army and Bechtel chose different tools to ensure effective project-team collaboration. In both cases, timely collaboration was critical to effectiveness. OA made significant value-added contributions to the success of each project.

Human-Resource Management

Having considered the effects of OA on line, staff, and project managers, we now turn our attention to global people-management issues. This section considers problems that affect entire organizations. These cases will be of great interest to top executives and human-resource staff groups that are concerned with the management of people throughout the organization.

The first case illustrates a challenge that every organization faces from time to time: reorganization. The second case shows the use of information tools to advise line managers on personnel budgets and plans. The third case considers the role of OA in implementing an early retirement program.

Restructuring the Defence Department

Company-wide reorganization efforts often take on massive proportions, with project-management problems compounded by the sensitive nature of the task. The project team must deal with massive amounts of detail in the form of organizational charter statements and job descriptions. Timing is often critical, since the announcement of the new organization must be well-coordinated and rumors must not be allowed to spread.

One example of a large reorganization is provided by the Ministry of Defence of the British government, which had the task of implementing a plan developed by the secretary of state for major changes in the top management structure of the ministry. The permanent undersecretary (the permanent civilian head of the ministry) chaired a steering committee, and assigned the role of developing the plans for reorganization to a team led by Michael Bell, director-general of management audit.[4]

There were two major problems associated with this project. First, the time scale was highly accelerated. The entire reorganization had to be completed by January 2, 1985. This, according to Bell, was an "absolutely immovable date." This gave the department nine months in which to plan and implement this major restructuring. The last major restructuring of the department in 1964 took longer, even though in some respects it was less fundamental. Furthermore, the 1964 reorganization resulted in a staff increase of 70; it was a requirement of the 1984 reorganization that numbers should not increase.

The second problem was that the reorganization was not a universally popular move. It would change the power structure, and there was likely to be opposition from those who would lose power. Some involvement in the planning from those affected was desirable in order to ease subsequent implementation.

The team of 30 military and civilian personnel produced a consultative document (issued by the secretary of state) that enabled the affected managers to react to the proposed changes. This document had to be produced in the first four months of the project, because the secretary of state wanted to publish a "white paper" describing the reorganization before the end of July, when Parliament recessed.

The magnitude of the project was impressive. The team had to think through the basic philosophy of the organization, and as far as possible discuss that philosophy with the staff concerned, in order to validate the details in the consultative document. They had to develop or confirm in detail every job description from that of a general down to a clerk — a total of about 1,500 positions. They had to work out an accommodation plan involving over 1,000 staff to ensure that the relevant people were collocated.

Bell explains, "In the government, if it's not on paper, it doesn't exist. Paper is the vehicle for determining and formulating policy. Also, these are very complex issues that the committee was discussing — it would have been difficult, if not impossible, to discuss them with a lack of documentation."

During the nine-month project, over 50 major reports were presented in 14 meetings of the steering committee. Thirty-six of these papers were produced in the first four months in order to get concurrence on the policies. Using feedback from the steering committee and the secretary of state, the team continued to discuss and change the drafts throughout the project.

When manual, labor-intensive processes were used in the past, each modification to a paper would take at least a day. This project team used word processing provided on a local area network to produce and edit the documents. Revised papers were often produced in a matter of hours. This turnaround capability was an important benefit, considering that there were a limited number of committee meetings in which to discuss the documents. Amendments were incorporated during the morning, and the committee had a fresh draft to work with in the afternoon.

With the help of the word processor, the white paper was completed on schedule in July, and the entire reorganization was effective by the January 1985 deadline. Bell says that, based on his experience with the manual production of paperwork, the mechanics of continual revision would have been impossible without word processors, at least with the secretarial and clerical staff that were available.

The benefits of reorganizing the U.K. Ministry of Defence are difficult to evaluate. Given the mission, however, the impact of the tools on the effectiveness of the project team is clear. Deadlines set forth by the secretary of state would have been difficult to meet without additional staff. Even if additional staff had been hired, the effectiveness of the reorganization would have suffered because the level of participation would have been limited.

Word processing helped the team with its critical success factors: the ability to deal with a huge volume of detailed documentation. By allowing more frequent revisions, word processing enhanced the team's ability to involve those persons affected by the reorganization.

We estimate that if lack of support by Parliament or ministry officials had added just one day to the implementation of the reorganization—that is, another day of confusion before the new organization began effective operations—the cost of the lost productivity would have paid for the word-processing system many times over. The value-added leverage was great because a few people controlled the destiny of the entire organization; the payoff was large because the tools directly addressed the critical success factors.

Personnel Cost Tracking

Day-to-day people-management issues that affect the entire organization usually are handled by the personnel or human-resource management staff group. In many of these activities there is significant potential leverage. The next two cases show the use of OA in human-resource management in ongoing personnel cost control and on a project-oriented assignment.

Managing payroll costs is a responsibility of line management, and the human-resource staff can assist by helping with staffing decisions. An example of the role of OA in this area is provided by a city government department.

For many years, the New York City Department of General Services struggled to manage its personnel within its budget. Typically, the department ran over budget in spite of careful controls and management concern, and in most years it was not able to meet the last two of the 26 payrolls without incremental funding. In 1982, for example, the department exceeded by almost 8 per cent its $54 million personnel budget, representing a $4.2 million overrun.

Fred DeJohn, deputy commissioner of the department, recognized that a significant part of the problem was the lack of information available to divisional managers to support their personnel decision making. When employees leave city jobs, they may not actually go off the payroll until their accrued vacation and compensatory time is worked off. Lacking accurate information, division managers tended to replace departing staff when they left their jobs rather than when they were actually taken off the payroll, and the personnel budget was exceeded.

DeJohn wanted to give the divisional managers a "checkbook" that would let them accurately monitor their use of personnel budgets. Information on hiring plans, payroll accounting, and attrition were scattered among various computer and paper tracking systems. Each division had personnel liaison officers, but they were unable to aggregate information in real time and made decisions as best they could — based purely on anticipated headcount rather than on the status of budgets.

Dean Plummer, director of local processing services, credited the use of a word processor with custom programming with giving the liaison officers the tools they needed to process personnel actions quickly and to simulate a divisional "checkbook" as envisioned by Dejohn. Since the personnel liaison officers were able to track budgets and spend more time understanding the managers' needs (rather than just processing paperwork), they felt comfortable allowing divisional managers more freedom. For example, local managers could delay some hiring to fund the immediate replacement of other jobs, or they could give up positions in order to fund job upgrades.

Without the use of office technology to expedite the implementation of the checkbook system, DeJohn believes, more resources (both manpower and money) would have been needed and more time would have elapsed before the desired combination of management flexibility and financial control could be realized. With these tools, he was confident of meeting the payroll budget; he did so in 1983, and has continued to do so every year since.

According to DeJohn, had these controls been delayed by just three months, an overrun of over $1 million would have been expected. That overrun would have been passed on to taxpayers. We assume that city services would have benefited slightly from the added expenditures. These added expenditures were not in the original budget, however, because the perceived benefits did not justify the cost. In other words, the added expenditures produced a net negative utility to taxpayers, the government equivalent of a loss. We might conservatively assume that this lost utility amounted to 10 per cent of the overrun, or $100,000.

The system cost about $40,000 to develop and utilized about $75,000 in capital equipment (25 per cent of a large word processor, plus five terminals, a disk drive, and a printer), for a total cost of $115,000. The system paid for itself in its first year simply by delivering financial controls sooner. Subsequent labor savings (cost-displacement benefits) and planning advantages can be considered as serendipitous (see Table 6.6).

In this case, most of the credit for better controls goes to DeJohn for his clever idea of the personnel "checkbook." We assume that he could have achieved the same end with an additional staff analyst, although this is not always possible in organizations concerned about staff reduction. OA, however, deserves credit for the earlier implementation of the project. The value-added benefits of beginning the project three months earlier avoided an overrun of at least $1 million.

From the taxpayers' standpoint, this additional expenditure is to some degree justified by improved city services. In our financial analysis, we do not assume that the $1 million was lost. To managers

Table 6.6.   Personnel Cost Tracking

Overrun if controls delayed three months	$1,000,000
Assumed negative utility to taxpayers	10%
One-time benefit from delivering controls sooner	$100,000
Cost-displacement benefit per year (estimated one person)	$40,000
Present value, five years, 10%	$152,000
Total benefit (cost-displacement plus value-added)	$252,000
Development cost	$115,000
One-year return on investment	22%
Five-year return on investment	120%

in the Department of General Services, however, a million-dollar overrun is a costly failure of financial controls. For them, the value-added benefits far outweigh the cost-displacement effects of this innovative application of a word processor.

Early Retirement Program

OA tools can be of great value to human-resource managers on special projects, often with highly leveraged results. In this case, we examine the role of interactive access to human-resource data in solving a temporary budget problem during a recession.

Olin Corporation developed an interactive human-resources database to replace its various data-processing systems. The database permits easy access by authorized staff to personnel data (addresses, pay reviews, marital status, etc.) for employees in all of Olin's domestic locations. The interactive database was built to assist decision making in EEO compliance, labor relations cases, personnel planning, and compensation as well as in the reduction of mundane work. They found that the system's operational costs were less than those of the manual systems, but the value-added benefits were far greater than cost savings.[5]

In August 1981, Olin executives decided to offer an early retirement program in order to avoid a layoff during the 1982 recession. The program gave full pension benefits and 20 per cent pay to employees aged 55 to 62. This amounted to about $30,000 per person, or about $13.5 million for the 450 people Olin hoped to remove from its payroll.

The program had to be carefully planned. Assuming some need to hire replacements for key people, at least 400 persons had to participate in the program in order to avoid layoffs. If more than 600 people participated, Olin stood to lose a great deal of money in replacing many of the retirees, and might also lose people that it wanted to keep.

Unfortunately, Olin was under considerable time pressure. The program had to be closed by December, because after January 1 a change in the accounting statutes would preclude spreading the cost of the program over 17 years. The $13 million impact on profits would be unacceptable, and the company would have to lay off workers.

John Ibberson, director of organization development at Olin, worked with human resources and benefits managers to generate

alternative terms and conditions, using the database to forecast what
the results would be. Olin chose a target segment of 600 people out of
the 1,200 eligible. The program was announced in October, and a
48 per cent employee acceptance of the program was attained (within
the target range). Of the 450 people who accepted the offer, only 100
had to be replaced, with a net of 350 people voluntarily taken off the
payroll.

Ibberson is certain that without the database Olin could not have
completed the planning and implementation of the program by
year-end. The program would then have reduced profits by over $13
million, and layoffs would have been unavoidable. With the retirement program in place, Olin was able to avoid any layoffs during the
recession.

Of course, Olin would have removed people from the payroll in
either case. But a layoff would have resulted in an increase in Olin's
state and federal unemployment taxes of at least 1 per cent, which
would equal approximately $1.5 million in increased taxes each year.
This one use of the database paid for the entire $1.3 million (three-
year) implementation costs of the human-resource management system (see Table 6.7).

In this case, the human-resource managers were responsible for a
project that not only had significant impacts on the bottom line, but
also had significant impacts on people's lives. The cost of the time
that the interactive database saved them (the cost-displacement
benefit) was small compared with the money at stake on this project.
The success factor was the analysis of the data within a short time
period, and the value-added leverage was gained by precluding an
increase in the payroll tax on all employees throughout the entire
company.

Table 6.7.   Early Retirement Program

Impact of delay on unemployment tax	1%
Olin payroll	$150,000,000
Net benefit per year	$1,500,000
Present value, five years, 10%	$5,700,000
Development cost	$1,300,000
One-year return on investment (this one use)	15%
Five-year return on investment (this one use)	340%

OA and People Management

The cases in this chapter demonstrate the variety of ways in which OA can help to manage people. Line, staff, and project managers used a variety of tools, including databases, decision support systems, word processing, voice message systems, and electronic mail. These examples span a range of industries, including manufacturing, telecommunications, consulting, and government organizations.

In all of these cases, saving the users time was the least of the benefits. The value-added leverage resulted from improvements in managerial effectiveness, which in turn improved the productivity and effectiveness of many others in the organization.

Line managers can find opportunities for high-payoff use of OA whenever they plan their staffing requirements and allocate people to their workloads. Staff managers are good candidates for value-added applications when their services help others achieve their missions, or when they deal with the human-resource issues of the entire organization. Project managers benefit from OA whenever they face problems of collaboration, coordination, or decision making under time pressure.

Effective people management is crucial to the success of virtually every organization. It does depend greatly on interpersonal skills—the rare talent of the excellent manager. But as these cases demonstrate, the judicious use of OA extends a good manager's ability to get the most from the organization.

Notes

1. The authors thank Matthew Young for the introduction to this case.
2. The authors thank Matthew Young for the introduction to this case.
3. The authors thank Maurice Welsh of Bechtel Power Corporation for the introduction to this case.
4. The authors thank Matthew Young for the introduction to this case.
5. The authors thank Ben Graves for the introduction to this case.

Finance

"Finance" comprises a broad set of services related to money matters. Because finance serves an important function as management's "eyes and ears," it is of concern to all managers in every organization; this chapter will be of particular interest, however, to financial professionals, budget managers, and top executives, particularly in large organizations.

In this chapter, we look at four specific areas of financial management. The first section presents cases in asset management, and the second section considers financial controls on decisions made by decentralized line managers. Closely related to these is the third section on budget management, another means of guiding decentralized decision making. The fourth section examines a few sources of financial risk.

We have included a unique "futuristic" case from over a decade ago. Using a cybernetic model of the organization, a finance minister gained significant control of a country's unstable economy by using interactive information systems. This case demonstrates the role of financial information systems as the "nervous system" of an organization.

Portfolio Management

Financial staff are responsible for managing a corporation's financial assets. In this section we look at their two roles. In the first case, financial staff has line management responsibilities for investment portfolios. In the second case, financial staff are expected to provide top management with the numbers they need to manage international assets. In each case, OA tools improved the ability of decision makers to utilize their assets profitably.

Investment Asset Management

Portfolio management is not of interest only to financial service companies; almost every firm has liquid assets to manage, and many hold investment portfolios. In larger firms, portfolios such as employee pensions can represent large blocks of money that must be professionally managed.

Chuck Carpentieri, director of employee benefit asset management at Olin Corporation, uses a decision support system based on an econometric model to make more money with Olin funds—an employee pension fund, a fund that pays employee health benefits, a fund that makes charitable contributions on behalf of Olin, and an employee thrift plan. With his staff of two, Carpentieri monitors, evaluates, communicates, and develops strategies for investing more than $600 million of financial assets.[1]

Carpentieri uses an econometric model in conjunction with data from outside investment managers and a capital budgeting model to assist in investment decisions. The econometric model helps Carpentieri and the four external investment management teams make rational investment decisions. The capital budgeting model assists in the all-important task of allocating funds to stocks, bonds, and liquid assets. Carpentieri explains, "The models give us an outlook on stocks and bonds which is then compared on a relative value basis."

For the equity portion of its portfolio, Olin keeps about 100 stocks at any given time. The decision support systems help screen stocks on a continuous basis to identify those that meet Olin's criteria; these then become candidates for the portfolios. Similarly, the stocks that are currently held are regularly screened. If any do not pass the test, they are candidates for sale.

The ultimate test of the decision support system is Olin's rate of return on its assets (after administrative costs). The Standard and Poor 500 provides one benchmark for Olin's performance on the stock portion of the funds. In 1984, the S & P 500 grew 6.2 per cent; one Olin portfolio worth approximately $46 million grew 15.4 per cent, 140 per cent better than the market. The additional 9.2 percentage points of growth were worth $4.2 million to fund beneficiaries. In 1984, another of Olin's portfolios performed 55 per cent better than the market, and a third portfolio performed 53 per cent better. Overall, Olin's three stock portfolios grew by approximately $7 million more than a market index of equal size.

Another standard of performance used in the investment industry is the TUCS database of funds managed by banks and investment managers. In stocks, the median return was 1.3 per cent for funds in the TUCS database. This is rather surprising, considering that the S & P return was 6.2 per cent. Overall, Olin's three stock portfolios outperformed the median TUCS return by more than 10 percentage points, placing them well within the top 10 per cent of all equity funds managed.

When stocks and bonds are taken together, the funds included in the TUCS database had a median growth of 8.3 per cent in 1984, compared with Olin's overall performance (after administrative costs) of 11.2 per cent. These results placed Olin in the top 20 per cent of all funds managed. This difference between an excellent and an average performing fund was worth over $15 million to fund beneficiaries.

"As we continue to work with the model, it is becoming apparent that we are in fact increasing our probability of outperforming the S & P index," says Carpentieri. He has compared the forecast of the model with actual market performance in 1984. In his sample of Olin's portfolio, five issues were expected to outperform the S & P 500; four out of the five actually did outperform the index. Three issues were expected to underperform the market, and two out of the three did.

Carpentieri points out that his success can't be entirely attributed to the model: "It's not the panacea of investment management." The assets are managed by four independent money managers located in New York, the southwest, and the midwest, and are held by a master trustee in Dallas. Their knowledge, judgment, and research capability are important parts of the equation. The model can only point to appropriate decisions consistent with the fundamental investment information with which it is supplied.

But Carpentieri notes that "the asset manager that performed the best not only has an excellent research capability, but has embraced the model." Carpentieri feels that the model has helped Olin to maintain effective, forthright communications with its managers.

Carpentieri calls the model a "catalyst" for communication and clear thinking: "The model forces you to communicate about real issues." It raises questions that otherwise might not be asked, enforces an analytic discipline, and provides a structure for effective discussion of Olin's investment objectives and strategy. Also, Carpentieri points out, "The model has added another dimension in our goal to maintain a high level of communication with our managers. When you're hooked to them by the modem, you're always uppermost in their minds."

Olin has also invested in diligent research. "But the bottom line is that we perform better when we use the output of the research effort as input to the model," says Carpentieri. "Before we had the model, we had average rates of return. The model has spelled the difference between below-average performance and above-average performance. The assets of the pension plan have almost tripled in seven years, even though this mature program pays out more to retirees than it takes in in the form of corporate contributions."

Although it is difficult to trace what part of this superior performance can be credited to the model, we asked Carpentieri to estimate its value to Olin by offering him a choice of the model or a guarantee of an extra 1 per cent return on his portfolios. Carpentieri said, "Using the performance over the last several years (which of course is not an assurance of future performance), I'd pick the model."

By applying the 1 per cent Carpentieri is willing to forgo for the model against the more than $600 million portfolio that he oversees, it can be reasonably concluded that he feels the model is worth at least $6 million per year. When the annual cost of the system is subtracted, the use of the model has a present value over five years (discounted at 10 per cent) of $22.6 million. In this case, OA is a tough investment to beat in any market (see Table 7.1).

This case describes the use of databases and decision support systems in managing investment portfolios. This is one of the few areas in most companies where financial staff take on line management responsibilities. There are a number of success factors in this area, including economic analysis, portfolio analysis, and team collaboration. In this case, OA in the form of a decision support system enhanced each of these.

Table 7.1. Investment Asset Management

Return on portfolio equivalent to value of system	1%
Size of portfolio	$600,000,000
Expected annual value of system	$6,000,000
Present value, five years, 10%	$22,600,000
Development cost (worst case estimate)	$100,000
One-year return on investment	5,900%
Five-year return on investment	23,000%

As busy as Carpentieri's staff may be, this is clearly an area in which greater productivity is of relatively little value. With the size of the portfolio so many times greater than the cost of the staff, the quality of decisions is far more important than the quantity.

The Pulse of an International Company

In a broad sense, every manager is responsible for the assets of the organization. Particularly at the executive level, timely financial data is fundamental to every major decision. Value-added opportunities may be found by improving the financial information supplied to key line managers.

Black & Decker, a manufacturer and marketer of consumer power tools and small household appliances, does business in approximately 50 countries. In the past, each decentralized group of countries prepared its own financial statements, then submitted them to headquarters for corporate consolidation.[2]

In 1984, Black & Decker appointed a new chief executive officer. As a primary corporate strategy, he reorganized the company so that it would operate as a single global organization. In the process, he eliminated the group level of financial management. Now, financial data are submitted directly to corporate headquarters each month. Headquarters staff then consolidates the data, adjusts the currency-hedging position, and submits reports to management. This change was an important early signal to the organization that the CEO was serious about adopting a global perspective.

To close the accounting books each month, every office used to submit its financial data by data communications, telephone, and facsimile. This closing process took seven days, and was highly error-prone. In 1985, the company installed personal computers worldwide, with special software for entering and editing the financial reports. The international data are now sent by electronic mail to the United Kingdom, where they are forwarded to corporate headquarters for consolidation. Currencies are automatically translated into U.S. dollars, and errors have been significantly reduced. Now, according to Ken Kelly, director of accounting systems and policies, the entire process is completed in four to five working days.

One advantage of faster international data transmission is the ability to hedge currencies more efficiently. For example, when there are changes in the balance sheet in the course of a month, Black & Decker loses some of its hedging coverage. In other words, to the extent that international assets and liabilities change, the company is subject to fluctuations in foreign currencies. By eliminating two to three days of such exposure, the consolidated balance sheet—and therefore the stock price—is more stable.

Kelly points out that the system also gives management better control of international operations. Local management worldwide can use the system to track its own numbers (in U.S. dollars), and have easy access to trend data. Corporate management has access to more consistent and reliable data, and is now building a database that shows historic trends. Problems are seen sooner, so corrective actions are more timely.

"I don't see how we could run this business without it," says Ken Kermes, Black & Decker's executive vice-president for finance and corporate development. "We made the same decisions before, but I wonder how many decisions we *didn't* make because we didn't have reliable information [on problems and opportunities] ... I'd be willing to pay $2 million to $3 million for this system."

According to Jerry Townsend, director of data administration, the system cost $120,000 for hardware, $55,000 for software, and about $100,000 for consulting and implementation costs—a total of $275,000. Operating costs are somewhat less than they were with the manual system. The perceived value to executives is much higher than these minor cost-displacement benefits, however (see Table 7.2).

In this company, top executives make decisions on the use of their worldwide resources on an ongoing basis. These key decision makers create high-leverage opportunities for OA, since so much depends on so few people. The system does not save executives' time, yet they perceive it to have a high value. The executives' estimate of the system's worth is based entirely on their perception of value-added benefits.

Both of the cases in this section are drawn from manufacturing companies. Financial service companies are even more fertile ground for such opportunities, and have led the way in leveraging the thinking of their talented money managers. In any organization that controls significant financial resources, decision support systems can

Table 7.2. The Pulse of an International Company

Value of system to decision maker	$2,000,000
Development cost	$275,000
Return on investment	600%

help asset managers track their holdings, consider alternative portfolios, and make timely decisions about the reallocation of funds.

Controlling Costs

In general, a large part of an organization's expenditures are relatively small purchases made by mid-level line managers. Financial staff and executives review larger decisions, but have only indirect control over the smaller decisions through performance appraisals, policy, and budgeting. In this section we present cases in which OA motivated line managers to better control costs; budgeting applications are dealt with in the following sections.

The first case shows the use of interactive access to data teamed with performance standards to impress marketing and distribution managers with the cost implications of their shipping decisions. The second case shows the use of decision support systems to improve field managers' analyses, which in turn allows top management to delegate greater control to those closest to the problem. In each case, management has used OA as a means of motivating better decentralized decision making.

Shipping Cost Control

Every organization hopes that its managers make the best possible decisions to maximize profits. Indeed, decentralized line managers are well positioned to make good decisions, since they are closest to the problems and must implement the decisions. But good decision making in a decentralized organization requires good decentralized information, and the nature of the information that is provided gives line managers a clue to understanding what is important to their executives. Information systems can thus become a tool for enforcing policy.

A large consumer goods manufacturing company provides an example of a successful application that helped control the cost of shipping goods from plants to distribution centers. The project was initiated because top management felt that accountability was lacking. For example, marketing might request shipment by air because timeliness was important to closing a sale; the incremental shipping costs were borne by the distribution department, however, and the marketing staff never understood the costs of their decisions. As one might expect, marketing felt free to order air freight delivery frequently.[3]

In addition to accountability, costs were higher than necessary owing to a lack of coordination. For example, a truck has both weight and volume limits. If one department ships heavy goods, the truck will travel with empty space; if another department ships a load of light goods, they will fill the space but travel under weight limits. Coordination was also needed between shippers and facilities managers. For example, one plant in the midwest shipped only by rail because it had no truck docks. Although in recent years trucking has become relatively cheaper, the facilities manager had no incentive to install the necessary truck docks.

The problem was cybernetic: those who made the decisions were not considering the total impact on the company, but only the costs to their own departmental budgets.

In response, the distribution department analyzed the costs of shipping and implemented a database that tracked actual shipping costs against standards of excellence. This portion of the system involved routine transaction processing, the domain of traditional MIS. The company then went on to provide interactive access to decentralized warehouse managers—a tool of OA. It is this interactive tool that gives decentralized managers the information they need to make day-to-day decisions.

In the process, accountability has improved, since the system can allocate the cost of decisions to the appropriate departments. The system cost $50,000 to build (including the analytic work), and $30,000 to $40,000 per year to operate. By comparing shipping costs in 1982 to those in 1981, the company estimates savings of more than $5 million per year (see Table 7.3).

Data-processing reports proved insufficient to guide line managers in making their daily decisions. The addition of interactive query capability—an office information tool—had a significant impact on

Table 7.3. Shipping Cost Control

Difference in shipping costs with and without system	$5,000,000
Operating costs per year	$40,000
Net benefit per year	$4,960,000
Present value, five years, 10%	$18,800,000
Development cost	$50,000
One-year return on investment	9,800%
Five-year return on investment	37,500%

shipping costs. By allowing managers to monitor their own performance, the system guided behavior (a straightforward cybernetic effect). There was no attempt to save the plant managers time; rather, the entire focus of this application was on improved decision making, which resulted in multimillion-dollar value-added benefits.

Fighting Fires

If OA can improve decentralized decision making, then the next order of effect should be an increase in top management's trust and willingness to delegate decisions to first-line managers. The combination of good decision support systems and good decision making by people who are closer to the problem should improve the performance of the organization. This effect is illustrated with a case involving a government department.

Many managers joke about their "firefighting" activities, but the U.S. Department of Agriculture's Forest Service takes that job seriously. The Forest Service is responsible for fighting fires that threaten national forest lands. To do so, they spend an average of $130 million annually on firefighting staff and preventive measures.[4]

Once the firefighting has begun, the Forest Service is provided with an emergency fund for direct costs; they have drawn an average of $81 million per year for staff overtime and for the hiring of additional crews, helicopters, observation airplanes, and air tankers carrying fire retardants. These emergency expenses are not budgeted funds that would otherwise be spent elsewhere, but are true direct costs from a special fund that directly affects the U.S. treasury.

In many cases, even taking into account the value of lost forest resources, it is better to let a fire burn to its natural boundaries and then suppress it than to mount an immediate all-out firefighting campaign. In the past, however, the risk of losing control of the fire prevented decision makers from using such a strategy. The Forest Service had a policy of trying to contain each fire by 10 o'clock on the morning after it was discovered. The first 12 hours are critical, and after mid-morning the air temperature rises and fires spread more quickly, warranting this "all-out attack" policy. Such an intensive effort could cost as much as $10 million for a large fire.

For years, Forest Service fire-management specialists and outside research scientists have been studying the behavior of forest fires. Their research has been reflected in a series of computer models that predict the amount of debris that is available as fuel for the fire, the impact of weather and terrain on the rate and direction of the fire's spread, and the expected result of firefighting tactics.

A system called BEHAVE draws together state-of-the-art fire-behavior prediction technologies into one package. It consists of two subsystems, one for modeling fuels and one for predicting fire behavior. Components of BEHAVE are downloaded into hand-held programmable calculators into which firefighters enter local conditions such as type of terrain and weather.

As a result of the BEHAVE model, firefighters can forecast with far greater assurance what assistance will be provided by natural boundaries and conditions, how much time they have, and what resources are in jeopardy. This greater confidence level has permitted a change in policy: fires are now fought in the most economic way possible. For example, in July 1985, a fire in Idaho was stopped for less than $400,000; the cost of an all-out effort to suppress the fire was estimated at over $3.7 million. Another fire that same summer was confined for $300,000 instead of the $4.6 million immediate control would have cost.

Bill McCleese, assistant director of fire management and a 25-year veteran of the Forest Service, estimates that when fixed costs are filtered out (for example, the salaries of people who would be employed in any case) and the value of lost forest resources is considered, 1985 savings of tax dollars amounted to at least $10 million.

From this benefit, we must subtract the system's operating costs — about $80,000 per year for computing, and approximately the same amount for telecommunications. Thus, the benefit of the decision support system was over $9.8 million in 1985 alone.

The Forest Service anticipates similar savings each year. If the model continues to deliver similar benefits over a five-year period, the present value (discounted at 10 per cent) of these incremental savings of tax dollars is $37.3 million. The development of the model's software cost about $150,000; the hand-held calculators for every ranger district cost about $600,000. Total development costs were about $750,000, for a return on investment of nearly 4,900 per cent (see Table 7.4).

Again, a remarkable return on investment has resulted from equipping those closest to the problem with the information and tools they need to make good decisions. The benefit — significantly improved cost control — is clearly value-added, since it results from improving the quality of decisions.

Table 7.4. Fighting Fires

Cost avoidance per year credited to system	$10,000,000
Operating costs of system	$160,000
Net benefit per year	$9,840,000
Present value, five years, 10%	$37,300,000
Development cost	$750,000
One-year return on investment	1,200%
Five-year return on investment	4,900%

Budgeting

In the preceding section, information and the tools necessary to work with it were the means by which management motivated cost-conscious decision making. In this section, we turn our attention to the more conventional means of guidance: the budgeting process. Here, the effect of OA is indirect. By helping people forecast and allocate budgets, the budgeting process is made more effective, and the organization benefits from better utilization and control of its resources.

The first case in this section describes the use of tools to optimize budgeted resources. The second case shows the impact of better budget tracking. Together they demonstrate two sides of the same coin: the effective use of budgets to allocate resources.

Doing the Most Within Budget

Budgets cannot prescribe every decision; rather, they allocate the organization's resources to a variety of purposes, and leave decentralized managers to fill in the details as the year progresses. Line managers must use their funds so as to achieve their performance goals.

Again, the U.S. Department of Agriculture's Forest Service provides an example. Even when not facing a blazing forest, rangers in 645 districts are busy people. Each year, every ranger district is given a budget and a set of specific resource-management objectives. This budget is not a single sum, but is divided among as many as 20 separate funding allocations, each of which can be spent only for certain types of work. Within these constraints, district rangers must develop a work plan that achieves up to 25 targets in such areas as timber harvesting, grazing, recreation use, reforestation, wildlife improvement, and land improvements.[5]

As in any organization, funds are limited and targets are ambitious. In the past, district rangers typically spent four to five weeks manually preparing one plausible work plan, and an equal amount of time revising it mid-year. When they were given local computing capability, almost invariably the first thing the rangers did was develop a spreadsheet for their budgets and work plans. Now, using a spreadsheet, they are able to explore a variety of alternatives in only one or two weeks.

The few weeks of time saved by each district ranger are important, but are not as significant as the value-added benefits. Work projects that meet different objectives can be integrated, or multiple projects of a similar nature on the same or neighboring ranger districts can be combined to gain an advantage in better contract prices. For example, while a crew was out on horseback cutting a new trail, they also installed a "trickle tank" water-collection system to sustain big game in the area. Consolidating these tasks required extensive planning to ensure that materials, oversight professionals, and a dozen other details were coordinated. The scheme saved the ranger from having to send another crew out on a three-day ride to install the tank later. In another situation, two ranger districts were able to combine reforestation projects at 70 per cent of the cost of reforesting each district separately.

Pamela Case, a management analyst in the Rocky Mountain region, examined three ranger districts in detail. Working with the district rangers, she analyzed the difference between the first plausible plan and the final optimized work program. She determined that the tools allowed a 10 to 20 per cent improvement in the efficiency of the use of budgeted funds. Put another way, without the spreadsheets the district rangers would have required at least 10 per cent more money to achieve the same target levels.

According to Rex Hartgraves, associate deputy chief for administration, about one-half of the Forest Service's 645 districts are using spreadsheets for work planning. Their budgets range from $250,000 to $4 million, with an average of $1.2 million per year. About $386 million is currently being allocated online. If the average district ranger gains only a 2 per cent (rather than a 10 per cent) improvement in his budgeting efficiency, then U.S. taxpayers are receiving approximately $7.7 million per year in services they otherwise would not have had.

Table 7.5.   Doing the Most Within Budget

Number of district rangers with system	322
Average budget per district	$1,200,000
Budget being allocated online	$386,000,000
Improved efficiency in budget utilization	2%
Value of improved efficiency in budget utilization	$7,700,000
Operating costs per year	$1,000,000
Net benefit per year	$6,700,000
Present value, five years, 10%	$25,400,000
Development cost	$1,100,000
One-year return on investment	500%
Five-year return on investment	2,200%

The operating cost of these 322 work stations and the network services that support them is about $1 million per year, leaving a net benefit of $6.7 million per year. The work stations cost an average of $3,500 each, for a total investment of about $1.1 million. For only one year of operation, the return on investment is over 500 per cent. Over a period of five years, the present value of the benefits (discounted at 10 per cent) is $25.4 million, for a return on investment of over 2,200 per cent (see Table 7.5).

In this case, balancing targets and budgets is a complicated process. Rangers have a great deal of discretion in planning their yearly activities, and they use OA to develop better work plans. Although the spreadsheet saves time, the Forest Service is not attempting to reduce the number of rangers; rather, the challenge is to satisfy a variety of demands on the national forests within budgetary constraints. Put another way, the spreadsheet does not produce cost-displacement benefits through better utilization of salary dollars; instead, value-added leverage results from better utilization of the entire Forest Service budget.

Accurate Budget Tracking

Even with line managers making the best decisions they can on a local level, there is a role for corporate financial staff in tracking expenditures against budgets and spotting problems before they become crises. Deviations from the budget can represent an over-investment in areas with diminishing returns while other critical areas are starving for capital. When deviations occur, management must quickly spot the problem and understand the cause of overruns in order to take timely corrective action.

In General Telephone and Electronics' (GTE) General Telephone Company of the South, the budgets and results group demonstrates the impact of decision support systems on budgeting. In April 1985, the company appeared to be operating under budget. It was about to initiate a major construction program, and year-to-date indicators would have encouraged the company to proceed. The use of analytic tools, however, enabled staff to forecast expenditures based on a deeper analysis of year-to-date results and seasonal trends. They found that a $1.7 million budget overrun was already in the making, but would not be reflected in accounting data until fall. This early identification of a potential overrun allowed management to reconsider the construction program start date while taking other measures to control costs.

This one incident exemplifies the broader challenge of budget tracking. H. Bryan Edwards, the company's budget and results group manager, anticipates that without the early warning of the analyses, expenditures in 1985 would have been as high as $205 million, or $6 million over a budget of $199 million. Edwards believes that the tools will enable GTE to limit expenditures to $201 million. He credits the tools (in the hands of competent analysts who fully understand the financial operations of the company) with avoiding approximately $4 million in budget overruns in 1985.

While budget overruns are not necessarily reductions to profits (they may be investments that either pay off or are simply postponed), there are consequences to exceeding budgets that do have an impact on profits. Assume that all expenditures over budget would otherwise simply have been postponed one year. At a minimum, the firm would have had to borrow more working capital than expected. Assuming that it could borrow at 10 per cent, a $4 million overrun would have cost $400,000 in interest alone for the year. Given the ongoing problems of budget control, better budget tracking can reduce corporate working capital requirements each year (see Table 7.6).

The budgets and results group performs a critical watchdog function in the telephone company. OA helped them to improve the quality of their budget-tracking analyses, and to see trends much

Table 7.6.   Accurate Forecasts

Expected budget without OA to aid tracking	$205,000,000
Expected budget with OA and careful tracking	$201,000,000
Budget overrun prevented	$4,000,000
Rate of borrowing for extension to working capital	10%
Net benefit per year	$400,000
Present value, five years, 10%	$1,500,000
Development cost (estimated for 12 PCs and time)	$100,000
One-year return on investment	300%
Five-year return on investment	1,400%

earlier than they would have without the tools. This was not an issue of productivity: more analysts would not necessarily allow more thoughtful analyses. Rather than simply saving staff time, OA was used to leverage the thinking abilities of a few key people. The value-added benefits resulted from their ability to understand better the causes of problems and to influence decisions so as to prevent millions of dollars in budget overruns.

Minimizing Financial Risk

There are numerous other financial functions, each related to different sources of financial risk. In this section, the cases describe the use of OA to address three types of financial exposure. The first case shows the importance of external information in decision making. The application shown in the second case helps ensure the effective utilization of a fixed-cost resource. The third case demonstrates the value-added benefits of improving the tracking of purchase orders.

Purchase Decision Support

We often joke about the shoemaker's children who go barefoot, but this is generally not a problem in the OA industry. OA vendors often are leading users of their own tools. For example, EIC/Intelligence makes use of its own topic-oriented databases for daily decision making.[6]

In mid-1985, EIC/Intelligence decided to purchase a new telephone system. The most attractive proposal they received was presented for the president's signature. Before approving the purchase, the president, Jim Kollegger, requested a database search to learn more about the system's vendor. One of EIC/Intelligence's services is a database on the telecommunications industry called "Tele/Scope." It includes daily updates on corporate news, legal and regulatory actions, new products, and industry research and development. According to Susan Babcock, Tele/Scope product manager, the search revealed a number of indications of maintenance problems with the proposed system, as well as a general instability in the vendor company. In addition to the risk of additional maintenance costs, there was a chance that business could be incapacitated for a time if the system failed.

A broader search led to a new system, costing $9,000 more, that would permit dual-line calls. This feature would allow EIC to conduct remote demonstrations of its service. An internal analysis forecast a potential 40 per cent impact on the travel costs of their sales force, worth $12,000 per year, or a present value over five years (discounted at 10 per cent) of more than $45,000.

There is a chance that having better information led to a decision that was "better" by $36,000. According to Babcock, the search required no more than five minutes of time on the computer; if one already has a work station, the search would cost only about $10. A single online database search to support a reasonably significant decision can pay for a work station and the database service (see Table 7.7).

This purchasing decision represented a significant investment for a relatively small company, and therefore was of interest to the president. The few minutes spent in online research avoided a potentially costly choice and identified a more profitable alternative.

Table 7.7. Purchase Decision Support

Travel savings per year from more advanced system	$12,000
Present value, five years, 10%	$45,000
Incremental cost of more advanced system	$9,000
Net benefit of choosing more advanced system	$36,000
Development cost (work station plus search)	$2,000
Return on investment	1,700%

Whenever significant decisions are affected by factors outside the organization, external databases can improve the basis upon which judgments are made, and by doing so can reduce the uncertainty surrounding the decision. There is a chance that additional information will only confirm the choice that otherwise would have been made, in which case the tool turns out to be of little value. But there is also a chance that new information will change a decision, leading to a better choice and significant value-added benefits to the decision maker.

Filling the Classroom

Investment decisions are often based on assumptions about how the organization will behave. For example, a more capable telephone system is a wise choice only if people use its added features. Once the decision to purchase is made, the organization must make the best use of the asset. OA can help.

Many assets are time-related; for example, if you shut down a factory today, you cannot make up for it by producing twice its capacity tomorrow. In this way, professional development is much like a factory. Once you schedule a class, the costs of facilities, administrative staff, and instructors remain the same no matter how many people are in the classroom; empty seats are lost forever.

Like any large organization, Digital Equipment Corporation (DEC) invests heavily in training its employees. Classes range from technical topics to a variety of business- and management-oriented professional development programs. Unfortunately, owing to the pressures of business, there are a number of cancellations at the last minute. In the past, those empty seats were a wasted resource worth between $750 and $1,000 per day. On an annual basis, DEC lost as much as $350,000 worth of training because of last-minute changes.

To improve the utilization of its resources, DEC's field training coordinator uses electronic mail to allocate seats at internal seminars. Now, last-minute openings are announced regionally or nationwide by electronic mail, and in many cases DEC is able to fill seats that would otherwise be vacant. The responsible training manager estimates that DEC gained the advantage of $175,000 worth of training in the first year this procedure was in place.

In this case, better company-wide communications helped make better use of a sunk-cost resource. The benefits were in improving not the productivity of the training manager, but that of the training resource.

Invalid Purchase Orders

Another source of financial risk arises out of the contracting process. When a company issues a purchase order, the supplier is entitled to bill the company as the product or service is delivered. The company may not request delivery of the entire budgeted amount, however, and purchase orders do expire after a time. In these situations, the supplier may be under the impression that it has the right to bill the company even though the purchase order is no longer valid.

One department of a toy-manufacturing company installed a purchase-order database management system on a microcomputer. Although purchasing administration was handled centrally, each department manager was responsible for tracking his or her own budgets and suppliers. According to Sherry Simonek, then director of the department, the microcomputer gave managers better access to the individual purchase-order data, as well as to summary reports by supplier, budget center, and project.

In the course of the project, the managers learned to handle approximately $5 million of purchase orders more efficiently. On blanket purchase orders, they are now able constantly to track the dollar amount of releases (the portion of the purchase orders on which they have authorized delivery), thereby preventing the authorization of expenditures over the amount of the original purchase order and allowing a more accurate forecast of the need for new purchase orders. According to Simonek, this improved the managers' ability to process purchase orders quickly and gained a great deal of credibility with the controller and the vice-president of purchasing.

More important, Simonek's department identified $250,000 of purchase orders (5 per cent of the total) that were open but no longer valid. Even if only 5 per cent of the suppliers had billed the company for open purchase orders that were no longer valid, the costs saved would pay for the system in the first year.

In fact, these errors accumulated over time in spite of normal management monitoring. Since most purchase orders are valid for one year, most of the errors occurred in one year. The system eliminated any chance of similar mistakes being made in the future. Assuming that future years' errors are one-half the amount of the ones that were discovered, and assuming that only 5 per cent of the vendors actually bill the company for invalid purchase orders, return on the investment exceeds 100 per cent (see Table 7.8).

In this company, each department manager was responsible for ensuring that invoices from suppliers matched products and services

Table 7.8.   Invalid Purchase Orders

Invalid purchase orders discovered owing to OA	$250,000
Minimum assumed percentage that would be invoiced	5%
Financial loss avoided in first year	$12,500
Percentage of loss avoided in future years	50%
Net benefit per year	$6,000
Present value, five years, 10%	$29,800
Development cost (equipment and consulting)	$11,000
One-year return on investment (excluding time savings)	14%
Five-year return on investment	170%

received, and that the budgeted amounts represented by purchase orders were adhered to. Each manager's ability to track purchase orders was a critical component of financial control. A simple database of purchase orders, in this case organized on a personal computer, allowed better control of the entire department's actual expenditures.

Tracking invoices and purchase orders is not a time-consuming activity. Even if managerial productivity were doubled, the resulting savings would be insignificant. This case, like its predecessors, demonstrates the importance of effectiveness over efficiency, emphasizing the value-added benefits of the financial applications of OA.

Information as the Organization's Nervous System

One of the most far-reaching and futuristic examples of the use of information technology for financial control occurred in a relatively primitive environment. This case involves cybernetics — the extension of OA to organization-wide managerial information tools. The case gives real meaning to the concept of financial information serving as the "nervous system" of the organization.

In November 1970, Salvador Allende became president of the Republic of Chile. Allende faced a very difficult challenge. Owing to the rapid nationalization of industry and an emphasis on worker participation, many foreign managers had left the country and educated Chileans were following suit. The brain-drain was significantly accelerated by Allende's election and the panic induced by the opposition over the potential consequences of that election.[7]

The half of the population that was agrarian, poorly educated, and lacking technological tools was in the throes of land reform that was breaking large estates into worker cooperatives. The disruption caused by the rapid changes in land ownership caused a food shortage that increased the people's fears. Economically, Chile was in the process of massive redistribution of wealth from the rich to the poor. This sudden increase in the purchasing power of workers further unstabilized the economy, with increased pressure on the stock market, consumption, and inflation.

To make matters worse, other countries reacted negatively to Allende's election. Chile suffered from a blockade of spare parts and from attempts to close world markets to Chilean copper (which accounted for more than 80 per cent of the country's foreign exchange). In addition, there was a blockade on foreign credit.

Amid this turmoil, the government had the insight to reach out for scientific tools to help bring the economy under control. The British cybernetician, Stafford Beer, was hired to work with the minister of finance, Fernando Flores. Beer found financial data more than a year out of date. Telecommunications to remote factories were completely absent. These information lags tended to destabilize the economy even further. (Imagine, for example, that your home thermostat sensed that the house was getting too cold in the evening and turned the heater on at noon the next day; the resulting rise in temperature would trigger your air conditioner, perhaps in the middle of the following night.) Beer viewed information in the context of the cybernetic design as crucial to the survival of an already unstable economy.

First, Beer and officials from the Ministry of Finance visited key production facilities nationwide. In each, they identified key facts needed to manage the economy — for example, certain production rates and inventories. They offered the plant managers a telex terminal, a communications capability they had not previously had access to, on the condition that they would report those key data regularly. Over a four-month period, using a mixture of cables and microwave transmitters, key industrial centers were linked nationwide. Even with very primitive equipment (such as 50-baud teletypes) and people to pass on daily transmissions, the capital now had information on the state of the economy that was one day rather than one year old.

Again using primitive technology, they installed a computer system in the capital to analyze the data. An interdisciplinary team designed models of all of the major enterprises in the economy. These were greatly simplified but dynamic and effective representations of the key production processes. Based on the models, the incoming data were analyzed to see if they matched expectations. If a factory's output was significantly below expectations for more than a day, the model would statistically identify a problem. Management, rather than receiving a list of production figures, got a simple report that listed only the significant problems. Such a system might be termed a management attention system rather than a management information system.

Recognizing that even this level of filtering would bury the Ministry of Finance in data, Beer employed another basic principle of cybernetics: the concept of recursion. Viable (stable) systems are contained within broader systems. The challenge Chile faced was to isolate problems and maintain stability at the lowest possible level. The model would report the deviation from expectations to the lowest level of management that could deal with it. If the problem was isolated in a firm, the report would go to that company's management. If the problem was evident throughout a sector, the report would go to the appropriate sector manager in the Ministry of Finance. Within the ministry, branch managers supervised sector managers and dealt with broader or more serious problems. If the problem persisted for a fixed period, the model would assume that local management was incapable of solving it and that the problem was contained in a higher level of the system. The model would automatically elevate the problem to the next level of management. In theory, problems could be raised sequentially over time all the way to the minister of finance.

By this mechanism, top management was assured that it could permit decentralized decision making without jeopardizing the entire system. By delegating with confidence, senior managers were able to focus on systemic problems at their own level and more effectively manage a broad scope of activities. Additionally, given the lack of trained management talent in Chile at the time, the system substituted for experience in all levels in focusing management's attention on the crucial issues.

At the highest level, issues of strategy remained. To support the government's economy-wide decision making, Beer assembled a decision room. Although the room had the appearance of the control deck of a futuristic spaceship, it too used primitive technologies. It included chairs with buttons that would control a variety of screens. Participants could view any of thousands of 35-millimeter slides in order to understand data, factory processes, and other photographs. Another screen reported problems from the model. Still another represented a flowchart of the model itself. This room was the hub of the nationwide information system, and was used by Allende and the top executives in the Ministry of Finance.

A test of the systems occurred during a nationwide trucking strike. In an already unstable economy, this disruption could have crippled the country. But managers were able to send the few transportation resources that they had to the most critical bottlenecks and deploy scarce emergency resources where they were most needed. The minister of finance credited this information system with the country's surviving the strike with minimum damage.

Allende's innovative use of information systems effectively brought a volatile situation under control. Of course, the long-term effects will never be known; Allende's overthrow occurred soon thereafter. Nonetheless, this bold experiment serves as a guiding example of the power of information systems and cybernetics to manage complex organizations.

OA and Finance

Financial management is a natural area of opportunity for OA, since it depends on managers' abilities to obtain and analyze data. The cases in this chapter demonstrate a variety of areas of finance that lend themselves to OA. Users include money managers, line managers, executives, and staff advisory groups. Cases were drawn from heavy and light manufacturing companies, service companies, and federal and local government organizations.

The benefits of the financial applications of OA include a higher return on assets, compliance with and improved utilization of budgets, and control of expenditures and risks in decision making. The financial applications of OA tend to result in value-added benefits for two reasons. First, the resources at stake generally far exceed the decision maker's salary. Second, decisions usually require little time to make, and increasing productivity will have little effect. It is ironic that in spite of the natural emphasis on value-added benefits in financial applications, financial staff are often the most resistant to the value-added justifications of OA.

Opportunities for high-leverage applications of OA to finance can be found by identifying those persons in the organization whose decisions significantly affect the utilization of assets. Certainly, top managers are prime candidates; but in most organizations, the many smaller daily decisions made by decentralized managers add up to more than the few large decisions made at the top. OA can be used to support a key decision or to enable decentralized managers to implement financial policy on a daily basis. Once those who are responsible for high-leverage decisions are identified, OA investments can produce remarkable returns by helping them allocate and control the organization's financial resources.

Notes

1. The authors thank Ben Graves for the introduction to this case.
2. The authors thank Robert Holland of Holland Systems Corporation for the introduction to this case.
3. The authors thank James Herget of Lamalie Associates for the introduction to this case.
4. The authors thank Pat Riemitis of Data General for the introduction to this case.
5. The authors thank Pat Riemitis of Data General for the introduction to this case.
6. The authors thank Paul Zurkowski of the Information Industry Association for the introduction to this case.
7. Stafford Beer, *Platform for Change* (Chichester, U.K.: John Wiley & Sons, 1975)

Getting New Products to Market

Introducing a new product or service is an endeavor that cuts across all functional areas of business. The ability to deliver high-quality new market offerings in a timely manner is critical to the success of most growth-oriented companies. The project teams that transform the product from an idea to an actual source of revenue are central to the effectiveness of the organization, and the value of their work is highly leveraged.

These factors make new-product delivery teams ideal candidates for OA. In this chapter, we trace the contribution of information tools to each step of the process. The first section examines the process of invention, that creative stage in which the product concept is created and designed. The second section considers the quality of the collaboration within the team that develops the new product. The third section shows ways in which OA aids the project team in delivering results on schedule. Finally, the last section looks at the market introduction, where OA can help leverage marketing resources for the new-product announcement.

The Creative Burst

A new product or service begins with a creative idea. The idea may come from a variety of sources; in the cases in this section, ideas came from an executive, an engineer, and a group of research scientists. The idea must then be developed into a product concept. It is in this process of refining the idea that OA can help.

In general, a business has more opportunities than it can pursue. Only a few of the many good ideas that are generated are actually implemented. In the first case, OA helped an entrepreneur overcome the obstacles to implementing a good idea. Creativity is also essential to converting an idea into a product. In the second case, the engineer responsible for the design of a high-technology product used OA to enhance his creativity, and in the process invented two products instead of one. The third case shows the impact of OA on a research and development group with an ongoing responsibility for developing ideas into products.

From Idea to Action

Too many good ideas are left untapped because the practical issues involved in converting an idea into a product seem overwhelming. OA can make a significant contribution to this product-development process. An example is provided by an entrepreneur who had many more good ideas than he could possibly implement.

Stan Golomb is president of Golomb Group, a marketing consulting firm that serves the dry-cleaning market. His company produces a 16-page monthly report on new information and ideas for the industry, and helps clients with promotions by providing direct-mail services and market research.[1]

Golomb's business requires not only constant creativity but also the ability to implement his novel ideas. For example, Golomb felt there was untapped opportunity in the "women in business" market. He knew that working women are beginning to wear more suits and other items of clothing that require dry cleaning. He also knew that these same women wear pantyhose—a product that rips, snags, and is constantly replaced. Golomb felt that working women might be attracted to a promotion offering free pantyhose as a "reward" for patronizing a dry-cleaning establishment.

But Golomb's business was dry cleaning and marketing, not pantyhose. From whom would he buy the pantyhose? How were pantyhose packaged? Were certain styles and colors popular? What was the market like for pantyhose? What different qualities were available? At what price?

Golomb hired an information broker to search external databases in order to obtain the information quickly. "It was wonderful," says Golomb. "In just a couple of days, they provided me with a three-inch-thick report on the pantyhose market. I was better informed than most of the pantyhose sales representatives!"

Using the information he received, Golomb selected an appropriate manufacturer to sell him the pantyhose, which he in turn sold to his clients. The dry-cleaning establishments began their promotion; customers received a card worth 20 per cent off the price of pantyhose for each sale over five dollars. Five cards could be used to redeem a free pair of pantyhose.

"The program has been a real success," Golomb says. "Our monthly Hanes sales are now showing a continuous growth. More and more cleaners are getting on the program and, once on it, they go on and on ... Everyone is happy with this program—Hanes, my clients, their customers, and me."

In the year ending in November 1984, Golomb's net income from this project was $30,000. Golomb predicts that his profits will rise: "This is a very stable promotion. We rarely lose anybody and we will continue to add clients." Golomb is certain that the promotion will earn $50,000 in net income in 1985. He projected with 80 per cent certainty that the program will earn $100,000 annually within two years. He feels there is a 50 per cent chance that he will net $200,000 per year within five years. Taking the expected value of these probabilities and discounting (at 10 per cent) the earnings for the first six years of the project, we calculate a present value of about $350,000.

We asked if he missed another opportunity by following up on this one. Golomb responded, "This was a very favorable situation because it is a project that virtually manages itself, and we are a small operation with limited human resources. It also doesn't sabotage any of my other ideas." Golomb considers these advantages to be incremental profits to the business. "When you're an entrepreneur like me, you have lots of ideas—the key is which ones you follow through on. Sometimes you follow the line of least resistance and ideas are just dropped because they are too difficult to carry out. I would have had a difficult time selecting a manufacturer without the database information. The report did all of my legwork for me. Without it, I would have had to go to department stores and make less well-informed decisions about whom to use as a manufacturer. In fact, I would say that the chances are only one out of three that I would have carried through with this idea if I hadn't had the database search information."

Since the odds are 33 per cent that he would have undertaken the project without the aid of the external database, the expected value of the system is 67 per cent of those profits, or about $231,000. Golomb concludes, "That's not a bad return on a search that cost about $200" (see Table 8.1).

In this case, the critical success factor was Golomb's ability to implement a good idea. This case cannot be treated as one of cost-displacement by comparing the cost of the online search to the cost of library research. As Golomb states, it is the psychological cost of library research that is an obstacle to a busy entrepreneur. Remember that in the beginning Golomb had no way of knowing how success-

Table 8.1.   From Idea to Action

1984 profits from program	$30,000

1985 profits from program	$50,000
Present value, one year, 10%, 1984 dollars	$45,000

1986 through 1988:	
ODDS	PROFIT CONTRIBUTION
100%	$50,000
80%	$100,000
Expected value of profit contribution per year	$90,000
Present value, three years, 10%, 1984 dollars	$185,000

1989 and beyond:	
ODDS	PROFIT CONTRIBUTION
100%	$50,000
80%	$100,000
50%	$200,000
Expected value of profit contribution per year	$140,000
Present value, one year, 10%, 1984 dollars	$87,000

Present value, five years, 10%, 1984 dollars	$260,000
Present value, six years, 10%, 1984 dollars	$347,000

Improvement in odds of doing project credited to information	67%

Value of information, five years	$173,000
Value of information, six years	$231,000

Development cost (search services)	$200

One-year return on investment	14,900%
Five-year return on investment	86,000%

ful the promotion would be. If the project hadn't been relatively easy to do, he probably wouldn't have done it. OA overcame the barriers by making his research easy, which significantly improved the odds of turning a creative idea into profits. OA clearly made a value-added contribution worth hundreds of thousands of dollars to the Golomb Group.

Inventing One More Product Than Expected

The process of developing an idea into a product may take more than hard work. When product design is involved, creativity is essential to the development as well as to the origination of the product concept. The next two cases portray OA as a tool for creative thinking. We look first at an individual engineer in a small firm, then at a research and development group in a medium-sized company.

Alex Kukielka is an engineer at Artel Communications Corp., a small high-technology firm outside of Boston. He was assigned to a small project team that was to design and develop a prototype of a new, leading-edge local network product utilizing fiber optic cables.

Kukielka used a spreadsheet to forecast the number of electronic components that could be put on a custom integrated-circuit chip. Those components that would not fit on the chip would have to be placed on the board in the form of a much more expensive set of discrete components. The spreadsheet allowed him to look at a greater range of alternative circuit designs, and to consider different combinations of components that should be put on the custom chip.

As he began making selections of components and saw the impact on the number of discrete components, he was able to optimize the manufacturing cost of the board. Most important, Kukielka felt that the spreadsheet made him more creative: "I was able to explore flashes of insight and not worry about the numbers."

Kukielka designed a chip that supports not only the intended high-functionality product but also an unexpected low-cost version of the product. In addition, Kukielka feels that the spreadsheet made him better able to gain management support for his design decisions because of the level of documentation it provided.

In subsequent months, the computer market softened significantly. Artel's marketing management decided to introduce the low-end product first, and save the high-end product for a follow-on announcement when the needs of the market and its ability to pay increased. Kukielka believes that the low-end product satisfies an entirely separate market need, and thus will not cannibalize sales of the more expensive product.

While the incremental profits of this low-end product strategy are impossible to decipher, the odds that this low-end market entry will bring at least one incremental sale are virtually 100 per cent. The spreadsheet made possible profits from at least one sale that otherwise would not have happened. Considering the financial contribution of the product, this one use of the spreadsheet will more than pay

Table 8.2.   Inventing One More Product than Expected

Profit contribution of a small sale	$5,000
Odds of one more sale due to low-end product strategy	100%
Minimum expected value of OA	$5,000
Development cost	$5,000
Return on investment, one incremental sale (one use of PC)	0%
Return on investment, 10 incremental sales	900%

for the personal computer and the spreadsheet. Of course, for every additional product sale that would not have occurred with the more expensive product, the rate of return on the personal computer investment will go up 100 per cent (see Table 8.2).

In this project, Kukielka himself was essential to the successful development of the product, and he presented a high-leverage opportunity for OA. The spreadsheet saved him time, but with the team working late every night, that time was certainly not taken as a cost saving. The time saved may have accelerated the project schedule by a day, but with all of the other steps on which product delivery is dependent, this day could easily be lost later in the project. The additional creative thinking that OA allowed had a tangible impact on results. By giving customers and marketing staff more flexibility, Kukielka's creative design is likely to be worth many times the cost of the personal computer.

From Labs to Market

A similar case occurred halfway around the world on a somewhat larger scale. Here too OA assisted in the creative thinking involved in developing new products.

Gori is a Danish producer of wood-protection products. The company has a laboratory that does the research necessary to create and evaluate products. Prior to installing a computer, all mathematical research calculations were performed by hand. The difficulty of performing these calculations meant that only a limited number of new products could be developed.[2]

Mogens Paludan Larsen, Gori's data-processing manager, installed a personal computer with mathematical packages in the research laboratory. By focusing the staff's attention on the creative rather

Table 8.3.   From Labs to Market

Average revenue per product per year	DKr10,000,000
Present value, five years, 10%	DKr37,900,000
Profit margin (conservative estimate, not disclosed)	10%
Present value of profit contribution per product	DKr3,800,000
Incremental products developed per year credited to OA	0.5
Profit contribution per year credited to OA	DKr1,900,000
Present value, five years, 10%	DKr7,200,000
Development cost	DKr70,000
One-year return on investment	2,600%
Five-year return on investment	10,000%

than the mundane aspects of their work, it allowed them to do more research — research that Finn Imsgard, one of the laboratory managers for Gori, says would not have taken place without the computer. In addition, the tools improved the quality of their work. For example, the decision support system allows laboratory personnel to run advanced tests comparing Gori products to competitors' products for efficiency and durability, generating product improvements with a significant marketing value.

Imsgard estimates that mathematical programs on the personal computer allowed his staff to do 30 to 40 per cent more research than they would have been able to do using manual calculations. He conservatively estimates that this extra research probably results in one additional new product every two years.

A successful new product grosses more than DKr 10 million per year over the course of a five-year period. Over its product life cycle of at least five years, each product has a present value at its time of introduction of DKr 37 million. Clearly, just one such innovation will more than pay for the DKr 70,000 personal computer (see Table 8.3).

The research scientists at Gori are essential to the success of the company, and the results of their work are far more valuable than the cost of their time. Thus, they presented a good opportunity for value-added applications. A key consideration was the scientists' ability to develop the mathematical models that are necessary to design products. Decision support systems were the natural answer.

If the time that OA saved the scientists was used to reduce the size of the research and development staff, or if more products could have been developed simply by adding to the staff, the benefits would have been measured as cost-displacement. Gori, however, notes an improvement in the quality as well as the quantity of research and development, ensuring that new products are profitable. The value-added approach to management is therefore appropriate.

Project Team Collaboration and Product Quality

In addition to individual creativity, larger projects depend on the ability of product-development teams to work together. In this section, we present cases in which OA tools improved collaboration within such a team.

Collaboration takes place both in meetings and between meetings. The first case describes the use of teleconferencing to support meetings, and the second portrays the use of a voice message system to exchange ideas between meetings. In the first case, the project team resided within one metropolitan area; in the second case, the team was spread across two continents. In both cases, better collaboration improved the quality of the resulting product.

Engineering an Airplane

Large engineering projects typically divide the tasks into modules; each module is assigned to a team of engineers. Working in parallel, the teams develop the modules, and the entire product is then assembled. Close collaboration among teams is essential to be sure that the many modules fit together into a working system. Such complex projects also involve a wide range of specialists who must work closely together to meld their various disciplines.

An airplane manufacturer used full-motion video teleconferencing to assist in the development of a new commercial airplane. The system tied together 12 conference rooms in three sites, separated by as much as 38 miles, linking its engineering offices, manufacturing facilities, and the air field.[3] Before the teleconferencing system was implemented, selected engineers would travel for up to an hour each way to work with colleagues and to meet with the test pilot at the airport. With all departments represented at the briefing before and after each daily test flight, key engineers were tied up for half a day in just maintaining communications.

With the use of full-motion video teleconferencing within the metropolitan area, the pilot directly briefed all engineering departments simultaneously. All staff members could hear the test results and ask the pilot questions. Briefings were kept short. One meeting of 98 people lasted only seven minutes; in this case, teleconferencing is estimated to have saved 300 person-hours. Furthermore, since more people at each site could be included in the briefing, less time was lost communicating within each department. With the time saved by avoiding travel and internal communications, more changes per flight were turned around.

The improved quality of collaboration had value-added impacts. Design problems were identified as parts produced by various engineering groups were assembled into systems. In one case, a problem was identified by a group during a review meeting. The team might have gone ahead with the project because of test-flight scheduling requirements rather than waiting anywhere from one day to two weeks to convene the experts who would resolve the problem. Instead, the group used teleconferencing to bring the key engineer, who was the expert on a particular component, into the meeting. He identified the design flaw and corrected the problem immediately. Had the problem not been corrected until later in the project, management estimates, it would have cost the company approximately $1 million.

An engineering manager (who was originally skeptical about teleconferencing) recalls that two such incidents occurred in the course of developing the new airplane. Thus, video teleconferencing eliminated extra efforts worth $2 million in savings. Furthermore, the resulting airplane design was 7 per cent more fuel-efficient than expected; this major competitive advantage was credited to better engineering collaboration through teleconferencing.

The combination of time savings (cost-displacement) and better collaboration (value-added) resulted in an airplane that was ready for FAA testing two weeks ahead of schedule. Project development costs are estimated by industry observers to be at least $1 billion over the course of the four-year project. Of this, we might assume that one-half was fixed cost of materials and fixed-price component subcontracts. Thus, internal Boeing expenditures might have averaged $2.4 million per week.

Even with the relatively slower pace of expenditures late in the period, project costs could easily have been over $1 million per week. Completion two weeks ahead of schedule saved at least $2 million in project costs, far more than the simple cost-displacement effects. In addition, some competitive advantage was gained when the airplane was introduced into the market earlier than it otherwise would have been.

Boeing estimates that its annual costs, including transmission, salaries, and equipment depreciation, were about $355,000, or $1.4 million over the four years. The profit contribution of OA was over $2.5 million (see Table 8.4).

Table 8.4.   Engineering an Airplane

Better collaboration:	
Two problems identified earlier in design process	$2,000,000
Delivered product sooner:	
Time savings	2 weeks
Development cost per week (estimated, not disclosed)	$1,000,000
Savings in project costs	$2,000,000
Gross benefit during four-year program:	$4,000,000
Operating costs (four years at $355,000 annually)	$1,420,000
Net benefit (profit contribution) over four-year program	$2,580,000
Development cost (estimated)	$168,000
Return on investment	1,400%

In this case, better collaboration helped to identify systemic problems early in the design process, when they were relatively easier to fix. The $2 million saved dwarfs the travel-cost savings. The company credits teleconferencing with enabling the engineers to complete the design sooner than they otherwise would have. Weeks of development costs were saved, not just the time of those involved in the teleconferences (cost-displacement) but of the entire project — the value-added leverage.

This is an excellent example of the value-added concept. Simply adding more people could not have solved the problems that teleconferencing addressed; in fact, more people would only have exacerbated the problems of collaboration. The tools did more than just save time; they improved the quality of the design process. These value-added benefits were clearly the largest and most relevant contribution of OA in this case.

Bootstrapping a Product to Market

Whenever a project team divides tasks into modules, the team is dependent on its ability to collaborate so as to ensure that the pieces will fit together. The airplane manufacturer addressed this problem with regular meetings. Another approach is to provide a means of collaboration between meetings. Voice message systems and electronic mail support this type of ongoing synchronous collaboration.

One of the early experiments with voice message systems (VMS) took place at IBM in 1981, as the company was developing its VMS product. IBM made its early VMS available internally to managers in the office products division. Participants identified a number of productivity gains from the system. One study measured a 75 per cent reduction in memoranda. IBM found VMS telephone calls to be more concise (since they lacked interaction): VMS messages lasted an average of four minutes, as opposed to six minutes for the average telephone call. In addition, participants felt they could control their time better, since they were less likely to be interrupted by a telephone call. In general, they subjectively estimated time savings at one-half hour per person each day.

Ron Paxton, then manager of administrative and office systems, notes that there were value-added benefits as well as productivity gains. The system was tested by the 20-person, three-division project team responsible for developing and marketing IBM's VMS product. The experimental system was used by managers in Franklin Lakes, New Jersey; product development engineers in Boca Raton, Florida; marketing staff in Atlanta, Georgia; and research engineers in La Gaude, France.

The VMS permitted more frequent communication between locations in spite of the difference in time zones, thus speeding product development. Messages were of better quality. The system was used to broadcast messages to the entire project team as bugs in the project were identified. Meetings could be held the same day rather than one or two days later. Through better communications, the participants were able to fine-tune the product within the alloted development time, thus gaining a competitive edge.

For example, a few days before the team was required to freeze the system specifications, one of the participants noted that the system failed to say "goodbye" after taking a message, leaving new users wondering whether their message was safely recorded. Because the participants could communicate rapidly with one another, the change was made with time to spare. Paxton says the odds of being able to include that feature without the use of the VMS were less than 50 per cent. At the time, the IBM product was priced higher than the competition and competed on features; the "goodbye" feature (at that time unusual, now common) helped to distinguish the IBM product from its competitors.

To evaluate the contribution of the VMS to profits requires some simple statistical analysis and a few conservative assumptions. Each sale of a 10-port (1,000-user) system represented revenue of approximately $500,000 and profits of at least $100,000. If we conservatively assume that this feature made a difference of 0.5 per cent in product saleability, the feature would contribute profits of $500 per sale. Since the use of the VMS improved the odds of including the feature from 50 to 100 per cent, the expected value of the VMS is one-half of those profits, or $250 on every system sold.

Industry observers estimate that IBM sold at least 200 units, suggesting a return on the VMS investment of $50,000. At fair market value, VMS rental costs about $50 per person per month, or $1,000 per month for the project team (including overseas telephone charges). Thus, this one application paid for the project team's use of VMS for an entire year (see Table 8.5).

Paxton points out that the VMS was an important political aid. In one case, he recalls learning that his department director had changed the date of an all-day project review meeting to the following day by picking up his VMS messages from home in the evening. Paxton felt that, at that stage of the project, the risk of cancellation in that review meeting was very high; subjectively, he estimates that the odds of the director saying "yes" were only 20 per cent. By using the whole evening to prepare his presentation for the meeting, Paxton believes, the odds of approval were raised to 50 per cent. Incidentally, Paxton notes, the continuation of the project was approved.

While the entire project and its associated profit stream were at stake, from the manager's perspective a budget of two people for the year, or $100,000, was also at risk. The VMS improved the odds of a favorable decision by 30 per cent, for an expected value of $30,000. This case illustrates how timely communications can lead to better decision making.

This case points out the many small events that can add up to a successful project. The 20 people on the team were spread across several time zones, but they had to work closely together to design the product successfully. With the profitability of the product depending on their results, the quality of their collaboration was far more important than the cost of their time.

Table 8.5.   Bootstrapping a Product to Market

Addition of feature at last minute:	
Profit per sale (estimated)	$100,000
Impact of feature on odds of sale (conservative estimate)	0.5%
Improvement in odds of feature credited to system	50%
Expected value of VMS per sale	$250
Number of systems sold (estimated)	200
Expected value of impact of VMS on design collaboration	$50,000
Preparation for management meeting:	
Odds of favorable decision without OA	20%
Odds of favorable decision with OA	50%
Improvement in odds	30%
Value of decision (two positions)	$100,000
Expected value of impact of VMS on management	$30,000
Net benefit of VMS in two incidents	$80,000
Development cost (one year at $1,000 per week)	$52,000
Return on investment based on two incidents	54%

In both cases in this section, OA helped by allowing more frequent interaction between members of the project teams. The result was competitive products, lower total development costs, and timely deliveries to market. These value-added benefits are highly leveraged, because a select group of people occupy the critical path from a creative idea to a profitable product.

Getting the Product Out the Door on Time

In the preceding section, the emphasis was on the quality of collaboration. In this section, we examine the value of timely delivery of new products to the marketplace. Not every project works against a fixed deadline, but delays in product introduction usually mean lost sales opportunities. The cases in this section measure the value of speed in product development and introduction.

The first case is similar to those in the last section — using electronic mail in project-team collaboration — but its benefits are evaluated in terms of timeliness rather than quality. The second case addresses the problem of educating the sales force to sell a new product, a critical step in the product-introduction process.

New-Product Delivery Team

Electronic mail can assist a project team by allowing meaningful collaboration on a daily basis rather than in monthly face-to-face meetings. Electronic mail complements the telephone by permitting the exchange of working documents and allowing additional communications at off-hours. These effects can help a project team deliver results faster.

An international service company formed a team of people in New England, Florida, and the midwest to bring a new service to the market. They scheduled the project at 12 months' elapsed time—a reasonable estimate, based on prior experience with similar projects. With the help of David R. Lockwood, the team subsequently acquired an electronic mail system which was used heavily for team coordination between monthly meetings.[4] In addition to feeling that they had produced a better service through better collaboration, the team members got the service to market two months ahead of schedule. Members of the team credited electronic mail with this time savings.

It probably was tempting to multiply the two months by the participants' salaries to calculate a cost-displacement benefit as if that time would be used to reduce managerial headcount. Instead, the company took the value-added approach. The benefits were seen as two additional months of profits (at rates forecasted for one year after launch), because the advantage of an additional two months of market operations was gained. This is actually a conservative estimate; it ignores the competitive value of entering the market earlier. In this case, the incremental contribution to profits was worth $110,000. The electronic mail service cost $10,000 for the year, with a return on investment of 1,000 per cent (see Table 8.6).

Table 8.6.   New-Product Delivery Team

Time savings credited to electronic mail	2 months
Incremental profit credited to OA	$110,000
Development cost	$10,000
Return on investment	1,000%

Unless a product has a very limited market and life cycle, an earlier introduction means additional months of profits. Even in limited markets, earlier introduction accelerates the profit stream, and can be evaluated in terms of the time value of money. In either case, a competitive edge is gained, although this edge is more difficult to evaluate. Clearly, the value-added benefits of an earlier market introduction far exceed the cost-displacement benefits of managerial time savings.

Getting the Sales Force Up to Speed

Once a product has been announced, the sales force must be trained to sell it. Until sales representatives receive product training, their effectiveness will be less than ideal. A marketing consultant for a large mutual life insurance company in the United States provides an example. The company's disability insurance product was modified every two to three years. The consultant estimates that revenue dropped at least 20 per cent after each major change, until agency managers and sales agents were briefed on the product and its attributes.

In the past, the consultant was part of a team that traveled nationwide to brief the sales force. By meeting with four or five agencies each week, the team was able to reach the 50 largest agencies in 11 weeks, and all of them in 17 weeks. The average period between the introduction of the new product and the completion of sales training was 5.5 weeks. Average weekly new-business premiums were $135,000. With an average of 20 per cent lower revenue in the period prior to training, the loss due to the product change was $148,000.

The marketing consultant was instrumental in initiating the use of audio teleconferencing for agency briefings. By avoiding travel, the team is now able to brief the 50 largest agencies in 2.5 weeks, and all of them in just four weeks. Lost revenue has been reduced to $34,000. Teleconferencing has prevented the loss of $115,000 of new-business premiums following a product announcement by permitting more rapid sales training. If the disability policies stay on the books for an average of 15 years (typical for the industry), then, discounting at 10 per cent, this benefit is worth approximately $873,000. In addition, approximately $10,000 in travel costs is avoided. The costs of training by audio teleconference are $5,000, for an operating-cost-displacement of $5,000 per announcement.

Teleconferencing also saves staff time. Because the consultant is now able to spend an additional four weeks in his office, he is better able to help the agencies close complex sales. In one case alone, the consultant was credited by the sales staff with providing the critical difference that closed the sale of a policy that produces $10,000 in premiums per year. Its present value, therefore, is $76,000 (discounting at 10 per cent). The extra four weeks every three years in the office improved the odds of the sales rep's reaching the consultant by 3 per cent. The time saving can be valued at approximately $2,000 in this case alone.

The marketing consultant answers four or five calls per week, and feels he improves the odds of closing a sale by an average of at least 10 per cent. The four weeks of increased availability are likely to produce an additional 1.8 sales per year, with an average premium of $800 per year. The present value of these additional sales is approximately $11,000.

Since a major new-product announcement occurs once every two or three years, benefits can be divided by three to annualize them. In all, nearly $300,000 per year of value-added benefits in addition to direct cost savings is gained through a small investment in teleconferencing (see Table 8.7).

The marketing consultant was a key resource after each new-product announcement, since the sales force depended on him for training and advice. By speeding the training process, teleconferencing helped the company avoid a protracted period of less productive selling time, and thus generated additional revenues. Even the straightforward time savings had a value-added impact. Time saved was not taken as cost-displacement, since the marketing consulting staff was not reduced. Rather, the time was used to provide additional field support, which in turn generated more revenue. Thus, all of the benefits were value-added.

Educating Buyers

Much of the work of marketing lies in educating customers on the merits of a company's products and services. These promotional activities are especially important when a new product is announced.

Teleconferencing allows a company to reach many people worldwide very quickly and cost-effectively. In this section, we consider two examples in which buyers were informed about the merits of the new product. In the first case, educational programs were delivered via audio teleconferences that significantly increased customer awareness. In the second case, audio teleconferencing was used to

Table 8.7.   Getting the Sales Force Up to Speed

Value of speedier training:	
Effectiveness without training	80%
Premiums per week	$135,000
Premiums lost per week owing to lack of training	$27,000
Time to train largest agencies without teleconferencing	11 weeks
Average time from announcement to agent training	5.5 weeks
Lost premiums	$148,500
Time to train largest agencies with teleconferencing	2.5 weeks
Average time from announcement to agent training	1.25 weeks
Lost premiums	$33,750
Net savings of premiums due to faster training	$114,750
Present value, 15 years on books, 10%	$873,000
Value of increased consultant availability:	
Extra time in office	4 weeks
Sales consulting telephone calls per week	4.5
Extra calls per announcement	18
Improvement in odds of closing each sale	10%
Expected value extra sales per announcement	1.8
Average premium value of a sale	$800
Present value of a sale, 15 years, 10%	$6,000
Net benefit per announcement of increased availability	$11,000
Total net benefit per announcement	$884,000
Announcements per year	0.33
Net benefit per year of faster training	$295,000
Present value, five years, 10%	$1,100,000
Development cost (estimated equipment and planning)	$5,000
One-year return on investment	5,800%
Five-year return on investment	22,000%

educate the consulting community, which in turn influences customers and the press. In both instances, increased awareness has improved product profitability.

Teaching Physicians to Use a New Drug

In some industries, customers must be educated before they can use a new product. This is especially true for pharmaceuticals; doctors must understand every aspect of a new drug before they will feel comfortable prescribing it.

In one innovative pharmaceutical company, audio teleconferencing was used to speed the customer product-adoption process. In conjunction with an announcement of a new drug for the treatment of heart disease, nationwide teleconferences were held for half of the clinics that specialize in heart disorders. The meeting described the drug and its applications; speakers included a recognized authority on heart disease and the scientists who invented the product. Clinicians heard one another's questions answered, and were able to interact with their counterparts across the nation.[5]

The teleconference was well received. Fifty-eight per cent of the participants rated the teleconference a "superior" way to learn about new products, and 88 per cent found it at least "somewhat better" than traditional product-information methods.

In parallel, the company held a series of teleconferences with its sales force in lieu of a sales convention. Company officials felt that in addition to saving a significant amount of money, product sales were accelerated by informing the sales force more quickly about new products. In addition, the meeting motivated the field through interaction with top executives. Managers, in turn, were able to gain direct feedback from the field; as a result of the teleconferences, they made quick modifications to marketing programs rather than waiting for disappointing results to trigger remedial action. Sixty-eight per cent of the sales representatives who attended felt the experience was at least as good as a face-to-face conference.

Subsequently, the firm studied the clinicians who attended the first teleconference and the control group that had received the traditional marketing approach for product introductions. Significant differences were found in product awareness (100 per cent versus 89 per cent), brand-name recognition (100 per cent versus 70 per cent), brand-name recall (79 per cent versus 58 per cent), recall of specific conditions of use (68 per cent versus 49 per cent), and recall of dosage (71 per cent versus 49 per cent).

The key question, of course, is whether this improvement in marketing effectiveness translates into sales. According to the post-teleconference survey, clinical participants prescribed the drug for an average of 4.71 patients each; the control group prescribed the drug for an average of 3.44 patients. A 37 per cent potential increase in sales can be credited to the use of teleconferencing for this product introduction.

The importance of customer education was clearly recognized in this market. Audio teleconferencing provided a fast, cost-effective way to reach key customers nationwide. Its value-added leverage is its ability to affect a key customer decision criterion more effectively and more quickly than conventional marketing approaches.

Informing Consultants Who Influence the Sale

Independent consultants are often called upon to help customers make decisions, particularly with regard to new products—for example, in computer purchases. Their studies not only assess the customer's needs, but often go on to recommend one or more vendors. It is important that consultants be well informed about new products and vendor strategies.

Digital Equipment Corporation (DEC) recognized the important role of consultants, and felt that DEC was not being considered in user decisions because consultants did not fully understand the strength of DEC's product lines and strategies. In many cases DEC's systems were not being recommended even though they offered the best product for the customer.

In May 1983, DEC established a consultant-relations program under the direction of Craig D. Zamzow. Zamzow is an innovator who believes in practicing what he preaches. He instituted the use of audio teleconferencing to brief selected industry consultants in conjunction with DEC major product announcements. In these briefings, DEC marketing and engineering staff explained in detail the products being announced, giving the consultants a unique opportunity to talk with DEC inventors and executives.

In fiscal year 1985 DEC's sales force identified $12.6 million worth of sales that were significantly influenced by consultants involved in the program. Of course, even when a consultant is involved, not every customer asks the consultant's advice on vendors. In 1985, however, at least three deals—two for $2.5 million each and one for $2 million—were closed because DEC was recommended by consultants who were involved in the consultant-relations program. In total, Zamzow estimates, consultants were the major factor in vendor selection in 75 per cent of $12.6 million in sales (and some percentage of other sales not reported by the field). Thus, at least $9.45 million in sales were heavily influenced by the consultants who are served by the program.

Of these sales, some might have gone to DEC with or without the program. Zamzow notes, however, that many of the consultants involved had not recommended DEC in the past. Without the program, Zamzow estimates, between 10 and 25 per cent of the selected consultants might have recommended DEC, as opposed to the 100 per cent who actually did. Thus, the program can be credited with the difference of at least 75 per cent of the recommendations, worth $7 million in additional revenues. Using DEC's annual report, we estimate that this represents an incremental contribution to profits of $2.7 million.

Zamzow and his staff conservatively estimate that the teleconferences represent about 7 per cent of the impact of their total consultant-relations program. Thus, the teleconferences alone can be credited with $190,000 in contribution to profits by convincing consultants that DEC is worth recommending.

In addition to recommending DEC products to customers, consultants participating in the program are making better-informed and more positive statements about DEC in the trade press. Zamzow's group has tracked press coverage of DEC, and rates each mention based on its tone, its position in the magazine, and whether or not the company is mentioned in the article's title or illustrations. On the assumption that editorial coverage is at least as valuable as paid advertising, the advertising costs in each magazine are used to convert the editorial-coverage rating into an advertising-cost equivalent. With this formula, the group identified over $1 million worth of editorial exposure involving consultants who participated in the program in fiscal 1985.

Again, the consultants' comments may not have been affected by what they learned in the program. However, the sample of articles was chosen to reflect cases where the impact was greatest. Many other mentions in the press were not included in the $1 million sample. Zamzow estimates that the consultants' program influenced at least 75 per cent of the articles measured.

The influence of the consultant-relations program affects the tone of the article, which accounts for about half of the rating scheme. Since only those articles that were felt to be affected by the program were tracked, Zamzow believes that the program can be credited with much of the favorable tone of the articles. He cites specific examples of consultants who made unfavorable comments before they were educated about DEC's product line. In the $1 million sample, Zamzow estimates, at least 75 per cent of the points for "tone" would otherwise not have been awarded. In other words, the consultant-relations program is credited with 75 per cent of the tone, which represents half of the rating in 75 per cent of the articles. Multiplying these percentages, the program as a whole is credited with 28 per cent of the favorable editorial coverage in the $1 million sample studied, worth $280,000 in advertising-equivalent coverage. Again applying the 7 per cent that the teleconferences represent to the overall impact of the program, the audio teleconferences are worth $20,000.

The impact of audio teleconferencing to inform industry consultants in total was worth an estimated $210,000 in fiscal 1985. The cost for the year was approximately $10,000, for a return on investment of 1,900 per cent (see Table 8.8). What's more, this was the second year of the consultants' program; as momentum is gained, Zamzow believes, the same budget will produce returns in future years that are between two and three times the 1985 results. An OA tool used in an innovative way has produced remarkable leverage during new-product introductions.

Audio teleconferencing and one-way video teleconferencing have been used for press conferences to extend coverage far beyond those who can be wined and dined in a single city. In each case, it helped to make those who are instrumental to the purchase decision — press and consultants as well as customers — aware of the new product very quickly. In these cases, teleconferencing is not being used to reduce travel; it is used in addition to traditional approaches such as trade shows and private seminars. Its benefits are calculated entirely in terms of value-added. The value-added leverage results from accelerating the product-adoption process — bringing in incremental revenues during the crucial few months just after a new product is introduced to the market.

OA and New Products

In the process of creating and introducing a new product or service, a number of functional areas and skills are utilized, and each may benefit from the use of OA tools. The cases in this chapter involve creative thinkers such as entrepreneurs, engineers, and scientists; product-delivery teams include marketing and manufacturing staff. Marketing takes the lead during the introduction of the product by offering sales training, customer education, and press and consultant briefings.

Table 8.8.   Getting Favorable Reviews

Consultants' recommendations:	
Sales in which consultants were involved	$12,600,000
Portion that consultants influenced	75%
Sales heavily influenced by consultants	$9,450,000
Odds of recommending DEC without program	25%
Ratio who recommended DEC	100%
Improvement in odds due to consultant relations program	75%
Expected value of sales credited to program	$7,000,000
Revenue less direct costs (from annual report)	39%
Expected value of profits credited to program	$2,700,000
Portion of program influence credited to teleconferences	7%
Expected value per year, consultant recommendations	$190,000
Value of consultant comments to the press:	
Editorial value in sample	$1,000,000
Portion heavily influenced by consultants	75%
Importance of tone in calculation of editorial value	50%
Percentage of tone points that would not have occurred	75%
Editorial value credited to consultant-relations program	$280,000
Portion of program influence credited to teleconferences	7%
Expected value per year of consultants' comments to press	$20,000
Total expected value per year from teleconferences	$210,000
Operating costs per year	$10,000
Net benefit per year	$200,000
Present value, five years, 10%	$760,000
Development cost (first year's cost, assuming no benefits)	$10,000
One-year return on investment	1,900%
Five-year return on investment	7,500%

At each of these different stages, and for all of these different people, OA offers significant value-added potential. External databases and decision support systems help capture and develop ideas. Teleconferencing, voice message systems, and electronic mail build the collaboration required to make an idea into a product, and help communicate the product announcement to key decision makers and advisers. OA has been credited with improving the odds of products reaching the market, improving the design of the products, and delivering the profit stream sooner.

Applications of OA to new-product ventures can be found in two ways. First, the key individuals who are on the critical path must be identified for each step in the product-development process. OA applications can be defined in the context of their critical success factors. Second, those who influence the purchasing decision can be identified. OA may help explain the new product to them, give them a better feeling for its strengths and weaknesses, demonstrate the company's interest in working with them, and accelerate market adoption. All of these benefits contribute directly to a company's bottom line.

Notes

1. The authors thank Riva Basch of Information on Demand for the introduction to this case.
2. The authors thank Jan Bender of Digital Equipment Corporation (Denmark) for the introduction to this case.
3. *TeleSpan*, April 15, 1982, at 13. See also R. Johansen, *Teleconferencing and Beyond: Communications in the Office of the Future* (New York: McGraw-Hill, 1984).
4. David Lockwood, "Piloting Computer-Based Message Systems," presentation made to the Diebold Automated Office Program, June 19-20, 1979.
5. Thomas W. Hoff, "Case Study: Audio Teleconferencing in Marketing," presentation to the Diebold Automated Office Program, working session 80-4, December 2-3, 1980.

Winning Negotiations

Negotiations are a part of everyone's business day, but they are especially important to the success of senior executives. Common topics of negotiation include acquisitions, lawsuits, government regulations, and deals with customers and suppliers. Information, of course, is the primary commodity in a negotiation, and the payoff of OA in this context can be very high.

In this last chapter of Part 2, we look at the variety of ways OA can help with negotiations. The three sections consider three success factors in negotiating: holding stronger cards, controlling the timing of the process, and presenting the case in a convincing manner.

Holding Stronger Cards

The strength of one's position is, of course, one of the primary success factors in negotiating. A negotiating position includes many elements, such as the relative subjective cost of a delayed or unfavorable settlement, the respective resources of the parties, and third-party influences. OA can do little to affect these external factors. But one key element of a negotiating position — the evidence the negotiator can present to validate his or her position — is amenable to OA support. Our first case demonstrates the value of information in the courtroom, a traditional negotiating environment; the second case makes use of internal data in a negotiation with the government. In both cases, superior access to information made a significant difference in the outcome of the negotiation.

Winning a Lawsuit

Much of the practice of law involves negotiating. Lawyers are skilled at the art, and recognize the value of information. Law firms and corporate legal departments are already users of external databases and word processors, and are beginning to explore other OA tools. The example of a corporate lawsuit illustrates the value of access to external databases.

A conglomerate bought a small company that turned out to be bankrupt. The conglomerate sued for stock fraud. The defense hired an expert witness—a prominent finance professor known for his work in portfolio theory. This witness was to testify that the company was worth something when the conglomerate bought it, and that the conglomerate subsequently drove it into bankruptcy. The witness was well-chosen; he had a proven track record on similar cases.[1]

During the trial, the conglomerate's law firm recognized that the witness would play a significant role in the outcome of the suit, and that their pretrial research had not developed a convincing rebuttal. They used external databases to search the literature on portfolio theory. The firm's manager of external databases looked up the professor's publications and found contradictions in them. She also searched for writers who had commented on his work, and found a number of critiques. Finally, she examined a cross-section of the broader literature on portfolio theory to identify alternative theories. As a result, the prosecution lawyers were able to challenge the expert witness with conflicting statements from his past writings and from other experts. In doing so, they weakened his credibility by showing that his testimony constituted opinion rather than fact.

The results were gratifying. The head of the law firm wrote to the chief executive officer of the conglomerate stating that a $600 external database search had made a material difference in the outcome of the $18 million suit. Quantifying the value of this application depends on the meaning of the term "material." Even if the external databases improved the odds of winning by as little as 5 per cent, this one search was worth nearly $1 million (see Table 9.1).

Table 9.1.   Winning a Lawsuit

Size of suit	$18,000,000
Minimum assumed "significant" impact of information	5%
Expected value of information	$900,000
Development cost (with time and terminal, estimated)	$3,600
Return on investment	25,000%

The information significantly strengthened the plaintiff's chance of winning by allowing it to enhance its position as the trial progressed. OA had an expected value of hundreds of times its cost. In this case, one could not substitute a week of library research for the few minutes of online database searching; the trial was proceeding and the time was simply not available. A cost-displacement analysis of the benefits is completely inappropriate here. The tools clearly added value that could not have been purchased in any other way.

Avoiding Tax Problems

Access to internal corporate data can strengthen a negotiating position when the issue being discussed involves internal operating statistics. One example of this type of negotiation is labor contracts. Government negotiations often involve internal data, as in the following case.

Olin Corporation needed to measure its vacation liability. The company had no standard corporation-wide policy on vacations; however, vacation accrual had to be computed by December 31, 1984, for the company to be able to write the amount off for tax purposes.[2] Without the database, it would have been impossible to demonstrate to the U.S. Internal Revenue Service (IRS) what the accrued vacation liability was. Using its human-resource information system, Olin generated a report in one day which the IRS approved two days later.

According to John Ibberson, director of organization development, the company gained a $9 million tax writeoff that otherwise might have been postponed for a year. With an average tax rate of 10 per cent, this amounts to a time value of $900,000. Discounting at 10 per cent to the year before, when the system was built, this single inquiry into the human-resource accounting system was worth $818,000 to Olin (see Table 9.2).[3]

Since the wage bill is a significant part of most companies' expenses, human-resources staff often become involved with tax

Table 9.2.   Avoiding Tax Problems

Tax shelter from accrued vacation analysis	$9,000,000
Average tax rate	10%
Profit contribution of analysis	$900,000
Present value, 1984 dollars	$818,000

planning and negotiations. In this case, the facts were needed to capitalize on a significant opportunity. Because of its ready access to human-resource data via interactive office work stations, Olin was able to improve profits by over $800,000 with a single use of the database.

Again, the situation can be analyzed only from a value-added perspective. With the year-end deadline, manual methods would not have delivered results in the current tax year. Thus, the database did not simply save clerks and analysts time; it tipped the balance in an important negotiation.

Timing Is Everything

Another critical success factor in negotiation is proper timing. Negotiators do not need OA to slow down the negotiating process when more time is needed. But when they are under time pressure or in a position to gain an advantage by accelerating the process, OA may be of service.

This section reports two cases in which OA assisted negotiators in readying evidence at the proper time. In the first, competitive bidding for an acquisition created absolute deadlines for finalizing a proposal. In the second, a set of government regulations meant that being a month too early or a month too late would cost the company millions of dollars. In both cases OA made the difference in the optimal timing of action.

Corporate Acquisition Through Telecommunications

Corporate acquisitions such as the one described in the next case take on a dramatic aspect when executives battle to gain a negotiating edge. In addition to strategy and nerves, information and management response time played a major role in winning this negotiation.

The management-services manager at one of the world's largest chemical conglomerates, located in Europe, was told by the chairman of the board, "I want to change the nature of the head office. I want people to be more responsive. Things are moving so quickly in our industry. Without modern communications technology, I think we'll be at a competitive disadvantage. How much will this technology cost us?"[4] The manager didn't know how to respond; he guessed, "Three million dollars." The chairman looked at him without blinking and said, "That's petty cash if you can really accomplish my goal."

The value of the electronic mail system that was installed as a result of this conversation became readily apparent. The conglomerate wanted to acquire a U.S. company. A superb opportunity came up: a U.S. company decided to sell its chemical division because it was short of cash after an acquisition of its own. The division produced a unique line of advanced materials for the aerospace industry. This made it an enticing investment for chemical companies around the world; international competition for the acquisition was fierce.

The European conglomerate assembled an acquisition team located in New York, supported by a U.S. regional office, to prepare its bid. Documents pertaining to the deal were transmitted from the word processor in the U.S. office to the European headquarters via electronic mail. All the negotiations took place in top-secret conditions, and messages were sent with a high level of security in order to close the deal before competitors had time to respond.

The U.S. team was able to deliver drafts the following morning in Europe and receive answers by the time work began the next day, thus turning the time difference to their advantage. According to the manager of acquisitions, "the system gave us an added edge over European competitors, and put us on a par with American competitors."

As negotiations proceeded competition filtered down to a half-dozen major candidates. A date was set for the submission of final bids. The acquisition team felt that competitors were capable of outbidding them, and recommended a pre-emptive strategy. The team worked late Wednesday night to prepare a final acquisition paper, and after midnight (early morning in Europe) transmitted it. It was distributed to the board of directors on Thursday morning. On Friday, the acquisitions manager flew back to Europe on the Concorde, and (for only the third time in the history of the corporation) the board of directors held a Saturday meeting at which they approved the pre-emptive bid.

Their $750 million bid was made on Saturday afternoon, and detailed negotiations began in the United States the following Monday. The purchase agreement was signed in the early hours of Thursday morning, one day before the final bidding deadline. Although the price was high, the synergy value of the acquisition was substantial, and the purchasers were delighted to have acquired the business. The acquisitions manager says, "It would have been far more difficult to make this pre-emptive move without the fast communications through the system." The management-services manager reports a similar statement from the chairman of the board.

Asked if the system was worth $2 million (its entire cost) to the negotiating team, the acquisitions manager responded, "I'm certain it was worth at least that. Its value was immeasurable—we got the deal." As in many other cases, the electronic mail system paid for itself with one use.

Because a small team of people was responsible for such a significant project, the case was an ideal candidate for the value-added applications of OA. The critical success factor was the team's ability to respond quickly, which included obtaining approvals from the board of directors. In these circumstances, electronic mail was just the lever the team needed to compete effectively with other bidders.

It is likely that the synergy value of the acquisition was tens, if not hundreds, of millions of dollars above its price. Some small portion of this surplus value must be attributed to electronic mail, since the chief negotiator credits OA with enabling the winning strategy to be implemented. When so much depends on management effectiveness, the value-added leverage of OA can be immense.

Negotiating with the Government

Issues of timing are not restricted to such dramatic situations. In many negotiations there is a cost to delayed settlement. In the following case, a cost was associated with being too early or too late, making timing one of the critical components of success.

When a utility filed an application for a rate increase with the government, the documentation included over 850 pages of numeric tables. The utility was under considerable time pressure; even if only $10 million (less than 15 per cent) of the requested increase was granted, a one-month delay would have meant an estimated loss of profits of $375,000. In this case, however the consequences of delay would have been even greater. If the voluntary rate application was not filed on schedule, the company would have been forced to file under a different regulation that allows less latitude in determining what costs and investments can be included in the application. The different regulation also measures the level of capital investments as of a date three months before that of the normal filing. The company books a major portion of its capital investments in those three months due to construction schedules and administrative delays. Thus, the alternative filing would have excluded an estimated $30 million of investments. If the carrying costs of that incremental capital had been excluded, $3.4 million in profits would have been lost.

Table 9.3.   Negotiating with the Government

Cost of late filing:	
Revenue increase granted (conservative forecast)	$10,000,000
1 month of revenue	$833,000
Profit contribution (after 45% direct costs)	$375,000
Capital equipment not included in late filing	$30,000,000
Carrying costs	$3,400,000
Total cost of filing one month late	$3,775,000
Chance of missing deadline without OA	50%
Expected value of OA if analysis begins on schedule	$1,900,000
Cost of starting analysis one month early:	
Capital investments excluded from early filing	$10,000,000
Carrying costs, December capital investments	$1,000,000
Total cost of beginning filing analysis one month early	$1,000,000
Lesser of two evils	$1,000,000
Development cost (five PCs)	$25,000
Return on investment (one application only)	3,900%

To avoid this situation, the company could have begun the preparation process a month sooner. It would then have had to justify its requested increase based on a year ending one month sooner. The government would not have recognized the approximately $10 million in capital investments made in that month. The carrying costs not covered in the rate application would represent profits of about $1 million.

The company was caught between a rock and a hard place. To begin preparations early would have cost $1 million. The alternative was to risk missing the deadline at a cost of $3.8 million; the manager estimated there was at least a 50-50 chance of this occurring, for an expected value of $1.9 million.

The manager of the team chose neither alternative. Instead, he installed five personal computers with spreadsheets. "The PC was an invaluable tool in making this filing," he says. "The spreadsheet allowed the team to enter the information and make corrections easily without recalculating the entire document by hand. It also cut down on the time needed for proofing and retyping handwritten work sheets. I believe that, with the staff we had, it would have taken us at least an additional month to file this case without the help of the PC." In this case, the value-added leverage is in the ability of a team to respond quickly under pressure in a situation where timing was critical to the way in which they accounted for millions of dollars of capital (see Table 9.3).

The manager feels the value may be even higher: "The spreadsheet allowed us to analyze more alternatives, thus enabling us to present an even stronger case to the regulatory commission. Also, in subsequent settlement negotiations, quick response to settlement [proposals] allowed the process to proceed more quickly, which gave us a negotiating edge. We're sold on the PC."

The group responsible for filing with government regulatory commissions is always crucial to a regulated utility. Its success requires extensive data collection and analysis under great time pressure. These groups present a number of good opportunities for OA. In this case, the control over timing that the manager gained with the decision support systems was used not to reduce staff (cost-displacement), but to select the optimum time to develop the rate increase filing. Control of timing was worth $1 million, demonstrating the value-added negotiating edge that can be gained from OA.

Proper Presentation

Even the strongest arguments must be communicated in a convincing manner to be effective. The next section considers means of presenting evidence with greater impact. Computer printouts—or the computer itself—can be a medium for high-impact presentations.

The first case demonstrates the impact of a computer model in a financial negotiation. This is followed by two short anecdotes about internal negotiations that were easier to quantify in terms of their subjective value than their contribution to corporate profits. Finally, we close the chapter with a case involving a corporation's position in a federal legislative committee discussion.

Collecting Insurance Claims

Many people have experienced negotiations with insurance companies at some time in their lives. Corporations face similar challenges on a much larger scale. This case shows that OA can help develop more effective presentations of the facts, which can lead to faster settlement of claims.

The risk-management department of Consolidated Natural Gas (CNG) is responsible for loss control on property and casualty insurance. When the company suffers a loss, it is the risk-management group's responsibility to negotiate with the insurance company's representative to determine how much money CNG will receive. This can be a very tedious process, because the insurance company requires extensive proof of the loss. Invoices must be reviewed, out-of-pocket expenses must be proven, and so on. A major loss can take up to a year to settle.

There is a subtle undercurrent in these negotiations: the claimant must establish his credibility with the insurance company's adjuster. Otherwise, the lack of trust translates into time spent proving the veracity of claims. If the adjuster sees things in the claims he doesn't like or doesn't understand, then he will not sign a proof of loss statement.

CNG recently suffered a multimillion-dollar loss from an accident. Until three years ago, all of the risk-management group's calculations were done by hand, but this time a spreadsheet was used to model the loss. The model enabled the group to determine what the actual production and revenue figures would have been without the loss.

As the adjuster asked questions, the information was fed into the model. The adjuster could see immediately what effects his assumptions would have. Most important, the adjuster realized that the risk-management group had made conservative assumptions in building its case. From his viewpoint, this increased the trustworthiness of claims. He quickly said, "Let's have a printout; I'm ready to sign off." It was agreed that the insurance company owed CNG $3 million.

Frank Tierney, assistant vice-president for risk management at CNG, conservatively estimates that this settlement would have taken 90 days without the help of the model. In fact, the agreement was reached in one day. Ninety days' time value on $3 million at 10 per cent equals approximately $74,000. The entire cost of his two personal computers, software, and hard disk was $15,000, for a return on investment from this one use of nearly 400 per cent.

Most important, Tierney says, the insurance companies now say that CNG's data are better organized and presented than those of other major insurance customers. He has been actively building CNG's relationships with carriers to gain continuous coverage at a reasonable cost, and he feels that the clear analyses and presentations made possible by the spreadsheet reduce the underwriters' perception of uncertainty. This perception of risk in turn appears in the cost of coverage, and in the risk of cancellation.

For example, in the summer of 1985, insurance was difficult to acquire. According to Tierney, "At CNG we've managed to maintain our coverage in an environment where others have lost theirs. The PCs are at least partially responsible for that success." If CNG were to lose coverage, it would cost significantly more in premiums while a working relationship with a new carrier was built.

Even if coverage was not threatened, Tierney says, the improved relationship with carriers has helped to hold down premium costs. As he puts it, "These subtle little advantages [in negotiations] can, over a period of time, make a significant difference."

Tierney is 95 per cent sure that the spreadsheet-based analyses and presentations have made at least a 0.5 per cent difference in premium costs; he is 75 per cent sure that they have made a 1 per cent difference; he is 50 per cent sure they have made a 2 per cent difference. The expected value of this distribution is a 1.35 per cent impact on the annual premiums of $10 million, worth $135,000 per year. Over a period of five years, the present value of this effect (discounted at 10 per cent) is $512,000. With these longer-term effects added to the benefit of immediate settlement, the rate of return on investment rises to 3,800 per cent (see Table 9.4).

In this case the tool became a medium for presentation in the negotiation, and the shared view of the financial model contributed to a collaborative rather than an adversarial environment. No additional staff could have provided the same value as the shared information tool in this negotiation.

This one use of the personal computer paid for the system five times over. In the longer term, the spreadsheet as a means of communication solidified CNG's relationship with a valued insurance supplier, a relationship potentially worth hundreds of thousands of dollars to the company. The key staff group manages that important external relationship; because their work requires analysis of many charts, the spreadsheet is the ideal OA tool for them. Its value-added leverage is its ability to gain a negotiating edge when large sums of money are at stake.

Negotiating with the Boss

Negotiations occur within an organization as well as with independent parties. In the course of our research we came across two anecdotes that deserve mention. While we can only approximate their

Table 9.4. Collecting Insurance Claims

Value of faster settlement of dispute:	
Time saved by OA	90 days
Size of settlement	$3,000,000
Time value of money, 10%	$74,000
Value of better relations with insurance companies:	
ODDS	IMPACTS ON PREMIUM COST
95%	0.5%
75%	1.0%
50%	2.0%
Expected value	1.35%
Total insurance premium costs	$10,000,000
Expected value per year, cost increases avoided	$135,000
Present value, five years, 10%	$512,000
Development cost	$15,000
One-year return on investment	1,300%
Five-year return on investment	3,800%

subjective value, they are interesting for their approaches and their widespread applicability.

A director in a larger service organization asked for more staff. He was surprised when a decision meeting was called quickly and on short notice. He knew that to get the additional staff he would have to gain management's understanding of the projects currently in progress in his department and the implications of the staff shortage for his performance objectives.

He used a spreadsheet and graphics system to prepare a presentation on the use of staff in his department. In addition to helping him develop a convincing presentation, it enabled him to complete his preparations in two days, giving him time to think about his presentation strategy and to make last-minute revisions.

As a result, the director feels, management understood the issues far better than they otherwise would have. He feels that the graphics tools raised the odds of a favorable decision from 40 to 65 per cent. Since the decision was worth about $180,000 (three staff positions at about $60,000 each), the improved odds had an expected value of $45,000 (see Table 9.5).

Table 9.5. Winning Budget Concessions from the Boss

Odds of favorable decision without OA	40%
Odds of favorable decision with OA	65%
Improvement in odds credited to OA	25%
Value of decision	$180,000
Expected value of contribution of OA to better decision	$45,000
Development cost (one PC and management time)	$7,000
Subjective return on investment	540%

This is not to say that the tools contributed $45,000 to corporate profits. The benefit of the OA tools is related to this manager's ability to use those three additional people profitably. To measure the profit contribution would require a comprehensive analysis of the value-added returns from the director's department. Nonetheless, the case bears out the common wisdom that a picture can be worth a thousand words.

Another case of negotiating with the boss demonstrates the value of a spreadsheet and word processor. A subsidiary was in serious financial trouble. Management turnover was high, and a reorganization was imminent. The subsidiary managers made commitments to the board of directors that did not materialize. Corporate executives were asked to make a status presentation so that the board could decide whether or not to close down the subsidiary, change its key management staff, change its marketing direction, change its line of business, or move people to new positions within the company.

This presentation and critical decisions had to be presented by the corporation's senior vice-president of planning, in conjunction with the chief executive officer of the corporation. They were supported by the controller of the corporation, the president of the subsidiary, and the controller of the subsidiary.

The team had two days in which to develop the presentation, working from corporate headquarters in New York, subsidiary offices in California, and executive residences in New Jersey and Connecticut. To make matters worse, it was impossible to pin down the CEO of the corporation for the entire two days because of his busy schedule. Had they not had OA tools, they would have developed one scenario which, according to the senior vice-president, they would

have "fine-tuned a little bit," and they would have made their presentations based on their intuition. Instead, they did nine budget scenarios using a spreadsheet.

After their numeric analyses, the senior vice-president wrote the
report to the board using a word processor. He believes that if he had
done it in longhand or by dictation it would have been far shorter and
would not have attained the level of detail required for the board's
decision: "The computer helped me to compose a document that led
to a far more organized discussion with the CEO. In the meeting, we
covered all the details rather than jumping randomly from point to
point."

During the meeting all nine scenarios on the spreadsheet were
considered. The senior vice-president says, "We were able to use the
models [in meetings with the CEO] to destroy some executive myths,
making the decisions more rational, less emotional, and less based on
personality. Even if we had twice as much time, there is no other way
we could have kept [the CEO's] attention, kept the meeting focused on
the problem, and considered as many alternatives."

A decision that was of strategic importance to the firm was made a
bit more rationally and thoughtfully; nine different alternatives were
considered rather than only one. Senior management was better
prepared for the board meeting, and faced a lower risk of an adverse
decision. The senior vice-president says, "The PCs were of critical
importance in developing our strategy with regard to the subsidiary.
There's no question [their use] was worth at least their $10,000 cost."

We must assume that in each of these internal negotiations the
users had valid reasons to think that a decision that was favorable to
them was also good for the company. The difficulty of validating this
assumption makes it extremely hard to quantify the contribution of
OA in such internal negotiations. We can only note that an information edge can be gained within an organization as well as over
competitors.

Influencing Congress

The following case combines many of the aspects of the earlier cases
in this chapter. A negotiating position was improved by gathering
the right information in a limited time and presenting it with flair.
This case was difficult to quantify, if only because the immense
stakes lent a significant value to even a small improvement in the
chances of winning.

The case involves lobbying the federal government. Virtually every company is affected by the decisions of lawmakers, but the banking business is more sensitive than most to legislative action. In the United States, the Bank Holding Company Act regulates and limits the activities of bank holding companies. Certain banking activities, such as the issuance of credit cards, can be performed by so-called non-bank banks without subjecting those companies to all the regulations that apply to bank holding companies. Numerous large organizations offer these limited banking services, including Beneficial's credit card division.[5]

There has been political pressure to eliminate non-bank banks and to force all such activities to be performed only by banks or bank holding companies, although whether this would serve the public interest is questionable. In 1984 Congress considered a bill to eliminate non-bank banking, which did not pass in that session of Congress. In 1985, the Senate Banking, Housing, and Urban Affairs committee began discussing the reintroduction of the bill.

On April 24, David B. Ward, Beneficial's senior vice-president of government relations, learned that the Senate committee hearing was to be held on May 15. In that hearing the committee would consider testimony that could lead to modifications to the bill. It was important to Beneficial that the bill include a "grandfather" clause permitting existing non-bank banks to continue; otherwise it would be forced to divest a profitable subsidiary that represented 18 per cent of its assets and 11 per cent of its profits. (Forced divestitures have happened in the past in similar circumstances.)

Ward had three weeks to prepare testimony for presentation to the committee by Beneficial's chairman of the board, Finn Caspersen. From his office in Peapack, New Jersey, Ward had to collaborate with Caspersen and others in New Jersey, other top executives in Wilmington, Delaware, and the company's lobbyists in Washington, D.C. The wording of the document was critical, and had to be agreed upon by all concerned. As important as this issue was to the company, it was only one of many items occupying Ward and the other executives, and could not entail a full-time effort.

In the past, Ward would have drafted a document and sent it out for review. Owing to the logistics of remote collaboration, he might have revised the draft once, after receiving everyone's comments — typically, a few days prior to the committee hearing.

Now, however, Beneficial's top managers are regular users of spreadsheets, word processors, and electronic mail. Luciano Corea,

Beneficial's vice-president of office automation, explains that executives from the chairman down use an integrated minicomputer-based system that is networked company-wide. By using the system, all of the relevant people are able to work together on a daily basis. In this case, the testimony was revised four or five times in the course of the three weeks.

Ward relates yet another advantage of the system. The day before the committee meeting, Ward was reading prior testimony on a similar bill. He found a statement from June 1983 that tied the whole argument together and strengthened its impact. Without the system, it would have been impractical to attempt to change the document in time to have it printed in New Jersey and delivered in Washington the following morning. By using the system, Ward cleared the idea with all three locations, modified the document, and had it printed in the Washington office that same day for delivery to the committee.

The result of working online was a better-quality document — that is, more convincing testimony. Ward feels that he typically gets three-quarters of the value of a document in its first draft, and that he can reach 85 per cent of its potential impact after one revision. He would have stopped at this point without the system, and the document would have been about 15 per cent less effective than it was.

The effectiveness of testimony equates to a lower risk of unfavorable legislation being introduced. Beneficial was one of about ten major lobbyists concerned with the grandfather clause, along with other large companies such as Penney's and Sears Roebuck. Beneficial's testimony, presented by Caspersen, was among the most influential. The company is the tenth largest credit card service in the country, and the largest non-bank bank credit card company. The operations in jeopardy represented a far larger part of the company's business than they did for the other firms concerned.

Ward feels Beneficial's work played an important role in the outcome of the hearings. The odds of the grandfather clause being included might have been 60 to 65 per cent without Beneficial's testimony; with its testimony, Ward feels, the odds of a favorable outcome were 75 per cent. Put another way, the company's testimony reduced its risk by at least 10 percentage points.

If the testimony had been 15 per cent less effective because the system was not used, the risk might have been 1.5 percentage points greater than it was. What, then, is the value of a 1.5 per cent chance of being forced to divest operations that generate $12 million in profits each year? If the operations were divested, the cash received might earn just as much in an investment portfolio. If the cash could earn $12 million for five years, divesting would have a present value (discounted at 10 per cent) of $45.5 million.

However, the operations in question represent a strategic growth area for Beneficial. The company's traditional lines of business are relatively stable. The credit card and banking operations are expected to contribute $60 million per year, which is more than half of the current level of profits, in five years. If we assume a constant rate of growth in profits (just over 49.5 per cent), the present value of the profits from keeping these assets is $111 million.

Thus, a forced divestiture would cost Beneficial roughly $66 million. Reducing the risk of this by 1.5 per cent through the use of word processing and electronic mail is worth nearly $1 million (see Table 9.6).

An effective presentation of its case to lawmakers was extremely critical to Beneficial. OA tools helped make its testimony slightly

Table 9.6. Influencing Congress

Quality of document after one revision (compared to actual)	85%
Improvement in document effectiveness due to OA	15%
Odds of favorable decision without testimony	65%
Odds of favorable decision with testimony	75%
Improvement in odds of favorable decision by testimony	10%
Improvement in odds of favorable decision by OA	1.5%
Present value, forecasted profits from retaining business, assuming constant growth rate to $60 million, five years, 10%	$111,000,000
Less profits per year from divestiture	$12,000,000
Present value, five years, 10%, of selling business	$45,000,000
Value of retaining business	$66,000,000
Expected value of improvement in odds credited to OA	$990,000
Operating costs (10% of total system annual expense)	$35,000
Net benefit, this application	$955,000
Development cost (10% of total system allocated to executives)	$50,000
Return on investment (this use alone)	1,800%

more convincing. Because of the amounts at stake, even the slightest improvement in odds is valuable. In this case, we roughly estimate the value of OA to be nearly $1 million. Such benefits can be evaluated only in value-added terms.

Executives at Beneficial use electronic mail for a variety of purposes. This case describes one of the many high-stakes challenges facing Beneficial's top management team. We will explore their use further in a study of Beneficial's chairman of the board (chapter 10). In this company, a well-implemented OA system supporting high-leverage people is continually generating additional value-added results.

OA and Negotiations

This chapter has examined a variety of ways in which OA can provide a negotiating edge. Those involved in the cases were, for the most part, top executives. We believe that the same principles apply at all levels of the organization, in many types of negotiations. The larger the stakes, of course, the greater the leverage on OA benefits.

OA tools in the cases in this chapter included word processing, decision support systems, graphics, internal and external databases, and electronic mail. Before selecting an OA tool to support a negotiation, one must analyze the critical success factors inherent in the situation. In many cases, an information edge will be apparent — in building a better case, gaining better control of timing, or presenting proposals in a convincing manner.

Negotiations provide rich opportunities for value-added applications of OA, but those applications are also among the most difficult to implement. In some companies, they may not command enough attention, since negotiations are only one subset of executives' concerns. Furthermore, the topics are extremely sensitive and difficult to discuss. Nonetheless, OA is clearly a bet the odds on which favor those progressive executives who understand the importance of gaining an information edge.

Notes

1. B. Gibber, "Applications of External Information," presentation to the Diebold Automated Office Program, Working Session 80-1, January 8, 1980.
2. The authors thank Ben Graves for the introduction to this case.
3. The total cost of the system was $1.3 million; other cases in this book

have noted other applications which justify the entire amount.

4. The authors thank David Cooper of Digital Equipment Corporation (Europe) for the introduction to this case.

5. The authors thank Pat Riemitis of Data General for the introduction to this case.

THE LEADING EDGE

Two OA application areas have particularly intrigued us: executives and management meetings. These two areas of opportunity are especially promising, yet applications remain scarce. There is much to learn by taking a closer look at successes in these areas. Part 3 represents a shift in the style of the book; here we take a more in-depth view of emerging high-payoff applications.

Executive Use of Office Automation

We believe that executives may offer some of the highest returns on OA investments; at the very least, they have as much opportunity to experience value-added benefits as any other contingent in an organization. Little has been written on the executive use of communications and computing tools, however. With the exception of a few articles in the trade press, it is difficult to locate information on the subject.

Executives ought to be very interested in OA for a number of reasons. First, their decision making involves high stakes. Any improvement to the quality of their decisions — for example, improving the odds of a good decision or reducing the risk associated with the decision — is likely to have a significant impact on the bottom line. Second, executives are under increasing pressure from external environments that are growing more complex and changing more quickly, as well as from internal management workloads that are constantly on the rise. These tools offer executives the opportunity to extend their thinking and management abilities. Third, executive actions have a ripple effect throughout the entire organization. Improving executive effectiveness can have far-reaching effects on many people in the company. The impact of OA is highly leveraged both in its direct effects and because executives are opinion leaders who can encourage others to find more effective and productive ways of working.

In fact, executives are now coming under competitive pressure to begin their exploration of OA in order to gain an information edge that puts their competitors at a disadvantage. Now that progressive executives have led the way, a more rapid evolution of OA into the executive suite is certain to begin.

One executive, David Davis, felt strongly enough about his use of computers to write a response[1] to a *Sloan Management Review*

"Forum" written by Professor John Dearden, who posited that computers would not have an effect on top managers' jobs. Davis is the president of Tate & Lyle PLC, a company with $100 million in assets. In his article, he discussed some common applications for which he and his top managers use PCs: tracking the price of a commodity that accounted for a major portion of the cost of his company's products; tracing trade-offs between capacity, cost, and output flexibility of complex catalysts affecting costs and competitive advantage; discovering a dramatic increase in revenues by using a linear programming model which called for a change in a product mix; and determining patterns in the marginal costs of production.

Davis went on to describe the difference local computing power made in his working environments: "I have had a senior position in a North American company and a company in the United Kingdom. Both companies were in the same industry, but in one PCs were available almost from my first day on the job. Bought almost on speculation, they have been instrumental in the use of a number of tactics and strategies that were simple to execute but extraordinarily complex to analyze. The examples show that these strategies have yielded more than $2 million per year. All of the above applications … allowed profit improvements of at least half a million dollars per year; all were *essentially* interactive exploratory processes involving the exercise of judgment; and none could have been done without accessible computing power."

The executives profiled in this chapter echo Davis's belief in the power of OA tools. This chapter is an exploratory look at the ways in which executives have used computing and communications tools in their own offices; it outlines some of the reasons they have found these tools beneficial.

The cases in this chapter are somewhat different from the others in this book. Other cases have sometimes involved executives (and much of the book is as applicable to executives as to any other user); but those earlier cases did not explore a number of key questions about executive use of OA tools. In contrast, the interviews in this chapter are much less focused than the others in the book. We have not attempted to isolate particular executive applications of OA tools with measurable value-added benefits. Rather, we describe the broad use of OA by selected executives in many aspects of their work lives. These examples clearly demonstrate that executives are using OA tools successfully. They also show the diversity of applications and impacts that reflect the diversity of priorities faced by these corporate leaders. We present in this chapter stories that illustrate successful applications. We hope they will be a source of encouragement and inspiration to others.

Because little has been written about the executive use of OA, a type of "folklore" has been created about how executives respond to the tools. Most people believe that OA helps executives by providing higher-quality or more timely staff work, or by helping them organize their time. Some also believe that OA increases the volume of incoming communications (most of them unimportant), and that this information bogs down the executive in even more wasted effort.

We did not expect to find executives spending most of their time crunching numbers or typing letters, since those activities would reflect an unrealistic view of their responsibilities. We did hope to find that OA helps to filter incoming communications to executives so as to separate the important from the trivial. Because this work is an exploratory effort, however, we wanted to let executives tell their own stories unhindered by our prejudices. We reserve a more rigorous examination of the value-added benefits to executives for another study. Here we have chosen to let executives describe what they see as the most important benefits accruing from their use of the tools. In the process, we explore questions that are of particular interest in encouraging the executive use of OA:

- What tools do executives need most?
- How does the executive use of OA affect corporate culture?
- To what extent are executives involved in the design of their own systems?
- Why do many executives seemingly resist using OA personally?
- What benefits do executives perceive from their own use of OA?

Real-Time Decision Making

From a corner office of the new $129 million complex belonging to Beneficial Management Corporation, a 43-year-old executive runs the corporation with a fresh perspective, using tools his predecessors hadn't imagined.[2] Finn M.W. Caspersen, chairman of the board and chief executive officer of Beneficial, says, "For me, the computer is a communication device, and the primary function of the chairman is to communicate." Caspersen routinely sends and receives electronic mail; he finds it to be a much faster means of running the company than paper memos and the telephone. "I use it both to send and receive all of my internal mail. I generate 90 to 95 per cent of my electronic mail by typing it myself, despite the fact that I'm a very poor typist! It allows me to operate in a whole different time frame. Instead of having a memo wind its way through the system for five to seven days, I can get a response in half an hour."

Online Board of Directors

Among the many people with whom Caspersen is in regular communication, some of the most important are the members of Beneficial's board of directors. The entire board has access to the electronic mail system through individual terminals. "One of the problems with a board of directors is ensuring that they always have access to information and can communicate with the proper people. Without such access they will tend to feel straight-jacketed to a certain extent," says Caspersen. "This system gives our board online access to all of the information they might need. I always like to have the board members at Beneficial know what's happening before they read it in the newspapers. For instance, we had a $100 million debenture offering this morning, and they knew about it within 15 minutes of the offering — there's no other way that could happen."

In addition to disseminating information, the system provides Caspersen with quick access to the board: "If we need a board action or an executive committee action, accuracy and speed are essential. For example, we had an executive committee meeting on the Tuesday after the Labor Day weekend, and we were not aware of the need for that meeting until the Friday before Labor Day. The meeting involved a very complex discussion of the divestiture of Western Auto. There were some options that presented themselves and the meeting had to be called immediately."

Electronic mail did more than simply call the meeting participants together, Caspersen explains. "We were required to analyze several detailed offers. Via the computer system, the board received the complete background on all of the offers. At the 8 A.M. meeting on Tuesday morning we didn't have to cover any of the fundamentals; we got right down to the business of the committee. The questions were all extremely educated. We managed a very fast turnaround on a major business decision. In two hours we were able to dispose of what otherwise might have taken us ten or twelve. We had [legal] counsel there, investment bankers, and people coming from everywhere. People were spread all over the country over the weekend, and in normal circumstances you never could have gotten the information to them in time. We couldn't have gotten the same results with a courier service, because this was an ongoing interaction. The executive committee had all of the base data, which they were able to query in an online manner. They could test assumptions or changes in those data. By the time each arrived here, they had the benefits of those queries. We simply could not have done this in any other way."

When asked if he met with any resistance from the board, Caspersen was candid: "The only way to do this is to jump in—you don't put your toe in. The reaction of the board is primarily a function of age. I believe the younger members use it more than the older members. But if they want to know what's going on, they must get on the system; otherwise, they simply miss out. The electronic mail system has a mechanism to determine if a message has been read. If I send a message out certified and it lies there for three weeks, that's not a very good commentary on the abilities of the board member, and they know that I know it hasn't been read."

Top-Down Implementation

The implementation of end-user computing at Beneficial has had strong support from top management, and particularly from Caspersen. "I was one of the leading proponents [of office automation]. The personal work station is of tremendous assistance to executive productivity. The higher the executive, the more productivity potential. Ironically, the higher the executive, the less chance he'll use it. But I've been very insistent about this. I want my executives to be as productive as possible. By the time an executive dictates a memo to a secretary and the secretary types it and the executive looks back over it for revisions, there has been an enormous waste of time. When I receive a memo that has been compiled in that fashion, I send it back to the person and ask him why he's doing it that way when it's wasting so much time. I've never received two of those typed memoranda from the same person!"

Caspersen explains the implementation process at Beneficial: "We started by hooking up the entire executive committee, which I don't think is what the textbooks tell you to do—but it worked! Soon, everybody down the organization started to realize that if he wanted to get our attention, he had better get on the system. Instead of having reluctance on the part of people to use the system, we faced the situation of having a queue." Now, all the members of Beneficial's top management team use the computer.

Changing Corporate Culture

Caspersen has been a controversial figure at Beneficial because he has been an agent of change in restructuring the corporate culture. Asked if the system is a tool in formulating that change, Caspersen responds without hesitation: "It will be a tremendous tool. It reminds me of the short op-ed piece that Peter Drucker wrote for the *Wall Street Journal* which was entitled 'The Information Symphony'—that is exactly what's going on here. We no longer need a many-tiered bureaucracy. People break down the hierarchy by necessity—I think that is very important in an extensive organization. If you have the office in San Diego, California, able to access the chairman by typing in his name, the concept of having six people between you and him doesn't make sense anymore in that environment."

Is Caspersen concerned about being flooded with messages from lower levels? "Well, our next step is to get the system into all of our field offices. I'm sure I will receive an influx of messages from the field at that time, but as long as they're valid that doesn't bother me. I already get many messages. You see, I haven't been on this computer for half an hour and I've got 17 messages. But that's fine, that's the way it should be. If someone wants to communicate with me, this is an open door invitation and frankly, I've always encouraged that. I want to make it easy and rewarding."

Caspersen finds that the memos sent by electronic mail are not only received more quickly but are also more succinct. "The value for me is the ability to communicate very clearly and succinctly, and to know what's happening both inside and outside the organization," he said. "In this way I can turn around and 'massage' that information and make a decision and implement it instantly."

Executive Databases

"Our lobbying office in Washington uses the system extensively for list processing," explains Caspersen. "We know how members of Congress and senators vote on given issues and what their performance has been like in the past. We'll be adding the capability of knowing how many employees we have in their district. If the Washington office makes a contribution to a given congressman, or if I make a contribution, that's all kept on record. We can find some common ground by knowing what those contributions were. That's a very valuable lobbying tool. That would be impossible without the system."

Electronic mail also helps Caspersen with government relations. In chapter 9 the lobbying case describes how even a very slight improvement in the chances of favorable legislation being passed can be worth millions to a company like Beneficial.

The Executive Information Edge

"I think this system has opened up a lot of communication for me," Finn Caspersen says. "I feel less harried. I communicate when I'm ready, not when somebody else catches me on the phone. It gives me more time to think. The phone is an interruption."

He firmly believes that the use of office systems is having a positive impact. "What you're talking about here is the productivity of your executives," he explains. "People are able to produce more, to react more quickly, and they also tend to work longer hours — particularly when they use their computers at home. The accuracy of the information they use is greater. All of these things have significant effects on executives. There were many skeptics in the beginning, but as far as I know there are no skeptics now. People can't live without it; they can just get so much more done in a shorter amount of time."

Caspersen is an avid user: "I have the terminal in my office, one at home, and a portable terminal to carry when I'm traveling. My office is where I have my terminal. We're operating in real-time decision making at Beneficial. I believe that this is not an accepted way of doing business [in other organizations]. Yet, it's an absolutely great method for doubling your productivity. I'd say mine has increased 50 to 100 per cent. I know that my counterparts in competitive organizations are not using the computer as I am, and that gives me an advantage over them."

Strategic Decision Making

John F. Dembeck, vice-president and treasurer of the Olin Corporation, is a typical executive in some ways; he gets in to work every morning at 6 A.M., and his paneled office is decorated with plaques. He is atypical in other ways, however. Dembeck is an executive who uses his personal computer.[3] Not only does he use it for making business decisions, but he also dedicates at least an hour a day to learning something new about it. That hour is spent either experimenting with new applications or reading about computers. He says, "I have a responsibility to understand the capabilities and potential of the PC. If senior management doesn't spend the time necessary to learn about computers, two things will happen: (1) they will lose their ability to understand their work force which is rapidly becoming computer-literate, and (2) they will lose their competitive edge as a company."

Dembeck has personally developed about 1,000 spreadsheet models on his PC; each has helped him understand the implications of a variety of decisions, including acquisitions, tax problems, and capital management. He keeps about 50 at a time, erasing files after he is done with them. Dembeck explains, "I review my stock of spreadsheets quarterly. This forces me to rethink the problem the next time around. The computer has served as a tool to stimulate my imagination. By creating new solutions to old problems, the creative process can thrive."

Acquisitions

How do computers help him do business? Dembeck remembers when the chairman of the board told him the board was interested in acquiring a company, and was trying to decide what price to pay. An ordinary executive would take days to respond thoughtfully, perhaps delegating an assignment to a staff analyst. Dembeck, in 20 to 30 minutes, developed a spreadsheet that showed the impact of seven variables that would directly affect the cost. "I used to spend nights doing this stuff," he says.

The acquisition situation comes up often. "A company that does a lot of business with Olin was of high interest to us. We were considering acquiring it. Within minutes and after many alternative scenarios, I could tell how long it would take to pay back the investment and achieve the target rate of return—in this case it was seven years of positive returns before we'd get our money out. The real beauty of the spreadsheet is that it allows us to examine more alternatives in less time. Timing is important. When an investment banker calls and tells us something is available, we're not the only one they're calling. By using the electronic spreadsheet, we can get back faster with a decision.

"Computers also help me not to miss elements or components of a deal. When structuring a credit agreement, I'm dealing with five to 10 banks, using up to a dozen different variable rate spreads. The spreadsheet allows me in a 'what-if' mode to see the effect of all of those alternative rates compared side by side. Missing the impact of one of those alternatives could easily cost us a million dollars. More important, if I miss that optimal alternative, an outsider's perception of management would be 'this guy can be had.' The fact is, that PC puts me ahead of most people out there."

Thinking back on his experiences using the spreadsheet for immediate evaluations, Dembeck says, "There are also some surprises. I've negotiated three deals in the same way and I've detected a pattern in our competitors' bidding. Believe me, I can use that information — and I have. I also use the PC in situations involving foreign exchange questions, such as hedging versus non-hedging. And I frequently use it in negotiations. While I'm talking to someone on the phone, I can run the numbers right there in front of me."

The Right to Play

"The chairman frequently comes into my office and poses a question or problem," Dembeck says. "We look at the screen together in order to evaluate the problem. In this way, we try a wide range of alternative scenarios. If an analyst were coming in here to make a presentation relating to a problem we gave him, we would probably be much more limited in how many alternatives we gave him. If we constantly changed our minds, he'd go crazy. And we might be embarrassed to ask for an analysis of some of our wilder ideas."

Asked about the importance of their large central computers, Dembeck replies. "I like having my PC. For me, I don't need the MIS data. The big mainframe is for payroll, accounts receivable, that sort of thing. The role of MIS today is database management. They should be creating databases that management can tap into in order to shorten the time and improve the quality of decision making."

The Value of the PC

We asked Dembeck what he would be willing to pay for his PC. "When we make decisions that this company might profit from, we want confidence in the fact that the decision we make is the best. The PC opens up a wide spectrum of new alternatives for me. What price do you pay to extend the mind? It's something whose value can only be determined by the creativity of the mind that uses and directs it. Management decisions are related to talent. My managers have to be able to manage the top students from places like Harvard, Chicago, Wharton, and Stanford — and those people not only use computers, they require them. Managers who use state-of-the-art tools and push them beyond their capabilities are pushing their own brains. This is what brings the entrepreneurial spirit into a corporation. I have instructed every person who reports to me to get a PC. I justify it from the standpoint of being and staying ahead. The person who has to have a number to justify purchasing a PC shouldn't be in management."

Extending Executive Vision

Ronald Compton, president of American Re-Insurance Company, directs the course of this $1.6 billion company from his office on the fifty-second floor of a building located in the hub of New York's financial district. The Statue of Liberty dominates a breathtaking view of the harbor. Compton's work station is unobtrusively placed in a wooden bookcase to the right of a large color monitor directly above a table. Five comfortable chairs surround the table. We asked Compton if he held meetings there using the computer. He smiled and answered, "Yes, and you'll notice this table is a rather unusual shape. Lots of people around here call it 'The Altar.' We hold meetings here all the time. I also have my phone here so that I can work directly from my PC. In every element of this business I'm somehow assisted by the computer. In my world the computer takes the place of pencils, paper, and hand calculators. I write messages on it, I do financial modeling, and I use it to inform others. I wrote some of the software myself. It's not difficult—anyone could learn to do it."

Access to Information

American Re-Insurance is in a business that involves numbers and that depends on everyone understanding the numbers. One of the tools Compton finds most useful is the executive decision support system that he uses for a wide range of decision making. This system, loaded from the mainframe, provides Compton with critical information about the company, which is formatted in either words or graphics.

Compton says, "The immediacy of the numbers and my understanding of the assumptions make working with those numbers much easier for me. For example, in a planning meeting, I might want to see what our surplus would be in 1989. I might also take a look at staff turnover by division in a graphic display. In the past it would have taken days to get that information. Now I push a button and it's there in readable, understandable terms immediately."

Compton points out that it is as important for his staff to understand the numbers as it is for him. "You'd be amazed at how the computer affects what I call the creation and establishment of value. When I'm looking at the cash figures then *everybody* is looking at the cash figures, and the numbers start to rise because we all focus on it. It's a tool in establishing culture." Compton adds, "I also find it very useful in board meetings to bring the directors up to date on historical trends and to show how we are meeting our non-financial objectives."

Non-financial objectives? Are they charting subjective data? "Well, yes," explains Compton; "the subjective data is handled by charting each objective as to the date it should be completed and how far work has progressed to date. I create project planning schedules directly online, and revise them frequently. As the principal planner and strategist for this organization, I can add changes and see where we are. At a glance I can see if someone's putting things off. I spent years trying to figure out if people were meeting objectives on projects I had given them. With this system, I can immediately determine how a project is progressing."

His work station gives Compton easy access to a variety of types of information. "The system also contains information on our competitors. We also have a chart of the entire company online. It's not a typical organizational chart — we have very specific descriptions of each person's responsibilities. Really, I can see just about any information I need. Of course I can immediately print it out in hard copy, overheads, or 35-millimeter slides."

Compton is enthusiastic about the value of the charted data. "I'm a very visual person — my first love is photography. So graphics are a wonderful tool for me. I can understand them quickly and so can others. I always say that graphics is a language you can teach anybody. I'll tell you, before we got this system, it could take an entire day to see the trends that are contained in that one graph you're looking at. This is management by exception — I can see variations and determine whether something has violated a precondition."

Implementing Executive Decision Support Systems

We asked Compton how executive use of office automation was initiated at American Re-Insurance. "I have a friend in the computer education consulting business. I had shopped around for an executive course but they were too hardware-oriented. I had my friend build the course and we made all of the top-level people here go to it.

Then we told them that if they thought a micro would help them in their work they could have one. We got a very good response."

We also asked Compton about the degree to which his personal involvement played a role in the design of the system. "To make this system useful to me, I had to sit down and create a factor tree of critical success factors to this business. I asked myself what I needed to see and, together with others, we built the software to give me that information. Too many executives let the systems people determine what information they receive. It is absolutely essential that these executives first determine what is necessary to running the business properly — that is, to determine critical success factors. Then the system should provide that information. I could let someone else do all of this for me. But I had a mentor once who said, 'Every now and then take apart the numbers for yourself.' By helping to create the software and by using the computer myself, I understand the assumptions that go into what is on the screen and in the reports. I used to have someone else do it, but now I'd feel very uncomfortable because it gives me a much more in-depth understanding of what's really going on in the company I'm in charge of."

In Compton's opinion, "There is a big difference in dealing with the data-processing people once you are a computer user yourself. Now whenever users have a request for DP, they have to format their requests so that the DP people can pinpoint questions. It has been a valuable exercise. Do you know that we found three different definitions of the words 'paid losses' that were being used in EDP? Well, of course all three are legitimate, but before we started this formatting process, we were looking at the data and there was no way to know which definition was being used because we didn't know that the problem existed."

The Benefits of Executive Tools

Compton has been using personal computers for two years. "An idea could come to me at any time," he says. "With a PC at home, a lap portable to carry along when I travel and when I'm on my sailboat, and one here in the office, it's always close at hand."

We asked Compton whether he felt the computer dehumanized management to any significant degree. He replied, "I feel that my communication with people is quicker and clearer. Sometimes I've heard the argument that sending written messages frequently is dehumanizing. Baloney. People have been using written communication for thousands of years."

Compton is quick to point out the differences between his and the computer's work. "Obviously, the computer is only a tool. I have to do the real analysis. There are really two things that concern me in the decision-making process: (1) what do I need to know? and (2) how can I get the information quickly and understandably? This puts the data in understandable form and helps me by organizing and formatting it."

What have computers done for him? "They've clarified my thinking, they save me time — both in thinking and in being able to send messages to many people at once. By using the PC myself, I have improved my understanding of the business. I see it in my performance, and all indications are that my boss sees that improvement as well. He was certainly happy in our board meeting yesterday! Computers have proved to be powerful tools in capitalizing on changes in the market — I think it's helped put us ahead of our competitors. As I look at our performance over the last two years since we got the microcomputers and the [mainframe] decision support system, I realize that relative to what our performance would have been without the tools it's much, much better. I am certain that without these tools we wouldn't be as good as we are; and if we had had them earlier, we'd be better."

Our session at "The Altar" ended when Compton's secretary stepped in to say that the helicopter was waiting for him. A final question: what would he do if someone came to remove the computer system? "Retire," laughed Compton, "and I'm serious about that."

Managing Internationally

An ocean away from Compton, John Zapf, director of European operations for an automated testing-equipment firm, agrees that OA is a critical part of his work: "The major functions at headquarters are to ensure that everything is running smoothly in the field, that the communication flow is ongoing and accurate, that the divisions produce on time, and the data that are accumulated are consolidated into reports. In order to work effectively, computers are an essential part of the whole process."[4] Zapf finds the combination of word processing, spreadsheet, and electronic mail useful. He prepares, reads, and files his own mail, and believes that typing his own drafts is more efficient than dictating them.

International Communications

Zapf explains that, even in a decentralized company, communication with headquarters is of great importance. "One issue I've had to face as a European executive," says Zapf, "is that it would be easy for me to get out of touch with what's going on in the divisions, at corporate [headquarters], and in the subsidiaries. I need to at least keep weekly contact with people in the U.S. divisions, and I often need daily communication with them. I'm in contact with corporate [headquarters] approximately 25 times a week. If I tried to do all of this by phone, I'd be on the phone all day. We're an international company, and when you have people in different countries, there are going to be language problems. When messages are typed they are clearer and there is less margin for error. Also, the time zone problem is alleviated by the electronic mail. We have a branch of the company in Japan that is the counterpart to this organization. Japan is now on electronic mail and it's like we found them again! We simply couldn't call them on the phone because of the time zone problem.

"Electronic mail is also excellent for the sales people. I'll give you a common example of how we use it. Let's say we're competing with another company for a customer and the salesperson in the subsidiary makes an important discovery about a weakness in the competition. He can broadcast an electronic message to the other subsidiaries so they can all take advantage of his information. That kind of communication just didn't happen on that scale on a regular basis before we had electronic mail.

"I spend a lot of my time on the road, keeping in touch with the field. I go to the United States for two weeks at a time and I visit every division as well as corporate [headquarters]. The electronic mail really comes in handy. If I am leaving for the United States and realize that I've neglected to give my secretary a very important message, all I have to do is type it in on my terminal and transfer it from home. While I'm over the Atlantic, she has checked her mail, knows what to do, and takes care of the situation. Then when I arrive in the States, I simply borrow a terminal and check in for a message from her explaining how she has handled the problem. I spend two weeks taking notes, and when I get home I take one day at my house where it's quiet, I clean up the notes, and I write a visit report on the divisions or on a particular product line. If a division has a problem with a particular subsidiary, I write a personal memo to try and get it straightened out. This is an important step in our company's communication flow because the subsidiaries are interested in the divisions and the divisions are interested in getting the correct data out to the subsidiaries. Sometimes the memo will be to a division manager telling him or her that an error was made, and other times it will be of a more general nature. When I do have to reprimand someone, I can be specific now; before it was difficult to take corrective action by slapping someone's hand in front of everybody else. In total, I usually end up writing about 35 memos per week. Often I'll attach a print file of my forecasts. Without electronic mail and the spreadsheet, I never did these memos."

Forecasting Demand

Another important part of Zapf's job involves the forecasting his department does for every division. A report is prepared on units by division by company, and is updated every two weeks. Manufacturing decisions are based on that report. With seven divisions producing multiple products, forecasting becomes complicated.

In some cases export licenses are needed. "In the past, we would sit down in January and try to project figures for the year. It was very difficult to track our projections before we had a spreadsheet. Now we can incorporate more data on a more timely basis. The spreadsheets help to make our forecasts more accurate. This saves time in manufacturing—we don't overbuild or underbuild—and we are building to the right configuration. The accuracy in forecasting lets the corporation know where to invest," says Zapf. "I find that I monitor a lot more information now than I used to be able to monitor. I can see from numbers on the spreadsheet and from electronic mail messages where problems are occurring in the divisions or subsidiaries. Now I can take action sooner when I see a problem is growing.

"In addition," says Zapf, "one of the best capabilities that the computer offers me is the ability to do graphics. I can make my own slides in an hour and then my secretary might help edit them. As a result of this convenience, I'm using more graphics now and the professionalism of presentations has improved drastically. Because there are usually both analog people and digital people in the audience, I prepare both graphics and simplified spreadsheets. Some will want to see a picture and some will want to see the numbers. This way I can split the screen if I have both types in the audience."

We couldn't resist the temptation to ask Zapf about the enormous pair of blue-tinted sunglasses resting on top of his terminal. He chuckled. "Well, you see, before we got the computer, our forecasts were a little optimistic. So I've got them there to remind me when I'm forecasting not to look through *rose*-colored glasses."

The Benefits of OA

Zapf also makes use of his PC outside the office. "I have a Rainbow at home for myself and another PC for the kids to play with. I use the one at home for all of the same things I use it for in the office: spreadsheets, word processing, and electronic mail. I often send data from home to the VAX in the office. Most of our executives have terminals at home now, and before long everyone will. I think we'll get 20 per cent more work out of our employees by providing them with terminals at home."

Zapf continues, "I have a lot of ways of gauging the computer's effectiveness. When I arrived here in 1978, we didn't have anything [computerized]. Since then the company has been growing at a phenomenal rate, but we're not adding many people. We are also making more sales without adding a lot of people." When asked about the benefits to him personally, Zapf says emphatically, "I'll make a simple statement to sum this up. If they took my computer away, I'd quit. It would be like taking my car away from me."

Public Affairs

Rupert Smith is vice-president of public affairs at the General Telephone Company of the South, and a confirmed computer user.[5] "The most important aspects of my job are planning, anticipating, and responding with speed. My PC has definitely helped me with all three," he says.

Corporate Communications

In his position as vice-president of public affairs, communication tools are important to Smith. "We've also done some video teleconferencing here. It's a very good tool for communicating the company objectives, positions, and activities. I think the interactions that take place between the executives and the employees in the question-and-answer periods really add a lot to the capabilities of the medium. When there is a lot of change going on in an industry or a business, there is a lot of concurrent uncertainty and resentment. You have to open up communications channels; if you don't, people lose their minds because they imagine all sorts of possibilities. We really have been impressed with the capabilities of teleconferencing to provide us with those communication channels. In fact, we have another one coming up in a couple of weeks."

Executive Work Climate

Smith finds that using a range of OA tools makes his work more interesting. "My PC is a great stimulus because it's a novel way to do my work. It definitely motivates me and makes me more productive. Some of this work could be really tedious without it. For example, I recently compiled a report from a spreadsheet which involved three sets of forms with 45 items per form. It helped tremendously to have the spreadsheet do the numbers work. With the assistance of the spreadsheet, I can do extensive modifications with ease."

Smith offers an example: "I have a meeting next Tuesday, and I want to show the executive committee some budget comparisons. There is a great emphasis on budget control here, and I need to be able to present this type of information with clarity and accuracy. I was able to create these graphs in a matter of 10 to 15 minutes as opposed to the couple of hours it would have taken to have them drawn by hand and reproduced. That freed the time to use my spreadsheet to look at different scenarios that I wouldn't have had time to examine, so I was better prepared for the meeting.

"It's a good collaborative tool as well. When I'm discussing something with someone, we can do 'what-if' modeling while we're in the meeting. I've only touched the tip of the iceberg in terms of my applications. I try to experiment daily with new ones. I exchange notes with the vice-president of human resources on what he's figured out about his PC. I really find the PC therapeutic—all the way down to the soft noise it makes. I think if it could talk, I'd shut my door and never leave!

"In public affairs, we have a personal computer for every single employee. I've noticed that they're producing more and they're having more fun doing it. I'm not aware of anyone who is intimidated by the computer in our department. As soon as they realized how useful it was going to be to them, fear was not an issue. Some people in other areas do seem to be a bit uncertain about it and they talk about trying to stop the proliferation of PCs, but I think that's like standing at the shore and asking the tide not to come in."

Staying on Top of World Events

Lee Paschall, the former CEO and president of American Satellite Company, is an executive who has been using computers for longer than many hackers. He says, "My hands-on terminal activity really began in the mid-1970s. I went to the Defense Communications Agency as the Director in 1974. I was using the computer to evaluate the Defense Communications System by examining the performance of critical communications networks that the DCA provided."[6]

In 1981, Paschall joined American Satellite Company. "At American Satellite, I became an inveterate daily user of computers," he says. "In particular, I was using an external database called Tele/Scope. Every morning when I went into the office at American Satellite, I accessed the database and scanned the topics that had been entered the day before. Typically, there were 70 items in the topical headlines and I would read five to 10 of them in detail."

The Benefits of External Data

"[Data accessing] enormously reduced the amount of paper I was reading. In the telecommunications industry, in particular in the satellite communications business, there are an enormous number of technical publications and a myriad of stories each day in the trade press. Moreover, this greatly increased when we went through divestiture. The database tracked an extensive number of publications—for example, the *Washington Post*, the *New York Times*, the *Financial Times* of London, as well as all of the trade press such as *Communications News*, *Aviation Week*, and *Data Communications*. It also tracked the public releases of the FCC and the state public utilities commissions. I simply could not have covered this many periodicals personally without the system."

Paschall reports that in a number of instances the timeliness of the information was particularly valuable. "For example, there was one situation where an FCC order was expected regarding the orbital spacing of satellites. The order could have had a direct effect on our planning efforts. The legal staff at American Satellite had not expected any early decision on this matter. A very small, easily overlooked paragraph in the *Wall Street Journal* indicated that such a decision was imminent. I was able to alert the legal staff and we were able to react much more quickly than we otherwise would have. Other examples like this were prevalent in tracking the status of new products from other vendors of satellite equipment and services. A competitor would announce a new rate or service and we were able to begin to react that same day rather than a week or so later when their press release finally would get around to us."

Impacts on Management

"After I came in very early in the morning and read the database, I posed questions to the staff in the form of short notes and got a further explanation or an elaboration of our view on that particular issue," Paschall explains. "This was often important if I was called upon by my board of directors or the press to comment on an issue, which often happened. Having all of that information first thing in the morning tended to give the staff a feeling that I was constantly well-informed on a variety of issues. A current and well-informed manager or leader generates respect, which is a primary managerial objective."

Like Finn Caspersen, Paschall notes a visible shift in the corporate culture owing to his use of computing tools. "In 1981, American Satellite was seven years old and had not made a profit. It was in what I'd call an adolescent stage of its corporate development. After I started sending out information from the database, I began to notice a greater awareness of the outside world. Up until that time, the company had an inward focus. They were struggling to make the company profitable and to make it grow. I tried to encourage them to be less myopic in their vision. An executive helps bring the company to maturity by forcing them to think about something other than tomorrow's work day."

Paschall also appreciates the value of internal data. "Internal data is absolutely essential for the day-to-day management of a company. There are few successful companies that don't acknowledge that fact. On the other hand, the knowledge of the external world is extremely important to strategic and tactical planning and to the development of new businesses and new products. I believe companies that spend most of their time looking inward are just not in a very good position to compete over the long term."

Paschall believes that his personal use of computers has encouraged others in the company to begin using computers. "When I got to American Satellite, I think the terminal on my desk was the only personal work station in the building. People were doing strategic planning with hand-held calculators. I told them to go right out and buy half a dozen personal computers. Some people wanted to do a long-range plan for a centralized MIS before we began end-user computing, but I knew that would take forever and it simply wasn't worth waiting for; I told them to get started."

Paschall describes the impacts on his financial staff: "We were able to look at more alternatives and there was a definite reduction in after-hours labor. The accuracy of our calculations was much improved. We were willing to ask more questions because we didn't feel guilty about the amount of time it would take to find the answer. This definitely led to better decision making."

An Informed Board of Directors

Paschall is currently a board member of American Satellite, and he still finds the database a useful tool. "In my 'elder statesman' role at American Satellite, I use the database to track trends in our industry. For example, I went back through the database for one year and keyed in on the term 'joint ventures.' I detected a trend and was able to quantify the size and magnitude of that trend toward joint venture activities in the telecommunications business.

"I also use Tele/Scope for research. For example, there is a lot of activity now in fiber-optic technology. Fiber-optic cable is seen as a competitor to satellite transmission. When we put together a long-range plan for American Satellite, I used the database to search through two years of information on fiber optics. It would have been hopeless to try and find all of this information by hand. We got a complete story of what has happened in fiber optics; we determined the plans, financing, and actual implementation of various fiber networks. I was able to give the board a very comprehensive report on where fiber optics is going and what they should do about it."

Executive Use of Computing Tools

Paschall not only uses computers at the office, but also has a microcomputer at home that he uses for his personal financial planning, financial analyses, and word processing. Paschall even eschews available secretarial help, preferring to rely on his own word-processing capabilities. "American Satellite supplies me with secretarial services, but to sit here and write something out by hand and then take it up to the office and wait for the signature, etc., is just far too time-consuming. I type it myself and find that it saves me an enormous amount of time."

How was he trained to use the personal computer? "Trial and error! It was a personal challenge to me to figure out how the thing worked. I simply taught myself, using the manuals and tutorials. As for the database, I also taught myself. I was proficient within a week after using it from 30 minutes to an hour a day. It's a very simple, straightforward, user-friendly system. The internal database at American Satellite took a little longer—maybe two weeks. In that case, proficiency is directly tied to how often you use it."

Paschall believes it is important for executives to use computers themselves, hands-on. "If someone else did my information screening by clipping articles that he or she felt were pertinent to me, I would lose a lot of control. That person would have to judge what's important to me, and he or she simply wouldn't have my level of experience to know what nuance in a story may have long-term implications. You can't hire somebody whose mind works exactly like yours. I've always felt more comfortable doing my own thinking than having somebody else do it for me."

Executives may find excuses for not using their own computers or not doing their own database searches, according to Paschall. "I've heard those who say, 'Hey, my database is to call out and ask somebody.' People can do that, but it takes time. It not only takes somebody else's time, but you have to filter what you've heard to determine whether or not the person really understood the question and whether you really understood the answer, and then if you have a follow-up question, it is likely that the person might not be available to answer it immediately."

Paschall believes that many executives are afraid to use computers for some very simple reasons. "I believe what turns the typical executive off is a simple, prosaic thing like not being able to type. I may not be the most proficient typist in the world, but with a word-processor capability and a speller, I just rattle along and let the speller catch my mistakes. Senior executives of my generation seem to have a mental hang-up because they may fear that it's demeaning to be sitting in front of a terminal, or it may just be that it's something new and people typically hate something new. I think the next generation of leaders will not have any of these fears or inhibitions. They don't seem to have the same reluctance."

According to Paschall, "I don't know of any other way to find out what computers can do for you other than to use them. I suspect there are some people who will never make that leap. But I believe the vast majority of senior executives who are accustomed to questions, answers, and alternatives that come from human beings can easily make the transition to computing tools."

Like John Dembeck, Paschall points out that executives needn't be concerned about publicly embarrassing themselves. "Executives can make mistakes in the privacy of their own offices, and the computer is never going to tell anyone. I can explore many more options, some of them seemingly ridiculous, without fear of what my employees will think."

What is Paschall's advice to executives who haven't used computers? Chuckling, he says, "Try it, you'll like it."

Observations on the Executive Use of OA

The responses of the executives we interviewed offer an excellent basis for exploratory analysis. The range of industries they represent is broad: financial services, chemicals, insurance, manufacturing, telephone equipment and services, and satellite equipment and services. Some had used computers hands-on for years, while others have begun only recently.

What Tools?

Each of these executives has a different style and different reasons for using OA tools. It is clear that there is no single "correct" tool to use in introducing executives to OA. Nor does the selection of a tool correlate directly to industry. The executives seemed to select tools based on their own management styles and the critical business issues faced by their organizations.

The ways in which the tools are applied can be categorized as follows: (1) they are used to obtain more information; (2) they are used to increase individual thinking power; and (3) they are used as an instrument of leadership. The primary tools used for obtaining internal information are electronic mail, access to organizational (MIS) data, and external databases. Caspersen and Compton provide superb examples of how these tools serve them in their attempts to gain more information about their companies; Paschall's use of external databases enables him to meet his need for information about what goes on outside the organization.

Zapf, Smith, and Dembeck use spreadsheets to increase the amount and complexity of information they are capable of handling and to enhance their thinking power.

All of the executives are strong leaders. Some use OA tools as a means of increasing their leadership capabilities through communication. Caspersen uses electronic mail to motivate his executives and board members and to elicit their feedback. Zapf uses electronic mail as a means of providing feedback to remote employees. Smith finds videoconferencing to be an effective leadership tool in helping employees to weather industry changes by staying informed.

Corporate Culture

Several of the executives mention ways in which OA has affected their corporate culture:

- Communication flows directly to those who need to know rather than up and down the formal organizational pyramid.
- Communication takes place more frequently in all levels of the organization.
- Written communications are more succinct and less formal.
- The use of OA encourages employees to work longer hours.
- Internal databases enable employees to focus on the issues the executive focuses on.
- External databases give employees a greater awareness of what goes on outside the organization.
- OA changes communication patterns between executives and their boards of directors.
- The use of OA tools by executives is causing OA to be implemented more quickly in organizations.

Both Caspersen and Zapf mention that electronic mail has cut through organizational boundaries. Caspersen says he gets messages directly from people many levels down in the organization. He values being able to get information directly from its source rather than after it has passed through levels of management, where it is filtered and delayed. Caspersen also notes that the written communications he receives are more succinct and less formal. Zapf says that electronic mail improves lateral communication between subsidiaries. All of these effects have been documented in other research on electronic mail.

With respect to the improvement in vertical communication, Smith mentions the use of teleconferences in which announcements are transmitted from top executives to all employees. This practice is becoming increasingly common, replacing expensive "road shows" and videotapes that don't allow interaction.

It is interesting to note the impact of OA on the boards of directors of many of these firms. Caspersen uses electronic mail to communicate with his board, and he keeps track of their contributions online by watching their use of the system. Compton uses his internal database and graphics tools as a presentation device to communicate more effectively with his board. Paschall reports that OA helps him in all of his tasks as an independent member of the board of directors.

With respect to information access, Zapf, Caspersen, and Compton say that they received more internal information after implementing OA. Paschall emphasizes that external databases help his employees gain a greater awareness of events outside the organization. We have no evidence that internal data are more important to executives than external data, or vice-versa.

OA is a strong motivator of the executives we interviewed and their management team. Smith explicitly states his enthusiasm about working online, and all of these executives are avid and regular users. Paschall and Caspersen note that their personal use of OA has encouraged others to adopt the tools. The same motivational effects are seen with regard to their employees: Zapf and Caspersen mention that employees seem willing to work longer hours since the introduction of OA. The system may also contribute to employees' sense of direction: Compton reports that his use of internal databases has encouraged employees to focus on the issues that are of most concern to him.

In a variety of ways, OA has impacts on organizational culture. As we begin to understand what is possible, OA may become a powerful catalyst for cultural transformation as executives fulfill their role as leaders of people.

Involvement in Implementation

Another common theme is stressed by the executives themselves: each mentions the importance of his personal involvement in the selection and design of his office information tools. Since only executives understand their businesses well enough to know where OA tools can help, their personal interest is essential to successful implementation. Without their investment of time in designing their office information environments, executive applications are unlikely to succeed.

Sources of Resistance

In many cases executives have been relatively slow to adopt OA tools. Some people believe this resistance is a function of age. Executives in large organizations typically rose through the organization's ranks prior to the widespread influx of computer and communications technology, and many have had no exposure to or unsuccessful experiences with computer technology.

While age may be a factor in some cases, we believe that in general executives tend to be curious about and open to new ideas — more so than their lower-level managers of similar age — perhaps because of their willingness to try anything that helps them achieve their goals, or because they feel secure in their jobs and their marketability. The executives we interviewed are of all ages; thus, while age might be the cause of some initial objections, these are quickly overcome when the executive finds the OA tool to be of value.

Another commonly cited reason for executive resistance to OA is the stigma of using a keyboard. In some cultures, the keyboard is associated with secretarial work, and it is seen as degrading for an executive to "type." Every one of the executives we interviewed uses a keyboard without any feeling of embarrassment. We believe that the stigma of the keyboard is a symptom of a lack of incentives for working online rather than an actual cultural barrier. Most executives would probably use a keyboard without hesitation if they became convinced that it would help get the job done.

A very plausible explanation for executive resistance to OA is lack of time. Many executives recite the cliché, "I don't have time to save time!" Indeed, executives do tend to have less discretionary time available for personal projects and exploring new ways of working. Their busy agendas rush them from meeting to meeting late into the night. It is true that new ways of working initially require time for experimentation. Before an executive is willing to invest time in learning to use OA tools, he or she rightly demands that those tools provide a high return on that investment. Value-added benefits are likely to be the only kind that interest executives personally; they are also the most difficult for an executive to imagine without a base of experience. As we observed in this chapter, once executives experience the value of OA, they *make* time to learn how to use it, even to the point of maintaining work stations in their homes.

A fourth explanation for executive reluctance with regard to OA is that excellent support services are already available from the organization. When people lack adequate support, they may turn to technology as a substitute. Executives are surrounded by people who normally respond quickly and effectively to their requests. Surprisingly, these same executives who have good support may forgo it for the sake of speed and because of a desire to do their own thinking, as mentioned by Caspersen, Paschall, and Compton.

The only real incentive for an executive to consider OA is the true value-added benefit of permitting entirely new activities and ways of working, and of giving the company a competitive advantage.

What Benefits?

Despite the differences in the ways these executives apply OA, all of them understand and believe in the value of the "information edge." They all view OA tools as a means of gaining competitive advantage through better management. With regard to their base of information, the interviewees note significant improvements in accuracy, clarity, timeliness, and relevance through the use of databases and electronic mail. Compton's involvement in designing his own database management tools has given him a better understanding of the assumptions behind the numbers, and ensured the maintenance of relevant internal data. Zapf notes an improvement in the quality of data for forecasting, the basis for his investment decisions. He monitors more information, and feels he can take action sooner with OA tools.

The executives use various OA tools to spot important trends. Dembeck and Smith used spreadsheets to spot trends in both internal and external data; Dembeck's trend spotting involved determining a pattern in the way Olin's competitors were bidding in certain negotiations, while Paschal used databases to determine trends toward joint ventures in his industry.

OA also encourages written communication in place of telephone calls. Caspersen, Compton, and Zapf all felt this tendency had improved their communication channels by virtue of the more succinct, clear, and timely news they received from their staff.

The executives feel that OA provides them with the ability to do their own thinking rather than relying on the capabilities of others. They appreciate the ability to test more creative alternatives, even speculative ones that they might be reluctant to ask of analytic staff.

All of the executives are pleased with the amount of time the tools save them, but this is not seen as a cost saving. They use the productivity gains to enhance the quality of their thinking and interpersonal relations.

Perhaps these executives are the exception. They are risk takers whose gamble with OA has paid off handsomely. They are successful individuals both inside and outside the corporation. They may be seen as mavericks, but they should also be seen as good leaders exercising good judgment and investing their organization's precious capital in its most valuable resource—the minds of its people.

Notes

1. "SMR Forum: Computers and Top Management," *Sloan Management Review* 25, no. 3 (Spring 1984) 63.
2. The authors thank Pat Riemitis of Data General for the introduction to this case.
3. The authors thank Ben Graves for introduction to this case.
4. The authors thank Mary Cooper of Digital Equipment Corporation (Europe) for the introduction to this case.
5. The authors thank Ron Kyle of General Telephone Company of the South for the introduction to this case.
6. The authors thank Susan Babcock of EIC/Intelligence for the introduction to this case.

Augmented Meeting Support

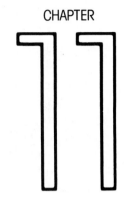

So far in this book, the case studies have described the use of OA tools by individuals or small groups.[1] While we have demonstrated that the impacts of OA may extend far beyond the single knowledge worker, the fact remains that most of the use of OA has been by individuals performing isolated tasks.

In practice, collaboration is an essential part of doing business. Much of our collaboration occurs in meetings — task-oriented gatherings of two or more people. With the exception of teleconferencing for geographically dispersed groups, we have seen little of the impact of OA on one of our most common working settings, the business meeting.

Improving meeting effectiveness is a challenge that most companies cannot afford to ignore, not only because managers spend between 35 and 69 per cent of their day in meetings,[2] but also because group decision making is part of the daily operation of most organizations. Group decision making brings a variety of approaches and perspectives to a problem, and participation facilitates the implementation of decisions.

Meetings occupy a relatively large part of the average knowledge worker's day. Yet people are commonly frustrated with the ineffectiveness of meetings: time is wasted in the actual meeting, and more time is wasted after the meeting in attempting to resolve remaining ambiguities and conflicts. Perhaps most important, meetings may fail to produce the desired results when significant business issues are at stake. This chapter describes a technique that applies OA tools to meetings to help improve group effectiveness on all of these dimensions.

Problems with Meeting Productivity

Creating a productive meeting environment is not easy. The diversity of perspectives present in any group, while potentially an asset, often makes understanding difficult. Often, each participant has his or her own agenda and leaves a meeting frustrated by a lack of results. Many people in business complain about the disproportionate amount of time taken by meetings and the unsatisfactory results that are attained. The same types of problems are cited repeatedly:

- Lack of creativity
  - Good ideas get lost
  - There is pressure to conform ("groupthink")[3]
  - There is premature closure before issues are resolved[4]

- Poor participation
  - Some people dominate
  - Some people don't participate
  - Participants fear conflict[5]

- Lack of focus
  - Discussions wander; points are repeated
  - Participants are overwhelmed by information
  - Participants are over-concerned with detail

- Lack of follow-through on decisions made in the meeting

Many of these problems can be remedied by training managers to lead meetings more successfully, but that approach is impractical in most organizations. Executives are reluctant to admit the need for such training or to allocate the necessary time and money resources.

Even when well-trained leaders are present, meetings are fraught with difficulties. Participants must share information and ideas, capture and meld their thinking, and negotiate solutions while dealing with complex issues that challenge everyone's thinking abilities. Office automation can help by making possible an "augmented meeting."

What Is an Augmented Meeting?

Augmented meeting support applies advanced OA tools to the traditional meeting. In addition to the usual table, blackboard, and slide projector, the meeting room contains a computer and a video projector (or a large screen) so all participants can see the contents of the computer monitor. The screen acts as a group "scratchpad" when the computer is used to present and modify materials and to take notes on the group's discussion. In this way all the tools of OA can be made available to meeting participants.

There is more to an augmented meeting than simply putting a work station in a conference room, however. Techniques have been developed to maximize group performance through the use of OA tools.

The computer is generally operated by a highly trained "chauffeur," who "drives" the system on behalf of the meeting participants.[6] The chauffeur uses various OA tools to take notes, perform mathematical calculations, and access internal and external databases. The tools are used for more than a simple presentation of data; they allow participants to develop their ideas interactively.

Office Automation Tools

As the group members discuss the agenda, the chauffeur records their thoughts in key words, thus building a complete structured outline of the discussion. This may be done using outline editors on PCs; we use a special system called "Augment" that is designed to operate "at the speed of thought."[7] Items can be added anywhere in the outline at any time, capturing the free-flowing discussion and recording each point in its proper place. Subsequently, participants may view and modify the structure on the video screen, reordering their thoughts and examining relationships between ideas. This structured text environment is far more effective than conventional word-processing systems.

When discussing figures, the group can interactively create and modify a model by devising a spreadsheet with rows and columns of their own choosing. Alternatives can be assessed by changing an assumption and watching the effects ripple through the spreadsheet. The structure of the model itself can be altered by changing the relationships between cells or by adding new rows and columns. In addition to using the familiar spreadsheet, augmented meetings may employ sophisticated decision support models to help structure and analyze complex problems.

Some people have experimented with the use of project management tools in augmented meetings. Others access information from the organization's internal databases or from external database services. Where internal systems permit, the group may access other documents on WP systems, or calendars and reminders on local office databases. Certain projects require more powerful or special-purpose tools, such as statistical tools, forecasting and planning models, and interactive graphics. Any of the wide range of information and communications tools may be brought into an augmented meeting.

Remember that meeting support tools need not produce polished documents or precise, complex models. Their role is to provide a group scratchpad to support intuitive, ad hoc structuring of the group's ideas.

Process Facilitation

While the chauffeur operates the OA tools, a process analyst (also called a process facilitator) may further increase group effectiveness by observing group interaction and providing feedback. For example, the process analyst may interject a comment when the discussion seems to be wandering or when relevant ideas are being ignored. Participants may ask the process analyst to help uncover hidden agenda items, to highlight the sources of misunderstandings, and to define disagreements. Judicious prompting of minority opinions helps avoid the groupthink phenomenon. The process analyst can ensure that issues reach an appropriate degree of resolution before the group moves on, to improve the quality of group thinking. The process analyst may also keep track of the time left for dealing with remaining agenda items and achieving the meeting objectives.

Impromptu Meeting Augmentation

Augmented meeting support has been applied in a variety of settings and to meetings of varying lengths. Early applications in the late 1960s involved a team of software engineers who were developing the tools used during their own planning sessions.[8] D.C. Engelbart and his research group at Stanford Research Institute used their structured-text editor and an early video projector in a variety of planning and decision-making meetings as they designed and built their industry-leading OA system.

The use of OA tools in meetings outside the research community is relatively new; in general, organizations evolve from individual to group applications of OA. In recent years, the technique has been applied to a range of meetings in corporate and government settings; topics such as strategic planning, venture start-ups, budgeting, project design, and key decisions affecting numerous departments are discussed. This chapter describes a few typical meetings, and summarizes the techniques that make augmented meetings successful.

Fast Response on Pricing Decisions

In some cases, people use OA tools in meetings without the aid of trained facilitators and special equipment. For example, chapter 10 described Ron Compton's use of his work station for meetings with his subordinates. Another example occurred at American Communications Services (ACS), a unit of American Hospital Supply Corporation that operates a 15-site video teleconferencing network.

In addition to managing the internal video teleconferencing network for its parent company, ACS provides communications consulting services to multi-hospital systems, including needs assessment, design, installation, and management of video teleconference networks. ACS also leases its video teleconferencing network to the parent corporation's major customers.

Frank E. Kavenik found augmented meetings to be useful in his decision making as vice-president of ACS. The system Kavenik uses for displaying spreadsheets is simple; a personal computer is connected to a 25-inch video monitor. He uses OA tools in strategy sessions on pricing policies, and for long-range strategic planning.

In the strategy sessions on pricing policy, a spreadsheet is displayed to examine detailed operating plans for specific projects. Kavenik and his colleagues can compare the ACS operating plan with their assumptions about competitors' plans. As the meeting progresses, a number of assumptions are tested. "As quickly as someone develops a scenario, it can be tested right before his or her eyes. In the past we would have had to adjourn the meeting and come back the next day in order to allow for time for the calculations to be made," explains Kavenik. "Now we look at many more scenarios, and as a group we receive quicker feedback. We are actually doing sensitivity analyses in real time."

Kavenik gives an example of a time-sensitive situation in which an augmented meeting had a substantial impact on effectiveness: "We were responding to a request for an updated pricing proposal. We were operating under a deadline, but, more important, we were in a competitive situation. The augmented meeting allowed us to respond much more quickly than we otherwise would have. I believe it allowed us to respond more quickly than our competitors. I think our

Table 11.1.   Fast Response on Pricing Decision

Estimated profit contribution	$200,000
Improvement in odds of closing deal	25%
Expected value of OA in impromptu meeting (one event)	$50,000
Present value if similar case occurs annually for five years, 10%	$190,000
Development cost	$7,000
One-year return on investment	600%
Five-year return on investment	2,600%

ability to work together with the spreadsheet increased our probability of success by 25 per cent on this project."

Based on the size of the project and industry-average operating margins, we estimate that this project contributed approximately $200,000 in profits. Thus, the expected value of the augmented meeting in this one case was approximately $50,000 (see Table 11.1).

Strategic Planning

ACS also uses an outline editor to augment strategic planning sessions. In the past, flipcharts and chalkboards were used to record ideas and issues that arose in these sessions. "Manually writing ideas out was a slow and tedious process; we couldn't go into as much depth on any one topic and we couldn't consider as many alternatives," says Kavenik. "Owing to the speed and ease of use of the outline editor, there were far more suggestions and the meeting was more free-flowing and spontaneous. We had a much higher level of detail than we normally have and we all walked away from each meeting with a copy of the outline to consider. We were doing good plans in the past, but now I believe they're even better. Now we are able to put more thought into the plans in less time."

Kavenik's presentation to his senior executives was based on the outline generated in the meeting. "When I presented the plan, I used the computer-generated table of contents as an executive summary. The more detailed 10-page printout was the basis for my extended presentation. The senior executives appreciated the fact that the plan was so well-organized and readable. They also commented on the depth of the supporting detail. After my presentation, it was very easy to incorporate their comments and suggestions on the computer."

How much did this augmented meeting support cost Kavenik? "Not much," he says. "You don't need expensive equipment; you just need what's necessary to get the job done. We did the strategic planning session with a $450 secondhand Apple II+ that our accounting department outgrew, a $250 monochrome monitor, and $125 worth of software. We did the spreadsheet calculations on a PC-XT [costing approximately $6,000, and acquired for other purposes] using the same monitor and $200 worth of software. You can get a lot of mileage out of a small expenditure.

"I keep the software and equipment in my office, ready for use in impromptu meetings when others stop by to discuss situations. The next step is to get a portable computer and a video projector so that I can do my presentation in real time and incorporate the suggestions of others on the spot. I believe that real time will have a tremendously powerful effect on the efficiency of the meeting. I'm evaluating video projectors right now."

There is no way of knowing how many creative users like Kavenik are holding augmented meetings on an impromptu basis. It is likely that they are growing increasingly numerous as users apply OA tools throughout their jobs. In parallel, specialized facilitators are advancing the techniques of augmented meetings as they support clients with their variety of approaches. Four consulting groups who facilitate augmented meetings are described here: our own firm (N. Dean Meyer and Associates Inc.), the Decision Techtronics Group at the State University of New York at Albany, CogniTech Services, and Halcomb Associates, Inc.

N. Dean Meyer and Associates Inc.

Our firm has conducted augmented meetings using Engelbart's structured text editor, Augment, as the primary tool. A number of these meetings were related to corporate and venture planning.

Strategic Planning

In 1981, the vice-president of strategic planning of a rapidly growing conglomerate worked with two of his staff to assemble the annual corporate strategic plan. The plan was developed based on subsidiary plans submitted by each of the operating companies and divisions. Two significant companies had been recently acquired; they did not begin to prepare their part of the plan until late in the annual cycle. Thus, divisional plans were not submitted to the corporate planning group until just a few weeks before the corporate plan had to be submitted to the board of directors.

The corporate strategic-planning group had to choose between waiting to see the divisional plans, or developing a corporate plan without input from two key divisions. By using a structured text editor throughout a week-long meeting, the corporate planners were able to incorporate all submissions into the final plan in one week, and gained greater support from key divisional executives. By working as a team online rather than splitting the plan into individual pieces, the corporate planning group produced a better plan for its board of directors.

As a result, the vice-president of planning feels that the augmented meeting significantly improved his chances of gaining funding for multi-million-dollar acquisitions in the coming year. An improvement of less than 0.5 per cent in those chances would pay the costs of augmented meeting support.

In another case, the president of an operating company met with 20 vice-presidents and their key staff for two days. A significant number of these people represented a subsidiary that had just been acquired. The president was concerned that they might not "buy into" corporate goals and directions. Before the meeting, the president entered into the system a rough draft of a consolidated plan in the form of both text and spreadsheets. He used the system to present the plan to the group. During his presentation, questions and comments led to modifications to the document. In just two days the next year's strategic plan was produced and consensus was gained. The effect of the augmented meeting was not getting the plan done, but building the consensus that led to action in the following year.

New Ventures

We have used augmented meetings to plan new ventures. For example, an entrepreneur had been performing research on display technologies that he hoped would produce a revolutionary video teleconferencing system. He hired five consultants from throughout the United States to plan the venture: experts in teleconferencing, office automation, video technology, sales and marketing, and accounting and business planning. The initial purpose of the meeting was to refine the product definition and the business launch plan.

The augmented meeting lasted two and a half days, and the team worked at a fast pace. They sorted through a multitude of facts and ideas, including the nature of the chosen and related technologies, other technological component requirements, assumptions about the marketplace, competitive offerings, and company resources. Midway through the meeting, it became clear that the original ideas were too far ahead of their time and that a successful venture was unlikely. Because the entire project team had participated in developing this analysis, the difficult decision to abort the project was made quickly. The remainder of the meeting was spent brainstorming alternative applications of their research. A number of ideas for more workable ventures were developed. It is unlikely that without the tools the group would have gotten to this stage, and the decision to cancel the original idea might have represented a total loss of the hundreds of thousands of dollars in research already performed.

Client Relations

We have also experimented with using structured text editors to augment larger groups. A committee of fifteen senior executives representing those who sponsored the Diebold Automated Office Program, a multi-client research program, allocated half a day to plan investigations for the coming year. The meeting was augmented by Dean Meyer; Dr. Tom Lodahl, director of the program, led the discussion. The broad-ranging conversation identified a variety of issues and structured them into six specific topics for study. The meeting documentation was presented online the next day to the 35 remaining sponsors for their comments and approval.

Without the augmented meeting technique, fewer ideas would have been presented to the larger group, and it is highly unlikely that they would have been well structured. The larger group would have been less likely to support the direction of the research program. If only one of the sponsors had left the meeting unsatisfied with the following year's plan and had dropped out of the program, the loss in profit contribution would have been twice the cost of the augmented meeting equipment and facilitators.

CogniTech Services Corp.

CogniTech Services Corp. is an independent consultancy in Easton, Connecticut. Its chairman, Dr. Tom Lodahl, and its president, Kay Redditt, have extensive backgrounds in office automation and apply their skills to a variety of business-planning requirements. On behalf of their clients they conduct augmented meetings using a spreadsheet and a word processor. We present two examples of their work: one from a small venture and another from a huge government organization.

Getting Equity for a Venture

With the increasing deregulation of industry in the United States, many banks are looking for non-traditional sources of income, and insurance is a prime target. Two principals in a new venture developed a way for banks to enter a new line of business by selling insurance.

Transforming the idea into a business required a significant amount of capital; to acquire support, a strategic plan and a prospectus had to be developed. The principals, creative thinkers, had not been able to structure their idea, analyze its potential, and agree on key decisions. Their venture was in danger of being prematurely sold or simply being dissolved. If they had sold at that time, they would have given up 50 per cent of their equity for a mere $200,000.

The key factor that changed the outlook of this venture was a series of augmented business-planning meetings. The entrepreneurs spent two weeks with Redditt over a period of a month and a half. They developed a market model using demographic data that forecasted the significant size of the market. They analyzed alternative capitalization structures that combined debt and equity, cash, and exclusive distribution rights. They determined the design of the product, how to market it to banks, how the banks could market it to their customers, the computer systems required to support the product, and franchise relationships that would maintain loyalty.

Once the model was built, the key investor manipulated it in another augmented meeting. The venture solidified his commitment by allowing him to change certain assumptions and elements of the strategy. In the process, the entrepreneurs found a way to launch the venture on only $1.4 million, rather than their original estimate of $7 million. This made it even easier to get funding, and allowed them to keep a greater share of the equity. As a result of the business plan and prospectus, they found five willing investors and selected one as a source of funding and distribution.

Profit forecasts for the company's first four years (ending in 1989) have a present value (discounted at 10 per cent) of $21.5 million. The investor acquired 15 per cent of the stock for $1.4 million. By dividing

Table 11.2.   Getting Equity for a Venture

Value of 15% of company actually sold	$1,400,000
Imputed value of 100% of company	$9,300,000
Portion owned by principals	85%
Portion that would have been retained without meetings	50%
Difference in percentage of ownership	35%
Equity value of difference in ownership credited to augmented meetings	$3,300,000
Development cost (estimated, for PC and consulting time)	$10,000
Return on investment	32,000%

$1.4 million by 15 per cent, we impute that the total current equity is worth $9.3 million. This is $9 million more than the estimated sales price of the concept before the business plan was developed.

Assuming that the venture would have grown to the same value with or without the augmented meeting, the augmented meeting is credited with retaining at least an incremental 35 per cent of the equity, worth $3.3 million (see Table 11.2).

Government Strategic Planning

CogniTech worked with a large government agency that used an augmented meeting to develop its annual strategic plan. In the past, such plans were written by a few high-level staff people, and there was little understanding or support among the agency's 90,000 employees. Planned programs had actually failed for lack of lower-level "buy-in." The executive in charge of planning wanted to continue to provide leadership from the top; at the same time, he recognized the importance of grass-roots support from regional management upward.

In August 1983, CogniTech met with seven top executives in a two-day off-site augmented meeting. Lodahl led and facilitated; Redditt chauffeured the meeting. The group received presentations on trends in society that would affect the agency, and brainstormed specific issues of strategic importance. Of the 11 major trends identified, seven appeared to be issues upon which they could act. As the participants talked, the meeting agenda evolved into an outline of the entire discussion, which in turn was transformed into a meeting report. This document proposed directions on key issues, to be acted upon by the entire agency. The document was then circulated to the next level of management for a critique.

One month later, Lodahl and the top management team met (offline) with 30 regional line managers and headquarters staff to review and revise the document. The group studied and modified the strategic trends, and formed a task force on each of the seven selected issues. Each task force developed plans in greater depth and determined budget requirements. The final strategic plan was published in May 1984, in keeping with the budget deadline set by Congress.

The participants credited the augmentation technique with enabling them to produce the document within the allotted few weeks. They felt it improved agency-wide comprehension of the issues and consensus on actions. The agency's executives feel that the high level of regional involvement would have been unlikely without the document produced with the aid of the augmented meeting.

Specifically, they estimate that the probability of successfully attaining agency-wide involvement in this planning program was 60 per cent (in fact, they feel it worked); based on past efforts, the odds of meaningful planning participation without the meeting augmentation would have been only 20 per cent. Thus, the augmented meeting support improved the odds of meaningful involvement by 40 percentage points.

The value of this participation is significant. Without it, as in the past, lower levels of management would not have effectively implemented ideas generated at the top, and ideas generated at lower levels would not have been heard at the top. As a result, the ratio of services delivered to tax dollars spent would suffer. Because of the scale of operations controlled by this agency, as little as 0.001 per cent less effective management of the agency could mean a loss of $9 million in tax dollars (see Table 11.3).

Decision Techtronics Group

The Decision Techtronics Group (DTG) at the Rockefeller College of Public Affairs and Policy in the State University of New York (SUNY) at Albany emphasizes quantitative decision-making techniques. Dr. Robert E. Quinn and Dr. John Rohrbaugh are experienced at meeting augmentation, having facilitated over 40 meetings for government and corporate clients.

Table 11.3.   Government Strategic Planning

Odds of successful involvement without augmented meeting	20%
Odds of successful involvement with augmented meeting	60%
Improvement in odds of successful involvement	40%
Potential impact of involvement on performance (assumed)	0.001%
Size of program	$900 billion
Expected value of involvement	$9,000,000
Expected value, augmented meeting performance impacts	$3,600,000
Development cost (estimated maximum, not disclosed)	$50,000
Return on investment	7,100%

The staff of DTG has employed five decision support models in augmented meetings: resource allocation, multi-attribute utility analysis for selecting among competing choices, dynamic simulation, social judgment analysis, and decision trees. Two DTG clients offered cases that demonstrate the importance of these decision aids.

Designing Curriculum

The New York state government, the twelfth largest employer in the United States, invests a great deal of time and money in training its employees on an ongoing basis. Don G. Giek, director of program planning and employee development in the governor's office of employee relations, is responsible for designing and managing training programs for professionals—scientists, doctors, engineers, and accountants—who occupy managerial positions. The eight six-day courses are conducted in accredited universities, and student participants can obtain college credits; each 36-class-hour course is specifically tailored to the state's needs and the students' jobs.

Giek agreed with the suggestion that the state would offer a better program if the program was designed by a panel of experts rather than simply delegated to a single university. A team of 24 educational experts from public and private colleges and universities in the state, various state agencies, union representatives, and nationally recognized authorities was assembled. Their job was to design the curriculum so that it would meet the range of educational needs within the allotted class time.

Prior to the meeting, online tools were used to perform a literature search, which produced a list of potential topics for management training. The panel members reviewed the list in advance, identified points of agreement and disagreement, and added thoughts of their own. The group then met at the DTG augmented-meeting facility for two days.

After Quinn's introduction, in which he explained the tools and the process to be used, the panel was divided into four groups representing four major topic areas. Each group concentrated on the two audiences for the topic—supervisors and administrators. They brainstormed until they were satisfied that they had generated a comprehensive list of potential course topics. For each topic they defined five steps in the teaching of the material: self-analysis, lecture, case studies, exercises, and role playing. For each of these steps within each topic, they estimated the class time that would be required and the relative educational payoff.

Each group then rated the relative importance of each topic. Based on this rating of importance, the time required for each step within a topic, and the relative payoff of each step, the computer calculated an efficiency index for the 36 course-hours.

Since the meeting facilitators recognized the value of the participants' intuitions and experiences, DTG helped the group make trade-offs, dropping entire topics or steps within topics, revising topic rankings, and reconsidering the time spent on each step and each topic.

Although there were a variety of opinions and perspectives, Giek notes, people were not contentious. "They were more at odds with themselves than with each other," he says. "They asked, 'Why am I being inconsistent?' There was more introspection and less sticking to ideas and positions." In spite of a multitude of difficult trade-offs, the panel members were satisfied that they had reached consensus by the end of the two-day meeting.

Based on his past involvement in the design of a similar program for a social service agency, Giek's alternative would have been to serve as a coordinator who repeatedly interacted with various advisory committees. Giek feels that this design process would have taken at least eight months instead of the month and a half in which the panel completed the design. In this case, the training program was a union-negotiated benefit that had been agreed upon one year before, and time pressure was mounting. Thus, the time saved was of significant value.

Table 11.4.   Designing Curriculum

Cost of training, per class of 30	$6,600
Classes per year	41
Training budget	$270,000
Extra class hours required by less effective design	25%
Cost of extra class hours for same level of training	$67,500
Additional days away from jobs per student per course	1.5
Average salary cost per year	$30,000
Average salary cost per work day	$120
Cost of time lost due to less efficient course per student	$180
Number of students (30 students × 41 classes)	1,230
Cost of lost time due to less efficient course per year	$221,000
Total benefit per year	$289,000
Present value, five years, 10%	$1,100,000
Development cost (estimate, average cost of meeting)	$10,000
One-year return on investment	2,800%
Five-year return on investment	11,000%

More important, Giek feels, the augmented meeting process generated a better educational program. There was more consensus and there were fewer concessions to minority-held positions than in the former advisory committee process. The result was readily accepted by the state, the unions, and the university administrators and professors. Senior professors are said to enjoy teaching the courses, and in many cases they feel the need to team-teach, evidence that the content is broader than it would have been had it been developed by an educator.

Giek estimates that had the program been designed in conventional ways, it would have taken between 25 and 50 per cent more time to teach the same material. The state spends $6,600 for each 36-hour class of 30 people and sponsored 41 classes in the first year of the program, for a cost of $270,000 per year. Thus, a 25 per cent gain in program effectiveness, requiring 45 class-hours instead of 36 to teach the same content, is worth $67,650 to the state.

In addition, time spent in school is time away from the job. One extra day and a half of school per person, with an average burdened salary of $30,000 per year, means that a less effective program would waste $221,400 per year in state employee's time. Giek feels that this difference of $289,000 per year is a conservative estimate of the value of the augmented meeting (see Table 11.4).

Allocating a Shrinking Budget

Another DTG user is SUNY itself. Each year, the university develops a comprehensive, specific financial plan for its $128 million budget. The university budget has been significantly reduced in recent years, although student loads and research activities have increased.

Of the total budget, about $17 million in support funds is allocated to departments through a bottom-up process. Of this, about $10.5 million is discretionary — that is, it can be allocated to departmental projects. Priorities are determined by the university president and five vice-presidents.

In the past, the executive-level decision-making process was a difficult one that required six or more three- to five-hour meetings over the course of a month. This high-level team discussed each project in depth — perhaps in too much depth.

Beginning with the 1983-84 fiscal year, the team tried an alternative process — the two-day DTG augmented meeting. In advance of the meeting, the executives individually ranked budget requests. Those rankings were entered into the decision support model the night before the meeting.

To avoid excessive discussion of details, participants agreed to bring no supporting documentation to the decision conference. As one participant says, "The bottom-up review process provided sufficient review of proposal and cost detail. The previous approach to financial planning was flawed by concentrating on such detail. The purpose of executive decision making is to set priorities, not to review departmental operations. That is best handled in another setting."

The computer model provided an aggregation of the individual rankings, and, using cross-matrix analysis, suggested an initial ordering of the projects. Those projects that rose to the top were generally agreed to be worthwhile, and those on the bottom were generally agreed to be postponable. The borderline projects in the middle were controversial, and the model focused discussion on these.

"In the past, the group would have drawn the line where the

Table 11.5.   Allocating a Shrinking Budget

Remove 20% from $100,000 above the line	$20,000
Percent of benefits for funding at 80% level (worst case)	80%
Lost program value	$20,000
Add to $100,000 below the line	$20,000
Percent of benefits gained for 20% of cost (conservative assumption)	50%
Gained program value	$50,000
Net gain in program effectiveness	$30,000
Staff time saved	$7,500
Total benefit	$37,500
Development cost of meeting	$7,500
Return on investment	400%

funding ran out," says a participant. "We would have struggled to get this far, and [would have] had no energy left to look at the projects just below the line."

In the augmented meeting, however, the team did look just below the line, at roughly $100,000 worth of projects that otherwise might not have been funded. They identified how $20,000 could be best spent among these projects. In most cases, they found ways to utilize the "80/20" rule, allowing them to achieve a large share of the benefits for a small portion of the cost by funding parts of a number of additional projects. They also considered projects just above the line — those that they intended to fund — for the same type of economies. By making such trade-offs interactively and seeing them reflected in the computer budget model, the team was able to agree on partial funding of some of these projects as well.

For example, in the 1985 process they found a project to improve graduate student recruiting that was funded at the fully proposed level of $7,500. They removed $2,400, primarily for recruitment trips, but left the budget for brochures and direct mail marketing intact, and felt that they retained most of the benefits. They spent the $2,400 on a program that originally was not to be funded at all, a $6,000 project to improve faculty recruitment. They felt that by concentrating on the neediest two of the six departments involved, they attained much of the benefit of the program for one-third of the original cost.

The university staff official responsible for financial planning credits the augmented meeting with the team's ability to make more effective use of limited funds. We might conservatively assume that the university in fact got only 50 (rather than 80) per cent of the benefit for 20 per cent of the funds ($20,000) below the line, and lost 100 per cent of the benefits for funds taken away from projects above the line. This optimization of the budget at such a detailed level would gain $50,000 of new benefits below the line for $20,000 in lost benefits above the line, for a net gain of $30,000. (To the participants interviewed, this estimate seemed conservative.) The staff official calculated that the time saved by the augmented meeting was worth $7,500, enough to pay for DTG meeting support. The value-added benefits, however, increased the return on investment from breakeven to a positive 400 per cent (see Table 11.5).

Halcomb Associates, Inc.

James Halcomb is a project planning consultant in Sunnyvale, California. For years, he has worked with new companies or new-product ventures on issues of project planning and management. He helped pioneer the augmented meeting support concept, using both a structured text editor and software that portrays program evaluation and review technique (PERT) charts. Halcomb has added to conventional PERT software the ability to track variances and risk through the PERT network. His software and his facilitating skills have combined to help numerous project teams achieve their objectives. Again, we report two exemplary cases.[9]

Designing a Product for Reproducibility

Quantum Corporation makes hard-disk drives for small computers. In this highly competitive market, their computer-manufacturer customers are sensitive to cost, quality, and ease of integration into their systems designs. In 1985, Quantum decided to offer a revolutionary new product that incorporates the controller in the drive itself rather than elsewhere in the computer. This would allow Quantum to build drives at lower cost since there would be no need to design in the ability to interface with a variety of controllers. They estimated an improvement in price and performance of at least 20 per cent. The new design also simplified their customers' jobs of designing computers to accommodate hard-disk drives.

James V. Parson was appointed program manager. He assembled a team of senior managers from manufacturing, quality control, marketing, production engineering, purchasing, receiving, and customer relations. They intended to design the product and a new manufacturing process from the ground up for reproducibility (ease of manufacturing, tolerance of variances, and in-process testing), in order to keep reject rates and costs low. This required collaboration from all functional areas throughout the project, so that the typical sequential design process that passes control from one department to the next was inappropriate.

Because of competition, Quantum was under time pressure. They had no choice but to pre-announce the product to give their customers time to design computer systems around it.

In a four-day augmented meeting facilitated by Halcomb, the team developed a detailed project schedule and, according to Parson, itemized at least 85 per cent of the departmental interdependencies. They began by using the structured text editor to determine what each department needed from others before it could do its tasks. These items were then put into a PERT schedule that reflected the interdependencies.

As a result, Parson says, each department knew exactly what was expected of it at any given time. This significantly speeded the development process. For example, in the past, specifications were typically documented after a working prototype was developed. If another department requested specifications earlier, the first department would produce tentative specifications—often grudgingly, because it lacked understanding of the interdependencies. The PERT chart contributed to greater interdepartmental collaboration, and allowed the team to overlap many steps in the process that otherwise would have been performed sequentially.

Halcomb's system of calculating time schedules based on the sum of variance-probability distributions for each step in the process allowed the team to forecast more accurately the time needed for completion. They estimated with 90 per cent assurance that they could complete the entire project in 15 months.

We asked Parson to consider the impact of running the project without the augmented meeting and the detailed understanding of interdependencies that resulted from it. He explained that, once the schedule was announced, the project would have been finished in 15 months no matter what complications arose. The quality of the product design could have suffered in the absence of the augmented meeting, however. This would have resulted in a higher scrap or

Table 11.6. Designing a Product for Reproducability

ODDS	IMPACT ON MANUFACTURING COSTS
95%	5%
85%	10%
75%	15%
30%	25%
Expected value	15%
Manufacturing budget	$3,000,000
Expected value, increased manufacturing cost without meeting	$450,000
Present value, five years, 10%	$1,700,000
Development cost (estimated, not disclosed)	$30,000
One-year return on investment	1,400%
Five-year return on investment	5,600%

rework rate, meaning higher manufacturing costs. Since the price of the product is fixed by the marketplace, higher manufacturing costs directly affect profit contributions.

Parson is 95 per cent sure that manufacturing costs would have been 5 per cent higher, 85 per cent sure of a 10 per cent increase, 75 per cent sure of a 15 per cent increase, and 30 per cent sure of a 25 per cent increase, for an expected value of 15 per cent. Considering the manufacturing budget, Parson credits the team's utilization of augmented meeting support with a $450,000 per year contribution to profits (see Table 11.6).

Getting a Product Back on Schedule

Chester W. Newell is president and CEO of Newell Research Corporation in Saratoga, California, a company that develops new high-technology products and sets up new business ventures based on their inventions. The company's focus has evolved from audio and video recording to computer memories of all types. Once a prototype is developed and a new product patented, a new company is started with the help of venture capital companies and state governments.

In one case, a product was developed and a company set up with the help of the Michigan Economic Development Authority. The new-company management then committed to moving from prototype to product release in 8 to 10 months rather than the forecasted 11

Table 11.7. Getting a Product Back on Schedule

Delays without the augmented meeting:	
Project planning	3 weeks

Design process:	
ODDS	PROJECT DELAY
100%	3 weeks
50%	5 weeks
Expected value	4 weeks

Total expected delay without augmented meeting	7 weeks
Cost per month of facilities	$200,000
Cost of expected delay	$323,000

Development cost (estimated, not disclosed)	$20,000

Return on investment	1,500%

to 13 months. The resulting pressure created such disorganization that, five months into the project, the company realized it was facing serious problems.

To get the project back on schedule, a decision was made to develop various pieces of the project in parallel as much as possible, while keeping manufacturing costs low so as to survive in a highly competitive marketplace. Halcomb facilitated a week-long meeting of about 15 managers and engineers, during which the team developed a detailed PERT chart that allowed them to find opportunities for parallel development steps. As it was, they released the product to pre-production within one month of its original schedule, 14 months after project initiation, and 12 months after they received their funding.

Without the meeting, Newell says, they still would have developed a PERT chart through a series of committee meetings. However, they would have had the disadvantage of fewer minds involved in planning, and less "buy-in" from those who had to perform the work. "Without that meeting, I doubt we could have done it," he says. "It set the stage, showed us where our problems were, and where to double up. If we hadn't done the [augmented] meeting, it would have taken more time to develop the project plan, and we would have had all kinds of surprises later in the project."

Newell is certain that without the augmented meeting, manual project planning would have taken at least three extra weeks. In addition, he is certain that development would have taken an additional three weeks, and is 50 per cent sure it might have taken at least five extra weeks, for a total expected delay of at least seven weeks.

The cost of this delay would have been significant. By June, the company had already bought land, built a plant, and contracted for staff. The plant would have been idle for an additional seven weeks, at a cost of $200,000 per month. Thus, the augmented meeting support probably saved the company an expected value of $323,000 in lost overhead (see Table 11.7).

OA Impacts on Meeting Productivity

These early applications of augmented meeting support suggest a number of OA impacts on group effectiveness. The observed patterns can be divided into eight broad categories: task orientation, degree of participation, cognitive styles, conceptual structure, volume of ideas and information, reduced repetition, greater continuity, and greater follow-through.

Task Orientation

Augmented meetings seem to result in significantly increased task orientation. Participants' attention spans are lengthened and they are better able to focus on the meeting objectives; the augmentation often generates a high-energy atmosphere because of the high degree of participation and the rapid progress.

Greater task orientation does not necessarily hurry the decision process. In fact, time for structuring the problems and creatively generating options (the divergent phase) is often cut short in conventional meetings for fear of not reaching a resolution. Augmented meeting support gives participants the feeling that subsequent convergence will be relatively easy, so they are more comfortable spending time in the creative, divergent phase.

This task orientation implies that the technique should not be applied to meetings whose purpose is building interpersonal relationships (for example, job interviews or delicate negotiations). Furthermore, the focus on task inhibits natural stress-reduction mechanisms (such as joking and breaks in conversation), while the increased pace of work raises the level of stress. Process facilitation can help participants cope with the resulting added stress. The technique seems most appropriate for task-oriented groups that are under time pressure.

Degree of Participation

In general, the degree of participation is enhanced in the augmented meeting. The instant recording of thoughts, regardless of group response, seems to encourage even reticent participants to offer their ideas. The increased focus on the group's common task and the recording of notes without attributing them to the authors disassociates personalities from ideas, encouraging the group to respond to all ideas as a team. The opportunity for an individual to dominate the meeting is lessened, not only by the tactful intervention of the process facilitator but by the slow and steady growth of the meeting notes.

Cognitive Styles

The medium seems to favor certain cognitive styles. Those who work well with concepts and structured outlines find their effectiveness greatly enhanced. "Receptive," fact-oriented thinkers may at first be confused by the rapid manipulation of concepts. Slower, contemplative thinkers may be lost in the swift interactions. Detail-oriented participants may be uncomfortable working with an outline that evolves from overviews through successive levels of structure.

But the technique may help to bridge differing cognitive styles (a problem in any meeting). The group's ability to move quickly between concepts and detail means that details can be recorded even when they are not on point, encouraging a tolerance of detail in those who work best with concepts. The ability to provide conceptual perspectives without losing touch with the details encourages more conceptual thinking in fact-oriented participants.

Conceptual Structure

When an outline-based text editor is used, the conceptual structure itself might be edited with commands such as "Show me the top two levels of our outline," or "Change this branch of thought with all its ramifications to a subset of that thought." The structure represents a key part of the communication process. Viewing the outline in varying levels of depth gives the participants a perspective on their thoughts, reinforces their understanding of the scope of the discussion, and allows them to specify explicitly the relationships between thoughts. Studying the structure of the notes can disclose flaws or gaps in the group's thinking, or reveal new options.

Similarly, structured numeric models help guide decision makers through a logical decision process. The staff of DTG notes that decision analytic models do not replace human judgments — rather, they aid judgment, build insight, and ensure decisions that are consistent with values and beliefs. The models allow decision makers to improve on their decision processes as well as on their assumptions. In both cases, the ability to work explicitly with the structure as well as the content of thoughts enhances group decision making.

Volume of Ideas and Information

In the course of an augmented meeting, all comments are recorded. This permits the group to work with more information and more concepts without being overwhelmed. Furthermore, no ideas are lost or overlooked. Even when they are off the topic, thoughts can be noted for later consideration. Thus, group members feel free to brainstorm without fear of losing the thread of discussion, creating confusion, or being censured for their non-sequiturs.

Since no effort is wasted in trying to remember an idea until it is appropriate to put it forth, participants quickly free their minds for new ideas. By reducing the time and psychological cost of exploring ideas, meeting augmentation encourages divergent opinions and creativity. This in turn encourages the group not to settle for the first feasible solution. In general, augmented meetings are most appropriate when groups must deal with complex issues and many facts.

Reduced Repetition

The emerging meeting notes provide an immediate view of the group's accomplishments. If the group returns to a topic that has already been treated (as too often happens), the screen can instantly display their prior work. This prevents their wasting time on issues that have been resolved. Participants simply note the new thoughts they wish to add to the growing meeting notes.

Greater Continuity

The meeting notes make it easy for the group to resume discussion where they left off after breaks. Participants can quickly get a perspective on where they are, what they have done so far, and where their present position fits in the broader context of the meeting. Better time management is encouraged by constant feedback on progress and on tasks remaining to be done.

Greater Follow-Through

The augmented meeting support technique seems to improve the likelihood of effective individual action, in keeping with group decisions, being taken after the meeting. The focus on visual meeting notes improves the retention of ideas exchanged in the meeting. It can also identify points of misunderstanding before the meeting is over, since the online notes are instantly available for editing, clarification of terms and concepts, and juxtaposition of related ideas.

After the meeting, detailed and accurate minutes are distributed. This immediate documentation avoids perpetuating any remaining misunderstandings about content and responsibilities. The notes also ensure that nothing is lost between the meeting and the implementation. Gilchrist, a participant in one of the DTG conferences, says, "When a vice-president comes in two months after a conference and says, 'Why can't I have the money for my new project?' I simply pull out the conference book and open it to the appropriate page."

The Future of Augmented Meetings

Important meetings need no longer be an expensive waste of time. Augmented meeting support is an opportunity for high-performance, high-productivity teamwork at a reasonable cost.[10] Research and widespread application will further explore the potential power of meeting augmentation. But there is no reason to postpone experimentation with this powerful use of OA.

Once the concept is more widely recognized, we expect to see the rise of "decision centers" with the right tools and trained support staffs, such as the DTG at SUNY Albany. After using such external facilities on a periodic basis, organizations will eventually build their own decision centers, staffed with specialists in supporting and facilitating decision making. As OA becomes common among all knowledge workers, we expect that every conference room will provide the basic facilities for augmented meeting support.

Notes

1. Portions of this chapter were originally published in N.D. Meyer and J.C. Bulyk, "Increasing Meeting Effectiveness Through Augmented Support," *Journal of Information Systems Management* 2, no. 3 (Summer 1985). Used by permission.
2. H. Mintzberg, *The Nature of Managerial Work* (New York: Harper & Row, 1973). See also M. Doyle and D. Straus, *How to Make Meetings Work* (New York: Playboy Paperbacks, 1976).
3. See I.L. Janis, *Victims of Groupthink* (Boston: Houghton-Mifflin, 1972.
4. See L.R. Hoffman and N.R.F. Maier, "Valence in the Adoption of Solutions by Problem-Solving Groups: Concept, Method, and Results," *Journal of Abnormal and Social Psychology* 69 (1964): 264-71.
5. See R.E. Hill, "Managing Interpersonal Conflict in Project Teams," *Sloan Management Review* (Winter 1977), 45-61.
6. Chauffeurs have also been used for individuals; see, for example, P.G.W. Keen and M.S. Morton, *Decision Support Systems: An Organizational Perspective* (New York: Addison-Wesley, 1978) and N.D. Meyer, "OA Chauffeurs: Driving the Executive's System," *Today's Office* March 1985.
7. Augment, a product of McDonnell-Douglas Inc., permits detailed note taking and conceptual outlining. Its structural capabilities permit much greater speed in moving the display through the notes and restructuring ideas than conventional word processors do. Thus, Augment might be termed a "semantic decision support system."
8. D.C. Englebart, et al., "Computer-Augmented Management-System Research and Development of Augmentation Facility—Final Report," final report of research funded by ARPA, contracted by Rome Air Development Centre, Rome, NY, publication #TR-70-82 (Stanford: Stanford Research Institute Research Augmentation Center, April 1970); see also D.C. Englebart with Richard W. Watson and James C. Norton, "The Augmented Knowledge Workshop," in *Proceedings of the AFIPS National Computer Conference*, vo. 42 (Montvale, N.J.: AFIPS Press, 1973) at 9-21.
9. The authors thank David Kaplow of Apple Computer Inc. for the introduction to Halcomb Associates, Inc.
10. D.C. Engelbart, "High Knowledge-Worker Teams," final technical report AF30602-80-0260-F, Rome Air Development Center (Rome, N.Y.: October 29, 1981)

IMPLEMENTATION METHODOLOGIES

Some of our readers are responsible for implementing OA within their organizations. These staff groups need concrete methodologies in addition to the research findings reported in prior chapters. Part 4 concludes the book with an overview of our method of implementing very high-payoff applications and measuring results.

Chapter 12 addresses the finding of these high-payoff applications. Its four-question analysis approach focuses the attention of implementors on those few areas of the business where success is likely to have the greatest impact.

Chapter 13 describes our methodology for measuring value-added benefits. It may be read in conjunction with Appendix A, an outline of a value-added assessment interview, and Appendix B, a review of techniques for interviewing when subjective judgments must be made.

Chapter 14 concludes the book with a discussion of the implications of adopting a value-added approach in an organization's OA program. Common obstacles and issues are addressed to help clear a path to value-added results.

Finding Value-Added Opportunities

Opportunities for value-added applications of OA are available to virtually every organization.[1] While not every user can offer returns as significant as those described in this book, each has a reasonable chance of finding a value-added application. Part of the art of finding value-added opportunities is enabling and encouraging creative user exploration of OA tools.

Staff groups responsible for information systems and executives who wish to improve their performance can do more to encourage value-added returns; they can actively seek value-added opportunities. Of course, to find such applications, one must look in the right places. The value-added approach to selection and application needs assessment is quite different from the tried-and-true methods of data processing.

This chapter summarizes our method of finding value-added opportunities. It is written for the OA implementor, whose job is to serve the needs of the user organization with new office information tools.

The Traditional Approach

Readers may ask, "Why do we need another approach? What is wrong with our usual approach to implementing systems?" A young telecommunications manager provided a poignant case example of the problems inherent in traditional methods. His president, having toured the experimental video teleconferencing facilities of an over-seas affiliate, had decided that his fellow executives should have the same capability, and assigned the telecommunications manager the task of implementing the system.

The telecommunications manager was delighted with this leading-edge assignment and receiving support from top management. He began by doing research: "What is teleconferencing? How do I choose between audio, audiographic, freeze-frame, or full-motion media? How can I locate and design effective rooms? What kind of codec and what kind of cameras should I use? Will we require multi-point or just point-to-point?"

Referring to expert opinions and to his own analysis of the organization's communication patterns, he defined company requirements for a teleconferencing system. With the basic design in mind, he was able to survey the vendors and estimate the price. When he informed the president of the cost, however, the president asked for a cost-justification study before allowing the project to proceed.

To justify the investment, the telecommunications manager had to identify the applications and their payoff. Travel costs are easily measured, and, while research evidence is mixed, vendors claim that teleconferencing will reduce travel. This provided a convenient basis for hard-dollar justification, and a convincing sales pitch for senior management. In this case, though, management wasn't convinced that the benefits were worth the costs, and the project still remains on hold.

In a similar case, approval was given and teleconferencing rooms were installed. Once the rooms were operational, the teleconferencing manager faced a challenge more difficult than gaining approval. Held accountable for the returns on investment in teleconferencing, he had to find users who were willing to reduce their travel time. Thus, the implementor was forced into the role of internal technology salesperson, with no guarantee of a justifiable business need for the technology.

The Failure of Tried-and-True Methods

These unhappy cases are only two examples of a relatively common occurrence: technology that has been installed but not implemented. The cost of such failures includes not only the price of the system, but also the opportunity cost of unrealized value-added gains. Hidden costs include organizational disruption and the loss of credibility of the implementor. In most cases, the fault lies not with the implementor, but with the implementation process.

Those responsible for OA often have successful backgrounds as managers of data processing or telecommunications. Implementation of these centralized technologies is based on systems analysis, the charting of information, and work flows. Systems analysis — a tried-and-true method for data processing, telecommunications, and word processing — is, unfortunately, not working well for OA. Results often fall short of expectations, and user indifference or resistance is not uncommon.

Assumptions About the Organization

The approach described above—define the technology, justify the cost, and identify applications and users—makes certain assumptions. Those assumptions may have been appropriate for well-structured applications such as transaction processing and routine typing. Now, however, they must be re-examined in the context of personal information tools for managers and professionals.

First, the justification of teleconferencing based on travel cost-displacement requires widespread usage, since only a portion of everyone's travel can be eliminated. Thus, we assume that OA can have a significant impact on people throughout the organization; that is, major organizational change is required before benefits are gained. Changing the way people work is not easy, and at best it is a gradual process.

Second, substituting teleconferencing for travel imputes a low value to the social interactions that occur during face-to-face meetings. The chance to smile, to drink and tell stories, and otherwise to build business friendships may be critical to the effective functioning of work teams. Indeed, most work teams explicitly schedule social events. This is an indication that they are willing to invest time and money in building effective teamwork. OA implementation methodologies must take into account the unique culture of each user group.

Third, justifying teleconferencing in terms of travel cost-displacement assumes that the current communication level is about right. In fact, it may be that the current level is too high, and that the real benefits are in encouraging delegation and decentralization of decision making. Alternatively, it may be that the communication level is too low, in which case there may be significant value added through more and better communication, collaboration, and coordination. These benefits are often far more important than travel cost savings. Value-added OA must be based on the users' unique missions and strategies.

The Problem with Selling Technology

The basic problem in the traditional approach is in the way staff managers view their roles—as internal technology salespeople rather than business advisers. If staff success (including status) is judged by the size of the capital equipment budget, technology managers will attempt to maximize the use of equipment rather than business benefits.

When a staff information systems professional approaches a user with a solution in search of a problem, their relationship is generally less than satisfactory. The user knows that the implementor is not there to serve the user's business needs, but to pursue his or her own interests. In these circumstances, the user is not likely fully to trust the information systems professional as a business adviser. If a project is defined, its implementation will be seen as the primary responsibility of the information staff. The user may not be committed to making the system work, and may even resist the change. The entire project could antagonize the very users it is supposed to serve.

Another danger results from the way in which the business problem is selected. The information systems staff must find a place to apply the chosen technology. Unless the technology is very flexible or of widespread interest, staff may not have a choice of which users to serve. Information systems staff must work with any user who can demonstrate a business need. Unfortunately, there is no guarantee that those users will have high-payoff, value-added application opportunities, or that they will be in strategic positions in the organization. Furthermore, it would be mere coincidence if the technology selected were of critical importance to a given user-manager's effectiveness.

To further compound this problem, the implementor who focuses narrowly on a particular technology may miss high-payoff applications of other OA tools that are just as easily available. Technology salespeople naturally view every discussion with users as an exploration of a particular type of tool. There is an old saying: "When you give a child a hammer, everything is a nail." The internal technology salesperson must walk away from opportunities that do not require the chosen technology. Otherwise, staff time may be wasted on applications that are tangential to business success, while critical needs (and the opportunity to demonstrate the payoff from OA) are ignored.

Technology-driven change is the antithesis of the value-added approach. It is not in the interest of the users, the information staff, or the organization. While exploratory research on new technologies is wise, staff should not "sell" a particular technology.

The technology-driven approach follows certain steps: technology, payoff, application, users. The value-added approach proceeds differently. First, the implementor determines what part of the

Figure 12.1. Approaches to Managing Technology

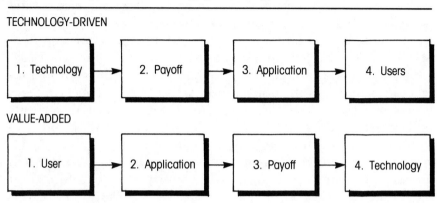

TECHNOLOGY-DRIVEN

| 1. Technology | → | 2. Payoff | → | 3. Application | → | 4. Users |

VALUE-ADDED

| 1. User | → | 2. Application | → | 3. Payoff | → | 4. Technology |

organization is of most concern to top management. Second, the implementor identifies an opinion-leading user whose support is of particular value and whose work is of particular relevance to top management. Third, an application is identified that is based on critical success factors, and the objectives and justification are phrased in business terms which management finds familiar. Figure 12.1 contrasts the technology-driven approach with the business-driven process.

Where to Begin?

OA staff groups are usually small. If they are spread too thin, they may not pay sufficient attention to each project, thus risking user rejection or missing important business benefits. Successful OA staff focus on a few key pilot projects.

Pilots are projects of limited scope — they represent small increments of change. Pilots apply a specific set of new *tools* to a limited set of *users* to solve a defined business *problem.*

Every OA project should be considered a pilot. The pilot approach avoids organization-wide projects that don't have identified users. Large systems-development projects build a "toolkit," but they are not the same as implementing applications. Without well-defined business problems and users, implementation projects are likely to lead to the installation of equipment that nobody uses. The surest way to deliver results is to serve a well-defined and willing user group.

The first few applications for users are the most critical to the success of an OA program. They must be carefully selected and designed to deliver relevant business benefits, advertise the opportunity throughout the organization, and build foundations for evolution. Serving those who volunteer, a common approach, may assure user support and ease the implementation process, but it does not guarantee either a high-payoff application or an experience that encourages others to try OA. We recommend that implementors focus their efforts on key areas of the organization, with confidence in their ability to implement worthwhile projects.

Another common approach is the "organization-wide needs assessment," generally in the form of a survey of major information requirements. This traditional approach also generally fails to identify value-added opportunities. By looking organization-wide, a survey generally cannot look deeply into the mission of each user group; it cannot identify value-added opportunities. Second, it tends to identify problems that people throughout the organization have in common; since each user group's mission is unique, the organization-wide needs assessment tends to focus on shared administrative problems. Thus, organization-wide surveys lead us back to administrative efficiency applications and away from value-added. Surveys are appropriate for gathering data to help define the magnitude of problems (later in the implementation process), but not for finding interesting problems in the first place.

A new approach is needed to identify value-added opportunities — one that considers the factors that are most relevant to success. An extremely important factor is the "centrality" of the users. Implementation efforts are best placed in departments that make the most significant contribution to the success of the organization. A limited set of departments or functions in an organization can be considered most critical to the success of the entire organization. These offer the greatest opportunity for value-added applications.

Thus, the first key question is:

1. Who in the organization is central — that is, which department has the most impact on total organizational success?

Analysis of centrality may lead implementors to focus on two user departments: one — the "cash cow" — that contributes the largest share of current profits, and another — the "growth star" — that is a key growth opportunity. In this case, it is wise to consider pilot activities in each area.

Business centrality can often be determined from the organization's strategic business plan. By considering the strategic goals of the firm, it may become clear which functions are responsible for the bulk of the task of implementing strategy and which will become central once strategic goals are met. In organizations that lack a strategic plan, a list of business-development projects can be ranked by their potential long-term profit contribution. Ongoing operations, also ranked by their relative profit contribution, can be considered in conjunction with strategic goals. Further depth can be added to this analysis by considering sources of risk on strategic objectives and on current operations.

Michael Porter's "value chain" perspective on the functions in an organization, summarized in Figure 12.2, can be a useful framework for determining centrality. If executives do not quickly name those departments and functions that are essential to the success of the organization, they might wish to rank-order the functions on Porter's value chain. In addition, they should be asked to look at the interfaces between primary functions along the chain of production, and between support activities and all of the primary functions. These interfaces may also provide high-payoff opportunities for OA.[2]

There is a cultural as well as a business aspect to centrality. Each company has its own culture — some emphasize finance, others favor marketing. It is telling to consider the background of key executives, and to sense which departments have the greatest political power and

Figure 12.2.   Porter's Value Chain

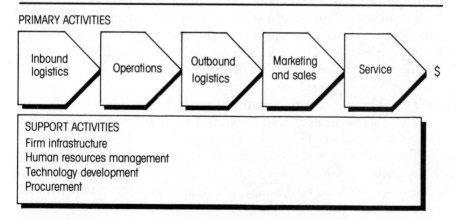

Adapted from Michael E. Porter, "How Information Gives You Competitive Advantage," *Harvard Business Review* 63, no. 4 (July-August 1985)

influence on others. In general, political power is synonymous with business centrality. When it is not, business and political factors must be balanced. (It may be wise to consider projects in two departments, one central to the business and the other the strongest politically.) Applications for these key departments deliver the most relevant business benefits, and are most visible to the user organization and, in particular, to top management.

The Politics of Implementation

Since change generally occurs in small steps, each successive step must both deliver benefits and contribute to evolutionary momentum. The second objective, building momentum, requires that the implementor select a user-manager who in turn can influence his or her peers.

The influence of a pilot on evolution depends on the strength of the users. If a user is not influential, a successful implementation will do little to convince others in the organization that OA is worthwhile. On the other hand, if OA successfully serves someone who is well-respected, word will spread and subsequent implementation efforts will be easier. Thus, the politically astute implementor must determine whom in the organization he or she would most like to serve. This is a critical decision, particularly in the early stages of establishing a new technology such as OA.

Furthermore, the users' credibility is an important part of gaining approval for a project. Many value-added measurements require a degree of subjective judgment. These estimates will be accepted as a legitimate part of the justification only if top management trusts the users who make the judgments. Similarly, after the project is completed, evaluation of results often depends on subjective judgments, and is only as believable as the user-managers. Ultimately, it is the users who must defend the project by describing its contributions to their effectiveness. Choosing whom to serve is equivalent to choosing one's allies; the implementor's credibility and influence will depend to a great extent on the power of the users.

Thus, early pilots should focus on the opinion leaders among the many potential user-managers. The selected user must have a business problem of concern and a willingness to explore new ways of working. In addition, early users must be well-liked and respected by their peers, successful, and seen as an integral part of the organizational culture.

This leads to the second key question:

2. Where in the central part of the organization is an opinion leader — that is, someone who is successful, respected, progressive, and with sufficient influence to bring about changes in working patterns?

The Payoff of Technology

Having selected a location for an implementation project, the next challenge is to find an issue that is of importance. Identifying a business objective for the project cannot be based on technology priorities alone. The greatest payoffs are those that are key to the users' success.

Because only users fully understand their business needs and goals, only they can identify the most useful applications. Value-added benefits are identified by listening carefully to users as they discuss their needs. Structured surveys can only measure the frequency of structured tasks; they do not work well at identifying value-added opportunities.

The third important question that an astute implementor will ask is:

3. How can I help the chosen user to succeed? Or, put another way, what does it take to get the user promoted?

The implementation process begins with a fact-finding session, which may be a one- or two-hour interview or an all-day workshop. In this brief initial encounter, the implementor attempts to gain the user's interest and involvement in identifying a high-payoff application. Once a critical need has been identified, structured data collection can contribute to the system design process.

During the initial interview, the implementor may encounter a variety of thinking styles. Some executives think systematically, using logical processes and structured concepts to make decisions. Others are more intuitive, considering many ideas at once and "feeling" their way toward the right solution. Neither style is better or worse, although each is appropriate for different business situations. Ideally, the implementor should be able to adapt the interview to each user's cognitive style.

We have found that a model of the "brain of the firm"[3] works very well to help analyze information needs with executives who prefer structured, systematic thinking patterns (see Figure 12.3). Based on

Figure 12.3.   The Brain of the Firm

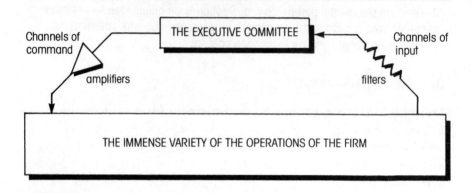

the work of Stafford Beer, the cybernetic model helps executives to focus on one of three areas of information needs.

First, they may feel the need for more (or more relevant) information from inside or outside the organization, focusing implementation efforts either on the capacity of the channels of input or on the appropriateness of the filters. These channels extend beyond the traditional scope of MIS to include all sources of input, structured and unstructured data, fact, and gossip, from inside and outside the company.

Second, executives may feel the need to improve the ability of the executive committee to deal with information and make decisions — for example, through decision support systems or augmented meetings.

Third, executives may feel that their commands are not being properly implemented by the organization, in which case they may request help with their channels of command (for example, in policy formation and communication). Information tools for writing and communication may improve the capacity, clarity, and focus of these downward channels.

Other executives think more intuitively, and prefer to work with concrete examples. To help them translate a business problem into an opportunity for OA, we offer a smorgasbord of "things OA can help with" (see Figure 12.4). Without concern for the technologies, this approach asks the executives to scan a list of critical success factors and pick the ones that most relate to their jobs and their personal success, and to order them by priority. This process typically guides the users into a discussion of their key projects and objectives.

In the early stages of an OA program, virtually every user can

Figure 12.4.   Critical Business Success Factors
(Copyright © 1984, N. Dean Meyer and Associates Inc.)

- Tracking activities
  - Business operations: status, problems
  - Projects: status, milestones, due dates, critical path
  - Appointments, commitments

- Staying abreast of current events
  - Who's doing what
  - How they see us
  - Marketplace status and trends
  - Investments, the economy

- Inventing, creating, and designing

- Making decisions
  - Brainstorming
  - Getting the facts
  - Organizing ideas and information
  - Analyzing and comparing alternatives
  - Forecasting
  - Allocating resources

- Presenting, convincing, and negotiating

- Leading, commanding
  - Documenting, writing, phrasing things properly
  - Formulating policy

- Working and communicating with people (inside or outside)
  - Knowing people
  - Reaching people
  - Teamwork and collaboration
  - Meeting
  - Announcing
  - Teaching

identify rewarding value-added applications for some OA tools. Most users are happy to talk about their business challenges. In fact, a discussion of value-added opportunities typically generates tremendous user commitment and enthusiasm. An implementor who is willing to listen can easily determine which applications will be most rewarding.

Because of the visibility of these focused implementation efforts, it is very important not to attempt to do too much. Usage should evolve in small and tangible steps. The implementor should ask the user to choose the highest priorities from the various business information needs that have been identified. Each step of change should be limited to one or two such objectives.

Allowing users to choose the problems to be addressed is the heart of the value-added approach, and the most straightforward way to assess needs. This step is crucial to the entire process. When it is done well, subsequent implementation is relatively easy. Users will not resist projects of their own design that address their primary concerns. When the equipment arrives, the users will know why it is there and will understand that it is relevant to their work. It is this defined problem-orientation that distinguishes the value-added approach from the technology-driven approach.

Tools and Technologies

Once priorities are set among the critical success factors, the business goals of the project will become clear. Only then can the users and the implementor select OA tools with value-added potential.

The implementor must be prepared to address whatever business problems the user sees as critical to success. For this reason, OA staff should have access to the entire range of tools. All of the tools are now readily available, easy to use, and cost-effective. There is no reason for a user organization to implement them in the same order in which they were invented. Neither is there any reason to implement the same tools for all users. The implementor must have the freedom to pick the tools that are most appropriate to the business problem.

With a toolkit at hand, the fourth key question is:

4. What tools will help the users achieve their business objectives?

The users' participation in this step of the process can be encouraged by showing them a list of OA tools and explaining the function of each (see Figure 1.1).

Once the required functionality is defined, the equipment and software must be chosen. These technologies should be selected with long- and short-term business and technological objectives in mind. Generally, the users are happy to leave this level of decision making to technical experts so long as they feel that their answers to the four key questions listed above are understood.

The "People Issues" of Change

Benefits are realized only if new technologies are adopted by users as part of their regular business practices. This may involve significant changes in individual working patterns, the social environment, and organizational (political) relationships. These changes do not come easily, but can be managed.

When it was first introduced, word processing frequently met user resistance because of mismanagement of the process of change. Many companies attempted to gather secretaries into typing pools to help justify expensive equipment. It made logical sense to staff the (then complex) machines with well-trained dedicated operators, and to keep the machines active at all times.

From the users' point of view, however, word processing destroyed working relationships between managers and secretaries. The secretaries were put in dead-end jobs, and perhaps were reporting to a former peer. Managers were demotivated by a loss of status caused by an absence of personal support, and found themselves (figuratively and literally) standing in line at the photocopiers. This destruction of an effective organization was done in order to gain efficient use of the technology, and the result was disastrous. The users' view of costs and benefits may be quite different from that of the implementor. Recall, for example, the teleconferencing implementors who attempted to stop managers from traveling. Their failure was easily predictable.

Figure 12.5 illustrates the differing assumptions of staff and users of various aspects of teleconferencing. The traditional approach is logical on the surface, but it ignores some critical dynamics of

Figure 12.5.   Two Different Views of Teleconferencing

STAFF	USER
Widespread change	Gradual change
Low value to social interactions	High value to social interactions
Travel is a boondoggle	Travel is a perquisite
Need same level of (but more efficient) communication	Need better collaboration through more communication
Goal is to spread technology	Goal is effective business

change. *People don't change unless they want to.* From the users' point of view, the cost of teleconferencing is immediate, while the benefits are longer-term and more abstract. The "subjective cost-benefit" to the user is quite different from the corporate perspective represented by the staff systems analyst.

Subjective cost-benefit is the primary determinant of successful organizational change. Just as people don't change unless they want to, users will work to make a system succeed when doing so helps them to succeed. Thus, the effective implementor seeks applications that are good both for the organization and for the people who must live with the system.

A true people-centered approach to implementation gives users control of their implementation projects. This goes beyond user participation in the usual sense; users should retain control of the project-management process, problem selection, systems design, justification, and measurement of benefits. There are at least three reasons why the value-added approach depends on user-centered implementation.

First, only users are in a position to identify value-added applications, since only they really understand what they are expected to accomplish. this understanding cannot be captured in structured surveys and brief interviews; it comes from holding a unique set of responsibilities over a period of time. The users must take the responsibility for identifying applications and defining business objectives. Technical staff can help with data collection and measurement methodologies, but cannot select applications for the users without the risk of solving irrelevant problems.

Furthermore, only the users themselves are responsible for measuring their business success. A personnel manager cannot do an employee's performance appraisal, but staff can guide line managers in developing ways to evaluate performance. Similarly, after implementing OA, the users should be responsible for measuring improvements in their own performance. OA staff can assist by explaining and evaluating a range of justification approaches and measurement instruments.

Second, only the users really know their office cultures — the social and motivational environment of the office. Managers are sincerely concerned about motivating their employees, and organizations often spend significant amounts on professional-development activities and improving the quality of working life. (Consider, for example, current investments in office carpets, the emphasis on management by objectives, and personnel counseling services.) If a technology is forced upon a user by staff groups, it is likely to damage the user's feelings of self-control. Furthermore, it may change the user's working environment in ways that are demotivational. Thus, users themselves are best qualified to design systems and new procedures that fit both their needs and their office cultures.

Third, to deliver significant benefits, users must work hard to make a new system successful. They must continue to support and maintain the system after it is installed. Elegant systems have failed for lack of user support, and technically poor systems have succeeded when users supported the project. To motivate user support, users must be put in control of the implementation process. The role of technical staff should not be that of a "doctor" who changes the users' work patterns, but rather that of a "counselor" who helps users achieve their objectives. Users are unlikely to resist projects that they think are in their business interests, particularly when they feel that they control the projects.

This user-centered approach is particularly important because OA addresses a higher level of users than earlier technologies. Managers and professionals are more capable than secretaries of resisting unwelcome changes, so OA is all the more dependent on effective handling of the people-issues of change. Top managers believe that the strength of an organization is in its people. They will not condone damaging people's effectiveness for the sake of technical efficiencies. To maintain support at all levels, implementors are well advised to facilitate a user-centered process of change.

After the First Few Pilots

Once an opinion-leader pilot has succeeded, the demand for OA tools and staff services usually grows rapidly. At this point, the same OA toolkit may be applied elsewhere in the organization.

OA staff may feel that extending an existing system to a new user group is routine, since these subsequent user pilots do not need to test the concepts or the technologies. Later implementation projects, however, do test the applicability of the tools to each unique business problem. Furthermore, every new user brings new challenges in managing change. From the users' point of view, each step in the evolutionary process is new, and thus to them is a pilot.

It may be difficult for OA staff to maintain a fresh attitude while implementing familiar systems. There is a temptation to package a standard solution and ignore the unique nature of each application.

Users are then left on their own to identify value-added applications. In this process, many high-payoff opportunities may be missed.

Retaining the value-added approach—that is, a series of well-focused, small-scale implementation projects even after the first few pilots—avoids many common implementation problems, and ensures attention to managing change. Smaller projects are less complex, and deliver benefits and build credibility quickly. Furthermore, multiple small projects allow more flexibility, making it easier to manage the organization-wide evolution of OA. To maintain their enthusiasm, implementors may find it useful to focus on managing the process of change rather than on system design. Existing systems may be seen as toolkits rather than as solutions. Indeed, the real implementation challenge goes beyond getting technologies to work properly, and involves generating a constant flow of contribution to profits.

The Value-Added Approach

In simple terms, value-added applications of OA are found by asking key individuals what they need to succeed. These high-payoff uses of the OA tools are found only in cases where the problem to be solved is both relevant and visible.

The value-added approach suggests that the most effective sequence of decision making for a business-oriented implementor is (1) payoff; (2) user; (3) application; and (4) technology. The approach begins with the application of tools to perceived needs in a few key parts of the organization. The tools are delivered to the key users by means of a people-oriented implementation process. In this process, the tools are defined and technologies selected with the assurance that they are appropriate to the user's business problem and office culture.

The value-added approach focuses on the unique problems of each user. Information centers can support the day-to-day needs of many users. Computing and telecommunications infrastructures can be built centrally, as a backbone for technology integration. Nonetheless, each new user should be treated as a new and unique implementation challenge. Successful use of this approach requires a facilitative attitude. Implementors should focus on serving individual users rather than on designing technologies.

After the first few value-added projects, opinion leaders begin to adopt more advanced tools, and the news of their successful early applications spreads to other users. Because it recognizes the incremental nature of organizational change, the value-added approach helps the organization move toward the integrated office of the future in solid business-oriented steps.

The value-added approach implies a different role for technical staff. Those who succeed view their task not as one of selling technology within the organization, but rather as one of solving identified business problems. The implementors whose careers progress fastest are those who are skilled at selecting the right problems to solve and who build credibility through evolutionary change.

The art of getting and keeping top management attention is best captured in a quotation from Ken Kesey, author of *One Flew over the Cuckoo's Nest*: "Put your good where it will do the most."

Notes

1. Portions of this chapter were originally published in N.D. Meyer, "Implementing Technology: The Quest for Support," *Data Communications* 12, no. 10 (September 1983)
2. Michael E. Porter, *Competitive Advantage* (New York: Free Press, 1985), at 36
3. Stafford Beer, *Platform for Change* (Chichester, U.K.: John Wiley and Sons, 1975)

Measuring Value-Added Benefits

CHAPTER
13

As organizations evolve toward high-productivity systems, OA will serve business strategy in a variety of ways; only a few of these are suggested by the cases in this book. This revolution in the way we do business will not happen overnight. OA will grow in a series of small steps, or pilots, each of which will address current business needs and possibly create value-added benefits.

To implement each of these steps requires investment; OA applications must compete with other capital requirements for a share of an organization's limited financial resources. Thus, measuring the payoff of OA is very important, both before and after each implementation project.

Before implementation begins, an understanding of the benefits is necessary to identify high-payoff applications and to justify investments in new technology. Particularly in the beginning stages of OA, top management typically requires a clear statement of the projected return on investment. After an application has been implemented, it cannot be evaluated without a knowledge of the business objectives it has addressed. Benefits analysis is basic both to justification and to evaluation.

Forecasting benefits before implementation is equivalent to objective setting. By discussion with the users, the project planning process should lead to a clear statement of the expected results of the proposed system. An evaluation interview can be done at the end of the design process, reiterating the objectives, refining the operational measures, and reviewing proposed changes in tools and business processes. This will lead to a pro forma statement of benefits for the project.

The pre-implementation measurement process is different from post-implementation measurement only in that one is dealing with objectives rather than results. The thought process and the equations are identical. In this chapter, we will describe the process of evaluation after implementation, since it is usually a more detailed undertaking. We will return to the issues of justification and budgeting in the next chapter.

After a project is completed, it can be evaluated by defining and measuring the actual impacts of the OA tools on business. The measurement of results reassures top management that investments in OA tools have been worthwhile, and the figures can be used to justify similar applications and identify opportunities elsewhere in the organization.

As discussed in chapter 1, relatively easy measurement of cost savings is often impossible or meaningless for managerial and professional applications. Value-added measures are more reasonable and relevant to top management. But value-added benefits are more difficult to measure than cost savings. Do not despair; remember that in the majority of the case examples described in this book, the value-added benefits were measurable in terms that management understood and appreciated.

The value-added approach to measurement is not a simple "cookbook" series of steps. There is no one right way to measure value-added benefits, just as there is no single way to measure a manager's worth. Value-added measurement is analogous to performance appraisals (and quite different from time-and-motion studies). In addition to being customized for each user, the evaluation process must incorporate a deep understanding of the user's business.

For these reasons, surveys and organization-wide studies are inappropriate. They look at a wide but shallow slice of the organization's business. Instead, the evaluation process should take the form of an interview with the key user. The implementor, through a series of probing questions, can help the user to define improvements precisely, and, once the improvement is clearly defined, the user and implementor together can place a value on it by linking it to the organization's profits or mission.

This chapter is intended to help implementors and users make the evaluation interview a creative and productive process of exploration.

An Example of a Value-Added Interview

The following conversation illustrates some of the common interchanges and obstacles that occur in the process of evaluating value-added benefits. It is based on the hundreds of interviews that went into the making of this book. Imagine that Diane, a member of your OA staff group, is interviewing John, a vice-president of sales in your corporation. Together, they are trying to understand the impacts of information tools on profits.

Diane: Hello, John. I understand you've been very creative in your use of the spreadsheet.

John: (with a nervous laugh): Well, I don't know, Diane. We're just trying to get our job done. But I don't think you can really measure what the PC is worth. This is going to be a waste of time.

Diane (ignoring John's pessimism): I'd like to understand just what the tools have done for you. But to do that, I need a bit of background on what you do for a living.

John: (with enthusiasm): Well, it's really complicated. I don't know if you can understand without being an engineer. But basically, we make bearings that go into real high-speed equipment—for example, turbines in cars and jets. To sell these things, we really have to tailor the specs to the manufacturers' needs.

Diane: By manufacturers, do you mean your customers?

John: Yes. We sell to the people who manufacture components such as turbines, who in turn sell to other companies, such as automobile manufacturers.

Diane: I take it you work on contract, rather than producing a standard product line?

John: That's right, Diane. All our products are custom.

Diane: Are these fairly large contracts?

John: You bet. You couldn't afford to have us design a custom bearing unless you were going to buy a heck of a lot of them. Oh, occasionally we get a job to make just a few of some design—for instance, for the space shuttle. But even those are fairly large contracts.

Diane: Okay, so what do you do with the spreadsheet?

John: Well, when we're bidding on a job, we have to estimate the costs of design and production. Also, we have to show the customer how our design will perform in his product. You know, there are lots of ways to make a bearing!

Diane: Why do you have to estimate your costs?

John: (thinking to himself, "you dummy!"): Well, we have to set our price.

Diane: You bid fixed-price rather than cost-plus fees?

John: That's right.

Diane: I guess if you estimate costs too low, you could lose a lot of money.

John: You bet. Don't quote me, but on one job we lost nearly $2 million!

Diane: How often did this sort of thing happen?

John: Oh, not too often. That one loser was years ago, and after that we were a lot more careful.

Diane: And if you estimte too high a price, what would happen?

John: We might lose the job.

Diane: To a competitor?

John: Sometimes. Or the customer might decide to redesign its product to use a standard rather than a custom bearing.

Diane: So how does the spreadsheet help?

John: Well, we can do all these calculations in a few minutes rather than days. It's saved a lot of time. I guess that's what you're looking for.

Diane: Whose time?

John: Our sales engineers are the ones who have to prepare the proposals. But they used to use our junior analysts to do all the calculating. Now, of course, the engineers do it themselves.

Diane: So it saved some junior analysts' time. How much per month or year?

John: Oh, we do about 30 proposals a year. On each one, it could have saved a few days of time—maybe a total of 75 days a year.

Diane: (thinking, "Seventy-five days of an analyst, costing at most $30,000 per year plus overhead—these time savings are worth $12,000 to $15,000—small change! Where's the real payoff?") So, John, it saved some analysts' time. Did it help the sales engineers at all?

John: Yes. They got the analyses back in minutes or maybe hours, rather than days.

Diane: What's the rush?

John: Well, we might be in a competitive situation. There's a deadline for submitting bids, and if we miss it, we're out of the running!

Diane: What portion of your revenues comes from situations like that with bidding deadlines?

John: Oh, at least half.

Diane: In the past, did you miss deadlines?

John: Once in a while, yes. You can't be everywhere with a small staff like ours.

Diane: Do you miss deadlines now?

John: We haven't since we started using the spreadsheet!

Diane: About how many deadlines per year did you miss in the past?

John: Gee, that's tough to say — maybe one or two.

Diane: Now that you have the spreadsheet, how many do you think you might lose?

John: Oh, now we can kick out a proposal in a few days if we have to. We like to spend more time, though, and really show the customer more alternatives.

Diane: But you still might miss one now and then, eh?

John: I really don't think so. If we want to bid, we can get the proposal out.

Diane: Are you saying there is no chance of missing a bid deadline?

John: Well, I suppose there's some chance. But I'm comfortable saying we don't need to miss any deadlines on projects we want to bid on.

Diane: Does this mean that the spreadsheet made the difference between possibly missing a deadline or making it, and that may mean one more proposal per year?

John: Yes, I think so.

Diane: I wonder what that proposal is worth. What's your hit rate? That is, how many proposals did you win divided by the number you submitted in deadline situations?

John: Well, that's tough to say. Last year, in that type of situation, we put in about 18 proposals, and we won 11.

Diane: That's better than 50 per cent!

John: Yes, we generally do better than 50 per cent.

Diane: So, you got in one extra proposal, and that gave you at least an extra 50 per cent chance of another contract. [Thinking, "Scored one! Now, onward."] Now let me go back a bit. You said there was danger in overpricing and losing contracts. Do you think the model has helped you win more contracts by not overpricing?

John: I think so. It's really hard to say …

Diane: Has your hit rate gone up?

John: Yes. But there's something else going on. The model really makes us look more professional.

Diane: How does it do that?

John: Well, now we can really show the customers the impacts of our design on their production costs. We can show them how their costs will look with our design versus their old one, or versus a competitor's.

Diane: Let me play dumb again. Why is that good?

John: Well, it lets them try out different designs to get their costs down. Sometimes we help them figure out a way to spend less money on us!

Diane: Now I'm really getting confused. Why is *that* good?

John: When we're in a competitive situation, we are more likely to win if we can find a way to give the customer the lowest total manufacturing costs. Also, customers are bringing us into their design process earlier now.

Diane: Why is that good?

John: In those situations, we are likely to get the contract without competition, or at least it gives us a foot in the door and a better understanding of the customer's needs. In some situations, the customer has a design already working, and we can show them how a redesign can help lower their costs.

Diane: So the model helps you optimize the customer's costs, design a part that better fits their needs, and maybe avoid competition. And in some cases, it helps you get a potential customer to realize they ought to be redesigning an existing product. Right?

John: That's right.

Diane: So the model should result in more sales because of all these effects?

John: It should. That's why we built it. And also it should help us build long-term customer loyalty because of our better support.

Diane: Would you say that the model improves your odds of closing a deal?

John: Gee, that's impossible to say. Every deal is so different, and there are so many factors that go into winning. And since these are such big projects, we don't do enough per year really to get a feel for statistics.

Diane: How many more sales per year do you think the model will bring in?

John: No, I really couldn't say. I don't think you can evaluate it that way. But we were able to justify it based on saving time.

Diane: Well, John, let me try one more angle on you. You do believe the model will help bring in sales?

John: Yes.

Diane: With what assurance can you say, "The model will bring in one more sale per year"? Fifty-fifty?

John: Oh, at least. I think it could bring in four or five sales.

Diane: Would you be more than 75 per cent sure that the model will bring in at least one more sale per year?

John: I think so. In fact, I'm almost sure of it.

Diane: 100 per cent sure?

John: Let's say 90 per cent sure.

Diane: Okay, what are the odds that it will bring in at least two sales per year?

John: I'm still pretty sure of that ... maybe two-out-of-three odds.

Diane: How about three sales?

John: I don't know ... Less than even odds, I think. Maybe 40 per cent.

Diane: Are you just talking about the effect of better proposals, or are you also accounting for the extra proposal you might get in under a deadline?

John: I was just talking about the higher hit-rate on proposals. That extra proposal will benefit as well.

Diane: (scribbling on the back of an envelope): Okay, given your probability estimates, the expected value of that higher hit rate is worth about two extra sales per year. We can add the 50 per cent (or better) odds that come from the extra proposal per year. That total is 2.5 extra sales per year because of the spreadsheet.

John: I can believe that.

Diane: John, how much is a sale worth to the company?

John: Well, that varies all over the map. Our deals range from $100,000 to $5 million.

Diane: What is a typical sale?

John: I'd say a typical sale would be between $500,000 and $1 million.

Diane: Let's be conservative and say $500,000. How much of that do you take to the bottom line?

John: Our average margins are about 20 per cent.

Diane: (furiously working her calculator): So that would be .2 times $500,000, or about $100,000. Since we expect the spreadsheet to add 2.5 sales per year, that means that the spreadsheet is worth about $250,000 per year. If we keep this up for three years, discounting at 10 per cent, that has a present value of $621,713. How much did you pay for that spreadsheet?

John: We have 10 sales engineers. Each of them got a $5,000 personal computer. And we spent about three months developing the model. I'd say we've invested about $70,000 altogether.

Diane: That's a 788 per cent ROI! That should make the controller happy! Now, John, let's go back over our assumptions to be sure we're being conservative.

John: Okay, but I think it's a reasonable analysis.

Four Steps to Measurement

Evaluation is like working backward through the four questions used to identify value-added applications, as described in chapter 12. (See Figure 13.1.) As the tools are traced back to the business objective, greater financial and logical rigor is applied until the linkage between information tools and profits (whether anticipated or measured) is made clear.

Figure 13.1. Finding and Measuring Value-Added Applications

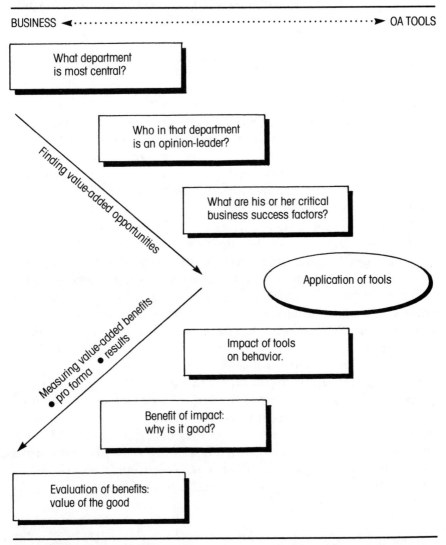

There are four basic steps to measuring value-added benefits. Remember that these four steps are useful both for evaluating anticipated returns before a project is implemented and for measuring results after a system is up and running (see Figure 13.2).

Figure 13.2. Four Steps to Measurement

---

1. Application: what tools are used, and for what?
2. Impact: how do the tools change behavior?
3. Benefit: why is the change in behavior good for the organization?
4. Evaluation: what is the value of the "good"?

These four questions can be answered by the users before implementation in a project proposal, or afterward in an evaluation interview. The first exploratory discussion may lead to other interviews — for example, with other members of the user group or those whom the user group serves (internal and external customers and the group's management). It may also necessitate surveys or research on what the user group actually does.

Note that the more structured measures — statistically valid surveys or time measures — are applicable only to well-structured tasks. In other words, they can only answer questions stated in terms of "yes" or "no," "this" or "that," or the percentages that meet specified criteria. They are best used only to fill in the blanks within a broader chain of reasoning that traces tools to the bottom line, not to find opportunities but to provide sizing data. While structured data-gathering techniques are the mainstay of systems analysis, they are only a small part of the value-added analysis.

The four steps in the evaluation process, and the suggested questions in each step, are offered only as a guideline for a semi-structured interview. In practice, the value-added interview remains to some degree an art. Experienced interviewers develop a "nose" for the linkages between tools and profits. It is hoped that this summary of our methodology will be combined with large quantities of personality, curiosity, business knowledge, and common sense.

What Application?

Before beginning any discussion of tools, we find it useful to gain some background on what the user does for a living. This information provides a fundamental understanding of the user's job in terms of both mission and daily tasks. It can be particularly informative to explore the basis upon which the user is measured—in other words, the criteria for success in his or her job. The user might be asked to think about what goes into his or her annual performance evaluation, what his or her key goals are for the year, what it takes to earn a bonus or promotion, or what his or her group contributes to the rest of the organization.

It should be noted that if the user is unable to articulate a business purpose, a serious management problem exists and the value-added approach is unlikely to be successful. In such cases we generally look for a user in a higher level of the organization, and we may address the problem of employee understanding of the company's mission along with our discussion of OA.

Given this background, the objective of the first step is to find business tasks that have been aided in significant ways by OA tools. The result of the first step in the measurement process, related to question 4 in chapter 12, is to gain a clear understanding of exactly what application is being measured. Any user is likely to utilize a variety of tools for a variety of needs. Each need, or business application, will require a separate measurement process, because each has a different business result. For example, an analyst might use a spreadsheet to track actual results against budgets and to forecast next year's budget. The value of better tracking must be analyzed separately from the value of more accurate forecasts.

Thus, the first step identifies the distinct business applications of the tools, each of which may warrant a distinct analysis of benefits. This series of questions begins with the tools that are used. For each tool, we ask what the user does with it. The discussion must be led away from the procedural level ("I use a spreadsheet to add columns of numbers") and back to business tasks ("I use a spreadsheet to track financial results"). It is these business tasks—both one-time projects and ongoing duties—that provide the basis for differentiating OA applications. The goal for this first step of the evaluation process is one or more statements that "this tool really helps me succeed at this particular task."

What Change in Behavior?

The second step in the evaluation process, refining question 3 in chapter 12, is to define precisely what it is that changed as a result of the tools—that is, the impacts of the tool on behavior. Put another way, step 2 compares the old way of doing business with the new, and documents the differences. This step moves the level of discussion out of strategic goals and down to specific work tasks such as producing documents, interacting with people, and making specified decisions. It defines the changes in the way people perform their daily work.

Step 2 may identify improvements in the individual tasks that make up a process. In other cases, improvements may be gained through the redesign of the entire process. A listing of critical business success factors is useful as a discussion catalyst at this stage of the evaluation process (see Figure 12.4).

By comparing the old and new way of doing business, the differences that result from the use of the tools can be listed. These differences may be expressed in a number of measures of work processes (see Figure 13.3).

Figure 13.3.   Task Differences Defined in Step 2

- Do tasks take less time?
- Are tasks completed in a more timely fashion?
- Are tasks not previously done being done now?
- Are tasks done with greater quality/success?
- Is there greater job satisfaction?

When tools are used to save time—that is, to improve productivity—the benefits may need no further analysis. This cost-displacement effect is measurable when there are reductions in expenditures or staff-to-volume ratios (either when the number of people is reduced or when future hiring is avoided). One may stop at a simple productivity analysis when the resulting savings are sufficient to justify the application.

Often, however, time savings are not used to reduce staff. Instead, the time is used to improve the quality of people's work or to do more business. The uses of saved time should be defined and then converted into one of the other types of benefits to develop a value-added analysis.

A second potential effect of OA tools is the completion of tasks on a more timely basis. In this case, the impact is measured in terms of response time to a request—for example, from management or a customer.

Very often, through the enabling power of the tools combined with the time saved on traditional tasks, the third effect is seen: users find themselves doing things they never did before. This is a particularly interesting effect. Sometimes the new activities may translate into increased quality in a task; for example, "what-if" analyses may improve the quality of a forecast. Alternatively, new activities may represent entirely new products or services for the user group to offer to its internal or external customers. These are among the most lucrative value-added opportunities.

The fourth effect, increased quality in the user's business outputs, may be defined in a number of ways. It may be measured in terms of accuracy of forecasts or decisions. Quality may be evidenced in terms of professionalism and motivational impact; for example, better presentations. In some cases, quality is measured in terms of a quantifiable variance from an ideal; for example, in manufactured goods. When the type of quality difference is unclear, the interviewee might be asked how one knows a good product from a bad product, or just why his or her work is better now than it was before.

Fifth, creative applications of OA may improve the quality of work life, in turn improving people's satisfaction with their jobs. This can be measured either through attitude surveys or by the subjective assessment of those who work with the affected people.

Why Is This Good?

Step 3 involves linking the change in behavior (defined in step 2) as closely as possible to the mission of the organization. This takes the discussion beyond the immediate effects on the user group to the secondary effects on the entire company. In essence, like questions 1 and 2 in chapter 12, this step identifies how the user contributes to company profits.

The goal of step 3 is to identify the logical connection between the behavioral impact and profits or other measures of the organization's success. (Estimating the size of those profits is reserved for step 4. For now, we concentrate on the logical linkage of behavioral changes to business goals.) The result of step 3 is a clear statement of the benefits of the tool.

Beginning with each change identified in step 2, one must keep asking questions such as, "Why is this good?" This line of questioning should end with a beneficial effect that can subsequently be quantified; for example, incremental sales or reduced risk. The questions below suggest a means of translating each of the types of impacts defined in step 2 into statements of benefits (see Figure 13.4).

Figure 13.4. Translating Impacts into Benefits

- Tasks take less time: where does the time go?
- Tasks are completed in a more timely fashion: what's the rush?
- Tasks not previously done are being done: why are they worth doing?
- Tasks are done with greater quality/success: who appreciates quality?
- There is greater job satisfaction: why pay for satisfaction?

Time savings, or productivity gains, in themselves are not value-added benefits. If the time saved is used to reduce costs, the benefit is simply the costs saved. If the time saved is used to do more or better work, however, there is potential for a value-added analysis. In step 3, one must ascertain how and where the free time is being used, essentially converting a time savings into one of the other categories of effects. (One may have to cycle back through step 2 at this point to clarify the behavior change that resulted from the available free time.)

When the impact is more timely results, the obvious question in step 3 is, "What's the rush?" When new tasks are being performed, the question must be, "Why is this task worth doing?" When the quality of work improves, one should ask, "Who cares about quality, and why?" Similarly, when there are improvements to job satisfaction, a decision-maker can be asked why job satisfaction is important to the organization. It may be important because it reduces turnover or absenteeism. More positively, it may be because management desires greater employee creativity and motivation. These objectives, in turn, must be evaluated by asking, "Why is that good?" In some (rare) cases, the motivating factor is altruism. If a business-oriented purpose is behind the desire to increase job satisfaction, however, this effect may translate into one of the other more measurable impacts.

Essentially, step 3 involves repeatedly asking, "Why is that good?" until each beneficial effect is completely defined. If a dead end is encountered, a shift in the style of questioning may uncover a new direction. For example, one might ask the user, "What are the consequences of this not happening?" Following this thread might lead to further questions such as, "Is there a risk of something bad happening?" or, "Is there an opportunity for something good to happen?"

By the end of step 3, the user should be able to say clearly, "The tool produced this benefit to the organization." The benefit at this point is not stated in monetary terms, but rather in business terms — for example, additional sales of a certain product in certain circumstances, or reduced risk of financial loss. Step 4 places a value on this beneficial effect.

While step 3 can be challenging and time-consuming, it generally is not impossible. Most users, when properly interviewed, can identify their contribution to the organization's goals, and hence the contribution of improvements in their effectiveness resulting from OA. Of the cases we explored that did not make it into this book for lack of concrete measures, very few dropped out at this step. Those evaluations that did not survive step 3 were generally technology- rather than business-driven applications. These wastes of resources might have been precluded had a value-added justification process been employed prior to implementation. More commonly, a precise statement of benefits results from step 3.

The Value of the Good

The fourth and final step involves placing a monetary value on the benefit. In some cases, we are able to measure hard dollars — that is, actual money brought into the organization because of OA. There are a number of sources of quantifiable benefits, as shown in Figure 13.5.

Bringing in More Profits

Increased revenues occur when the tools are used to generate sales. In some cases, OA may be traced to particular sales that otherwise would have been lost. This effect is particularly dramatic when OA enables an entirely new business activity to be undertaken.

In other cases, OA may be credited with increasing the odds of

Figure 13.5.   Quantifying Value-Added Benefits

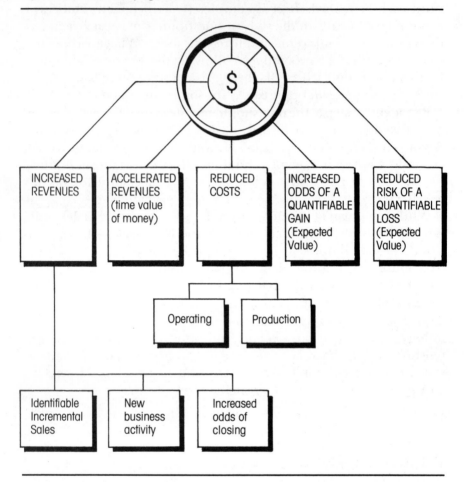

closing sales of a certain type, as shown in the dialogue at the beginning of this chapter. Evaluating the incremental revenues involves estimating the number of incremental sales that resulted from the tool and multiplying by the average size of each sale. Alternatively, the user may be able to estimate incremental revenues.

Incremental revenues can be converted to profits by an analysis of the marginal profit contribution. When margins are unavailable, contribution can be estimated using the average percentage of profit to revenue (taken from financial statements). For example, chapter 5 described a spreadsheet that generated an additional $20 million per year of profits by improving production quality and therefore market share. Chapter 8 described a situation in which an electronic mail application got a product to market two months sooner than would otherwise have been possible.

Increases in profits also occur when revenues are accelerated. In these instances, the value-added benefit is the time value of money. For example, chapter 9 described an example of an insurance claim that was settled earlier than it otherwise would have been.

Value-added impacts may also be measured by reductions, not in the costs of the office that used the tools — that would be simple cost-displacement — but in the organization's production or operating costs where there is significant leverage on gains. For example, in chapter 6 we saw that a database tool used by a telephone company reduced the cost of maintaining lines; in another company access to personnel data prevented the imposition of a $1.5-million-per-year increase in unemployment tax.

The Expected Value of Probabilities

Tools may improve the quality of management, but that improvement does not guarantee success. There is a difference between a good decision and a favorable outcome. A decision is good if it makes full use of available information to consider all reasonable alternatives and balances potential returns and risks. No matter how good the decision, all business results involve some degree of risk. Thus, the best possible decision can still lead to an unhappy outcome.

When evaluating the impact of tools on business, it is important to consider the impact on the probability of success, not on the actual outcome. For example, one might improve the odds of winning from 50 to 90 per cent, and then fail to win because of extraneous factors (the missing 10 per cent). Although the outcome may have been unfavorable, it would be unfair to discount the beneficial effect of the tools. Clearly, a 90 per cent chance of a reward is more valuable than a 50 per cent chance. For business decision making where risks are involved, one must consider the contribution of OA before the outcomes are known — that is, in terms of its impact on the value of the risky choice.

In instances where the outcome is uncertain, business decision making depends on a quantitative technique called "expected value." This simple mathematical calculation, well accepted for quantitative decision making, determines the value of risky alternatives (see Appendix B).

Figure 13.6.   The Time Value of Money

PRESENT VALUE OF A SINGLE PAYMENT

$$\text{Present value} = \frac{\text{Future value}}{(1 + i)^n}$$

January 1986 value of $1 paid at end of year, discounted at 10 per cent:

1986	1987	1988	1989	1990	1991
0.91	0.83	0.75	0.68	0.62	0.56

PRESENT VALUE OF A STREAM OF PAYMENTS

$$\text{Present value} = \sum \frac{\text{Payment}}{(1 + i)^n}$$

January 1986 value of $1 per year, discounted at 10 per cent

1986	1987	1988	1989	1990	1991
0.91	1.74	2.49	3.17	3.79	4.36

i = interest rate

n = number of years

Convert to Present Values

When the risk has been taken into account and the expected monetary impact has been calculated, that impact must be converted to present values. Money in the future is worth less than the same amount is now because of the time value of money. For example, if you were to put one dollar in the bank and earn 10 per cent interest, in one year you would have $1.10. Put another way, $1.10 in one year from now is worth the same as $1 today (it is discounted at 10 per cent). Similarly, $0.91 today is worth the same as $1 will be one year from now (again, discounted at 10 per cent). (See Figure 13.6.) To make fair comparisons, future benefits must be discounted into present dollars to compare to investments of present dollars.

Some applications pay off in one lump sum. For example, getting a product to market one month sooner results in one additional month of incremental profits. These profits can be discounted to their present value for comparison with the costs of the investment.

In other cases, the application produces ongoing benefits. For example, an OA tool may bring in one additional sale per year. The benefit of the tool is the present value of the stream of sales over the life of the tool. In practical terms, one might take the benefits over a five-year period.[1]

Throughout this book we have used a discount rate of 10 per cent. In practice, one should use a rate that approximates the organization's cost of capital (the weighted averge of inflation-adjusted debt and equity costs). While some organizations use a higher rate to adjust for risk, the proper way to account for risk is through expected values rather than the discount rate.[2]

Soft Monetary Measures

Cases that can be directly evaluated in monetary terms are the most convincing, but not all users can measure their results so clearly. The value-added benefits of OA can be measured in hard dollars when the users themselves are measurable in hard dollars. Many middle managers cannot accurately measure their contribution to an organization's bottom line.

But high-payoff applications that are relevant to top management should not be avoided just because they are difficult to measure. We must continue to focus on critical business success factors, and measure them as best we can.

In many instances results can be measured in terms other than monetary. For example, chapter 8 described a situation in which teleconferencing resulted in a better-designed airplane that is 20 per cent more fuel-efficient than planned. While we can measure the plane's fuel efficiency, we cannot identify which particular sales were credited to that competitive edge. Thus, the outcomes were clearly measurable, but management's subjective judgment is needed to put a monetary value on it.

The first step is to quantify non-monetary measures of outcomes; these are derived directly from the objectives of the user group. Some goals are difficult to quantify — for example, "improved community relations." This does not mean that the goal is of little value to the organization, but management judgment may be required to evaluate progress. When the gains are in terms of quality rather than quantity, concrete measures of satisfaction can be obtained from the users' clients (inside or outside the company) or the users' management.

In some cases, the users cannot measure their outputs in any terms. For example, it is difficult to measure a gain in competitive edge, the worth of increased employee motivation, or the quality of a strategic plan. When no business measures are available, we must resort to measures of the process rather than of outcome. For example, we can say that more people were involved in the plan, more competitive scenarios were considered, and more new opportunities were analyzed. Management can use its judgment to conclude that because the planning process was better, the actual plan was superior. Another measure of process is the satisfaction of the participants.

Subjective Judgments

After a non-monetary measure of results is developed, subjective management judgment can again be used. Subjective judgment is critical to most value-added measures. The less tangible the users' business product, the more judgment will be required. There are a number of approaches to assisting users with subjective judgments:

Figure 13.7.   Types of Subjective Judgments

- estimates of levels of outcomes;
- equivalent value comparisons;
- willingness to pay;
- minimum assumptions to payback.

The implementor may have to try each in turn; when the more common approaches are exhausted, the implementor must depend on the user for ideas of measuring the value of the work (and the improvements to it).

The first subjective measurement is the users' estimate of the total monetary impact of the tools. (Appendix B discusses how to convert probabilities of estimates into expected values.) Estimates of total impact are not always possible, however. In some cases, users may be able to identify other known benefits of approximately equal magnitude. When this line of questioning proves fruitless, the implementor may ask the user what he or she would be willing to pay for the benefit (a value that is often many times the actual cost of the project). Note that this judgment is far more reliable after steps 1 through 3 have precisely defined the benefit; in other words, it is easier for a decision maker to judge how much he or she is willing to pay for a business benefit than for an OA tool.

If a direct link is not possible, the implementor may identify the minimum assumptions required to justify the project. For example, in chapter 8 an engineer estimated that one sale of the new product made possible by the spreadsheet would pay for the entire system.

Are These Numbers Believable?

In reality, the measurement problem is not as difficult as it may seem. We do not really need to measure the benefits accurately. Rather, we need a critical mass of evidence to show that the application is worthwhile.

For example, instead of attempting to trace the sales that result from a value-added application, we might simply point out that it would take only one or a few incremental sales to pay for the project. It can be shown that the project is worthwhile even when the most conservative assumptions are used.

To convince ourselves and others of the importance and measurability of value-added benefits, small case studies are often better than large surveys. Stories such as those in this book portray the qualitative benefits that may be lost in detailed numeric analysis.

The need for justification of investments in OA changes as an organization moves through the stages of growth. In the initiation stage, when OA is new, it is not uncommon for top management to demand very strict justifications of the first few pilots. At this stage, applications should be sought in which the benefits can be measured in hard dollars.

Once the concept of value-added is proven by the first few applications, management relaxes its demand for measurement. During the "contagion" stage, when OA is spreading rapidly through the organization, management will approve those investments that deliver critical business benefits, so long as the user judges the benefits worth the investment.[3]

Later, in the consolidation stage, when OA is in widespread use, management typically accepts soft-dollar value-added measures, and in many cases approves projects based on a demonstration of need rather than return on investment.

Measuring benefits is very important to gaining approval for projects and documenting successes, but it is not an end in itself. Measures should be designed to answer questions put forth by decision makers. It is more important that the measures be relevant to top management than that they be detailed and extremely accurate.

To be relevant, OA applications and measures must focus on critical business needs. For example, consider the difference between a very accurate measure of typing efficiency and a rough measure of the benefits of getting a product to market more quickly. The odds are that your executive committee will always prefer the latter.

Second, measures must be understood by decision makers. They must be phrased in the language of business. It does no good to have detailed measures of work flows when management does not understand industrial engineering. Measures will have far greater impact on decision makers when they use language that is identical to that used in measuring the business itself.

What if someone gave you a choice between a coin and a handful of gold? It would be easy for you to determine the exact value of the coin, but some effort would be required to measure the value of the gold. Do you have a scale in your pocket? If not, your estimate of value of the gold will be inaccurate. Which would you pick?

If we implement OA only when we can accurately measure monetary results, then we are likely to be limited to administrative support applications that are of little interest to top management. Tangible measures of value-added impacts usually can be determined— benefits that are related to the users' business objectives. In many cases, subjective management judgments will be required to place a dollar value on those impacts. While measurement of value-added benefits is difficult, *it is better to measure significant benefits roughly than to measure trivia accurately*. For computers to become a part of business strategy and for the use of OA to grow among managers and professionals, we and our managers must learn to accept rough measures of relevant benefits.

Notes

1. For example, the present value (discounted at 10 per cent) of $1 per year for five years is worth less than an immediate payment of $5; each of the individual payments must be discounted into present values, for a total present value of the stream of payments of $3.79.
2. The authors thank Richard A. Rossi for his assistance with this section.
3. N. Dean Meyer, "The Office Automation Cookbook: Management Strategies for Getting Office Automation Moving," *Sloan Management Review* 24, no. 2 (Winter 1983) 51-60.

Adopting the Value-Added Perspective

Value-added applications are not uncommon. The cases reported here only scratch the surface of the range of successful OA applications that have been developed by creative implementors and users worldwide. We did not just report the "cream of the crop" or limit our research to leading-edge organizations. We find value-added applications in virtually every organization that we visit. We are able to measure the monetary impacts in about half of these cases, and we can find other measures of results in the remaining half. It is likely that every organization can find examples of value-added benefits among its current applications, and new opportunities for very high-payoff applications elsewhere in the organization.

Of course, not every application of OA produces such dramatic benefits. On the other hand, it only takes one or two million-dollar applications to pay for the budget of an entire OA program. Those ignoring the value-added perspective—either by demanding cost-displacement justifications or by focusing implementation efforts on administrative support—clearly are not serving the best interests of their organizations.

In the course of our research, we have seen some patterns among the organizations that are particularly successful at generating high-payoff applications. In this chapter, we suggest a series of policy changes that will maximize an organization's chances of gaining high-payoff value-added applications.

The Keys to Success

User Leadership

Because value-added opportunities for OA are derived from business objectives, their identification and measurement are business processes, not technical processes. They cannot be done by OA staff alone.

Understanding value-added requires participation from top managers and users at all levels who understand the mission and objectives of the business as only insiders can.

The organization's top managers provide the leadership for selecting and evaluating OA applications. They provide a definition of the overall business objectives, which form the basis for OA objectives. Furthermore, they must define the criteria they will use in evaluating OA proposals. Once they understand the concept of value-added and the range of measures — from hard to soft dollars — they must decide whether the organization will be very conservative and demand only hard-dollar benefits, or whether it will more progressively seek the higher-payoff applications that are more difficult to measure.

The users themselves play the most important role in the evaluation process, because they are responsible for the effective operation of their part of the business. In other words, users are responsible for improving their own effectiveness. It is the users' job to justify the resources they need to perform their mission effectively. Furthermore, only the users understand their business mission and the way they work. The users themselves must develop the measurement methodology that captures the nature of their business.

We have found that higher-level managers are more capable of identifying and evaluating value-added benefits. They are in a better position to understand the impact of their group's work on profits and their role in corporate strategy. Furthermore, executives and senior managers tend to be more able and more willing to make the subjective judgments that are likely to be required to evaluate value-added benefits. Our first recommendation is:

Let the users lead the implementation projects.

Freedom to Explore

It is important to note that many of the successful cases reported in this book occurred because innovative users experimented with the available tools, with little application-specific support from their information staff groups. This process of user innovation is extremely important. Implementing OA is an evolutionary process. We all learn as we go, and discover new applications in the process of solving recognized problems.

User innovation works to the advantage of those responsible for implementing OA. Oddly enough, many central information staff have become so concerned about the control of technology that they actually inhibit user exploration. To some degree, central control is desirable so as to make integrated networks feasible. However, central information staff who attempt to audit the data in every business analysis or use of the tools are being overly intrusive, and may preclude value-added discoveries. Our second recommendation is:

Encourage users to explore applications on their own.

Relax the Justification Climate

Excessive justification of investments in OA may stifle exploration and creativity. Furthermore, excessive controls are unprofitable. Consider, for example, controls that demand a 30 per cent annual return on investment in OA and accept only cost-displacement justifications. With such a threshold, an organization may spend $500,000 on personal and departmental computers, acquiring 100 work stations. On the other hand, without financial controls, that same organization might spend $1.5 million on 300 work stations.

For each 100 users, we expect to find from one to three value-added applications. Let's be conservative and assume that only one out of 100 users develops a value-added application. And let's conservatively assume that each such application produces benefits with a present value of just $500,000 (equivalent to the present value of $132,000 per year for five years).

With the controls, we expect $150,000 per year in cost savings that the 30 per cent ROI controls guaranteed. Over five years, these cost savings have a present value (discounted at 10 per cent) of $570,000. In addition, we predict one value-added application among the 100 users, with a present value of $500,000. Thus, the systems will produce a total return of $1,069,000, less equipment costs of $500,000, for a net contribution of $569,000.

Without such strict controls, we can still expect the 30 per cent return on investment from the first 100 work stations; to be conservative, let's assume that the other 200 users produce no cost-displacement results. We can expect three value-added applications among our 300 users. Thus, the 300 work stations will produce a total return of $2,068,000, less equipment costs of $1.5 million, for a net contribution of $569,000 — the same net result as with strict controls (see Table 14.1).

Table 14.1. The Cost of Controls—A Conservative Case

Work stations	100	300
Cost per work station	$5,000	$5,000
Minimum ROI per year	30%	30%
Number of work stations ROI applies to	100	100
Cost savings per year	$150,000	$150,000
Present value, cost savings, five years	$568,618	$568,618
Value-added applications	1	1
Value-added benefits per application	$500,000	$500,000
Total present value, value-added applications	$500,000	$1,500,000
Total present value	$1,068,618	$2,068,618
Development cost	$500,000	$1,500,000
Net contribution to profits	$568,618	$568,618
Return on investment	114%	38%

While the profit contribution is the same, without controls an additional 200 people have work stations, and they represent potential productivity gains and future value-added discoveries. In addition, we have avoided the cost (in time and pain) of enforcing tight restrictions. These intangible factors may balance the extra effort that will be required to integrate the technologies.

Consider, however, the upside potential of the less restrictive approach. If the users are as creative as most and find two value-added applications for every 100 work stations, then the controlled company will net $1,069,000 and the uncontrolled organization will earn $2,069,000—a million-dollar difference. With such upside potential, it is wise to bet on user innovation (see Table 14.2).

In general, all capital investments of significant size are subject to some justification requirements. OA, however, is often subjected to even stricter criteria than other investments. It is this additional obstacle to which we object. Our third recommendation is:

Accept subjective measures of relevant benefits as justification for investments in OA.

Table 14.2.   The Cost of Controls — A Realistic Case

Work stations	100	300
Cost per work station	$5,000	$5,000
Minimum ROI per year	30%	30%
Applies to number of work stations	100	100
Cost savings per year	$150,000	$150,000
Present value, cost savings, five years	$568,618	$568,618
Value-added applications	2	6
Value-added benefits per application	$500,000	$500,000
Total present value, value-added applications	$1,000,000	$3,000,000
Total present value	$1,568,618	$3,568,618
Development cost	$500,000	$1,500,000
Net contribution to profits	$1,068,618	$2,068,618
Return on investment	214%	138%

Budget for Reasonable Growth

OA managers must advise users and their executives on annual budgets for OA. The budget for maintenance and support is easily calculated based on the number of work stations and on past experience. The budget for new equipment, however, is more controversial. It is an important determinant of the pace of evolution of OA, and the rate of delivery of value-added benefits.

While statistical scenarios like the one above can be used to demonstrate potential value-added benefits, there is no way to measure value-added opportunities accurately at the organizational level. As discussed in chapter 2, econometric approaches have failed to provide useful measures. As discussed in chapters 12 and 13, organization-wide surveys cannot analyze the business of the user organization deeply enough to reveal value-added benefits.

It would be convenient if an organization-wide "scoping" of the potential value-added benefits could be used to justify OA budgets. Unfortunately, this is impossible. Budgeting for investments in OA beyond the more readily apparent cost-displacement applications requires a different approach.

Given the difficulty of measurement, it is recommended that the budget process not be used to substitute for the justification of applications. Rather, budget should simply be considered a valve on the pace of evolution. Each significant investment should be justified in the context of its application, not in an annual budget cycle.

In this light, progress with OA and its concomitant budget allocation requires *belief* on the part of top management in the value of OA. This is the key issue, with or without numeric analyses. If top management doesn't believe in OA, no statistics will sway their attitudes; once they understand its importance, budget should not be used to slow the rate of growth of OA or as a poor substitute for project justification.

Beliefs are built by experiences, particularly in the form of successes inside the organization. The cases in this book combined with documentation of value-added results can create a favorable budget environment — that is, one that supplies enough capital and expense monies to allow a natural pace of evolution. As a favorable environment grows, many organizations simultaneously relax the justification requirements of individual applications — also a sign of belief in OA and trust in the OA staff group.

To set the level of budget, then, the OA manager must estimate the natural pace of evolution of the organization. To do so, he or she can use the cumulative-normal S-curve of innovation.[1] In most organizations, it is safe to assume that 80 per cent of the white-collar workers will get work stations in the 10 to 12 years following the first OA pilot. Of course, each organization evolves at a different pace, and there is much the OA staff group can do to encourage a faster pace of evolution.

In summary, we recommend that OA managers:

Set the annual budget to accommodate a reasonable rate of growth.

The corollaries to this recommendation are:

Gain budget approval by building a favourable understanding of and attitude toward OA, not by using statistical justifications.

Justify investments for individual applications, not the entire budget.

OA Staff as Facilitators

OA staff groups should not be in the business of controlling user applications. As stated above, line managers are responsible for their own business performance. Thus, information staff should not be held responsible for justifying investments in other people's effectiveness. What, then, is the appropriate role of information staff groups?

OA professionals can help users with their justification and evaluation tasks. In addition to their implementation responsibilities, information staff can play two roles in the evaluation process. First, they can contribute their skills in measuring value-added — an understanding of what it is and of the methodologies for measurement (as outlined in chapters 12 and 13). Second, they can serve as facilitators of the process by helping users to define their objectives, gather relevant data, analyze and structure the data, and present their case to their management.

The outline shown in Appendix A can be used as a guide for the value-added interview. It must not be used as a questionnaire or survey. Every value-added application is different, and the evaluation process must respond to the unique business problem and use of tools. The value-added interview is a collaborative, exploratory process. This guide is offered to get implementors started on the path to high-payoff applications. As the implementor gains experience, this guide will fall by the wayside. The essential elements of a good interview can be summarized in three Cs: curiosity, clarity of purpose, and common sense.

Value-added implementors require a unique mix of skills. They must combine a broad technical background, excellent interpersonal skills, and a business perspective. Particularly in the stringent environment of the executive suite, implementors must demonstrate each of these traits to a high degree. Finding the right people for the job is not easy.

With regard to technical skills, a knowledge of OA tools is necessary. But value-added implementors need not be experts in technologies. They must simply understand the capabilities of the broad range of OA tools. Direct user experience and a logical mind may be all that is required.

Implementors must have the interpersonal skills necessary to keep the user focused on the effects of the tools, and to question the user's assumptions without being offensive. Interviewing is not easy. Users may become defensive or impatient when continually questioned about their responses. Implementors must have a great deal of creativity, the persistence to try numerous angles and trains of logic, and the sensitivity to know when to ease off and try again later.

Perhaps most important, implementors must have a solid grounding in business and finance, and an understanding of the workings of business in corporate or government environments. Some training in accounting and finance is a necessity. Exposure to decision science, business strategy, and economics is also required. Implementors should have the ability to create a budget, generate forecasts, perform research, and structure decisions.

When high-level users are involved, implementors must have the demeanor of executives. Their style will be evidenced in their dress, language, work habits, and business concerns. Implementors must be senior enough in the organization to be trusted with confidential information, and must maintain an extremely high degree of integrity and discretion.

Unfortunately, it is very difficult to hire trained OA implementors. Many firms find they must "grow their own." An MBA with a few years of experience in marketing or finance and a penchant for PCs may make an ideal candidate. An engineering or computer science background, while perhaps an advantage, is certainly not a necessity.

The key point remains: OA staff cannot be an expert at everyone's business. Referring to the user-centered process of change in our first recommendation, we suggest that the role of the OA staff group is to:

Listen, learn about the users' business, and find ways to be useful.

The Future of Value-Added

Value-added is the key to progress in OA. To consider only cost-displacement applications locks the industry into supporting secretaries and clerks. The potential of OA is far greater. It is not uncommon to find rates of return on investments in OA measured at 200 to 2,000 per cent.

Initially, most users seek local solutions to local problems. Thus, the first wave of value-added applications is likely to focus on the use of one or two tools by individuals and small groups. Most of the cases in this book fall into this category.

After gaining experience with OA tools, users will begin to explore new tools and applications. These too may have value-added potential. The first applications are likely to be the most rewarding (assuming they were well chosen and implemented), however, and subsequent individual applications typically face diminishing returns.

After a year or two of experience, users generally begin to explore a new class of applications: those that cross organizational boundaries.

Tools for telecommunications and sharing information become relatively more important at this time. An implementor need not wait to address interorganizational applications, but user awareness and receptivity will be greater after people have gained some experience with the individual tools.

These interorganizational applications open new horizons of value-added opportunities. Tools can help increase cooperation, coordination, and collaboration across functions, and thus improve organizational effectiveness at a higher level.

By this time, executives will have had firsthand experience with the power of OA to augment the minds of individuals and small groups, and subsequently to break down barriers to interorganizational synergy. As OA evolves, we expect even these interorganizational applications to experience diminishing returns. A new kind of application, so different that it might be considered an entirely new wave of innovation, will evolve. The next wave will be organization-wide applications—the science of cybernetics.

Cybernetics is the study of control mechanisms in systems. For example, the thermostat on a home heater is a cybernetic control that keeps the temperature in the house within a comfortable range. Similarly, the incentive structures and feedback loops embodied to a growing degree in information systems have a great deal of influence on the way people in organizations behave.

We believe that employees who misbehave—for example, by making bribes to government officials or polluting the environment—are doing so not because they are evil people, but rather because of the jobs they hold, their incentive structures, and the information they receive. Conversely, high-performance organizations have aligned their incentive programs, culture (intrinsic incentives), and performance tracking systems (information feedback) with their corporate goals.

Information systems today are a relatively small part of the cybernetics of an organization. As OA evolves, the role of computers and telecommunications technologies will grow. Eventually, executives will understand that to a significant degree they can guide the organization through involvement in the design of office information systems.

OA has potential far beyond the million-dollar applications described in this book. Today, creative implementors are finding ways to apply OA to issues that are crucial to the success of the business. In the future, OA may become the very fabric of the organization and a key tool for managing the entire company.

Conclusion

Value-added applications make computers a key part of business strategy—they create the information edge. In this book, we have seen examples in virtually every functional area, across a range of industries, utilizing a variety of OA tools. Value-added opportunities for OA are everywhere, waiting for creative users and astute implementors.

In chapters 12 and 13, we presented methodologies for finding and measuring value-added applications of OA. Using these techniques, OA staff groups can do far more than they have done in most organizations to date to deliver significant contributions to profits.

Yet even with willing users and enlightened implementors, policies may impede progress. This chapter has suggested a few of the most important policy issues facing the senior managers in many organizations. It is imperative that top management not only understand OA from a value-added perspective, but also become actively involved in creating a policy environment that encourages innovation.

There is much at stake, including the profits, growth, and long-term survival of the organization. OA offers an opportunity to gain an information edge by augmenting the intelligence of the organization. To initiate this wave of innovation and prepare for the next, we must stop measuring keystrokes and counting minutes; we must start seeking ways to improve significantly the organization's effectiveness with recognized impacts on the bottom line.

Notes

1. See Everett M. Rogers, *Diffusion of Innovations* (New York: Free Press, 1983), at 243.

Value-Added Interview Guide

Note: This interview guide is not intended as a questionnaire or survey. It should be used only as an outline for a semi-structured interview. The interview should be conducted with the appropriate user, and by an interviewer with the appropriate skills. See chapters 12 and 13 for a discussion of the value-added interview process.

Background Information

What is your title?
What are your job responsibilities?
How will you (or your boss) know if you are successful?
Describe your most important tasks/projects/goals.

Tools

Which tools are most valuable to you?
(Refer to the OA tools framework, Figure 1.1.)

Applications

What do you do with these tools? What task/activity/business problem do you use them for?
(Analyze benefits of each application, that is, the major combination of tools and tasks/activities/business problems.)

Impacts

What does the tool do? What are its tasks as opposed to yours?
How would you have done this task without the tools?
Exactly what is different now that you are using the tool?
   Tasks take less time

Tasks are completed in a more timely fashion
Tasks not previously done are now done
Tasks are done with greater quality/success
There is greater job satisfaction

Benefits and Evaluation

What were the benefits (not necessarily in monetary terms)?
Time savings:
  Productivity: What is the time you saved being used for?
    Doing more work? Does this mean that you have reduced or
    reassigned staff, or will hire few staff in future? (If so, take the
    burdened cost of staff time. If not, check to see if work not done
    before is being done.)
    Doing work not done before? (See below.)
    Doing a better job? (See "Improved Quality.")
  Timeliness: What's the hurry?
    Finish project and deliver its benefits sooner; for example, get-
    ting a new product to market: Does delivering the project sooner
    reduce its later benefits (for example, making the sale this year
    means we won't make it next year)? (If so, take time value of
    money. If not, take profits from extra period of benefits.)
Tasks not previously done:
  Exactly what are you doing that you otherwise would not have
  done? Why is this worth doing? What would happen if you
  stopped doing it? (Translate value of new work into one of the
  other benefits.)
Improved quality:
  In what ways is it better? (Analyze each way in which quality is
  improved, or else overall impact of quality improvements.)
  How much better? (See "Subjective Probability" estimation.)
  (Translate increased quality into one of the other benefits.)
Competitive edge:
  (Translate to increase odds of making a sale or market share.)
Increased revenue:
  Odds of winning a sale or deal (See "Subjective Probability" esti-
  mation.) (Multiply by average revenue/sale and number of sales/
  year, or by percentage of sales that are affected and total revenue to
  convert to incremental revenues.)
  Odds of identifying a market opportunity. (Multiply by present
  value of revenue from new business activity.)
  Incremental sales (per year) (Multiply by average revenue/sale.)

Incremental market share (Multiply by total revenue/year.)
(Convert revenue to profits by multiplying by marginal contribution to profits. Take present value of profits over conservative
period of operations.)

Reduced costs of business operations:
(Estimate cost savings per year. If savings will continue yearly, take
present value over conservative period.)

Accelerating benefits:
(Take time value of money, that is, the difference between the
present values of the profit stream at time of the actual start and at
the time it otherwise would have started.)

Reduced risk:
What was the risk when you used the tool? (See "Subjective Probability" estimation) What do you think the risk would have been
without the tool? How much money was at stake? (Multiply the
stake by the difference in odds to get the expected value of the
benefit.)

Job satisfaction:
Why is job satisfaction worth paying for? (Translate into one of the
other benefits.)

If All Else Fails

What would you be willing to pay for the system? (See "Subjective
Estimation.")
(Calculate minimum assumptions it would take to break even.)

Subjective Estimates of Increased Probabilities, Revenues

(See Appendix B.) What percentage increase do you think it has
made? (Prompt: 5 per cent, 10 per cent, 20 per cent. Record the most
the interviewee is willing to say, to nearest 5 or 10 per cent): "I will
make a statement and ask you to tell me what the odds are that this is
true: the system increased my business by (above) per cent. Would you
give 50/50 odds that this is true?"
(If yes, try 75 per cent, 100 per cent, etc.; record a comfortable number)
"What are the odds that the system has increased your business by
(above minus 10) per cent?"
(Lower the percentage and repeat until you find the amount interviewee is 100 per cent sure of.)
Convert probability distribution from cululative to discrete and
calculate expected value.)

Costs

What were the costs of the system?
  Initial:
  Ongoing:

Verification

(Review logical path and assumptions to be sure they are realistic and conservative.)

Expected Values

In choosing among alternatives when uncertainty is involved, a straightforward mathematical technique called "expected value" is commonly used. We use the technique throughout the book in two ways. Expected values are used to calculate the value of an uncertain outcome, and in particular to compare the risky decisions faced by the user with and without OA. We also use expected values to verify estimates made by users. This appendix explains the mechanics and application of the expected value calculation.[1]

Imagine that you are offered a choice between a one-dollar bill and a 20 per cent chance of a ten dollar bill; which will you choose? The value of the chance can be calculated at 20 per cent of ten dollars, or two dollars; in other words, if you were to take the chance frequently enough, you would average two dollars each time. In this example, you would be wise to take the chance:

The expected value of a chance to win =
$$\Sigma[(\text{Probability of outcome}_a) \cdot \text{Value of outcome}_a)]$$
20% chance of $10 =
$$(.2 \times \$10) + (.8 \times \$0) = \$2$$

Expected value calculations are used when the possible outcomes and their respective probabilities are known or can be estimated. Value-added benefits may be quantified through an expected value circulation when the tools increase the chances of success, or when they decrease the risk of a loss.

When the tools are credited with improving the chances of success on a business goal, the benefit has an expected value of the percentage improvement in the probability times the profits resulting from the goal. For example, if there is a 75 per cent chance that the tools brought in one more sale worth $1,000 in profits, then the expected value is $750.

Used in a slightly different way, expected values can be used to calculate a conservative sure value when one is not fully sure of a more optimistic outcome. For example, being 75 per cent sure that the impact was worth $1,000 is equivalent to being 100 per cent sure that the impact was worth $750.

Expected values can also be used when the tool reduces the risk of business loss. The expected value of the tool is the potential loss multiplied by the reduction in the probability. For example, chapter 5 describes a database that prevented potential losses through invalid purchase orders that were identified and eliminated.

In some cases, one must calculate the expected value of a distribution — a set of probabilities. For example, let us say that we are 90 per cent sure that the system brought in at least one sale, 67 per cent sure that the system brought in two or more sales, and 40 per cent sure that it brought in three or more sales. Since the stated probabilities are cumulative, we must first convert to discrete probabilities. The difference between 90 per cent and 67 per cent is 23 percentage points, so the chances of exactly one (and no more than one) additional sale are 23 per cent. Similarly, the probability of exactly two sales is 27 per cent:

$$\Sigma[(\text{Probability of outcome}_a) \cdot \text{Value of outcome}_a)]$$

a cumulative distribution of:
   90% chance of at least $1,000
or 67% chance of at least $2,000
or 40% chance of at least $3,000

means the same as a discrete distribution of:
   10% chance of less than $1,000, or of at least $0
+ 23% chance of $1,000-$1,999, or of at least $1,000
+ 27% chance of $2,000-$2,999, or of at least $2,000
+ 40% chance of at least $3,000

which equals at least
   $ 0
+   230
+   540
+   1,200
= $1,970 expected value of probability distribution

We are left with a 40 per cent chance that the system generated three or more sales. Let us say that the most we could credit to the system is five additional sales. In theory, the 40 per cent cululative probabilities must be distributed over three, four, and five additional sales. In practice, we can conservatively assume a 40 per cent probability of three additional sales and ignore the chance of four or five.[2]

Once the cumulative probabilities are converted to discrete values, the expected value is simply the sum of the probabilities multiplied by the outcomes. In this example, the expected value of this probability distribution is the value of one sale ($1,000) times the probability of one more, plus the value of two sales times the probability of two more, plus the value of three sales times the probability of three or more sales, or $1,970.[3]

In fact, most people are to some degree averse to risk. A 20 per cent chance of $10 is generally not as desirable as a certain $2. Utility value —that is, what people are willing to pay for the chance—is significantly lower than expected value when there is a chance of a devastating outcome (such as a financial loss far greater than the potential gain).

Likewise, there are situations in which people choose the alternative with the lower expected monetary value, again because of their attitude toward risk. The state-run lotteries are an example; the expected payoff is much smaller than the price of the lottery ticket, yet people bet on lotteries because they see winning as their only chance of getting rich. In other words, they place more value on a slim chance of getting rich—with all that implies about quality of life—than they do on the minor cost of the lottery ticket. Utility value tends to be higher than expected value when there is a chance of payoff far beyond the cost of any of the unfavorable outcomes.

The case in which utility is likely to be higher than expected values is common throughout most of the situations we analyzed, because of the tremendous potential payoff of OA. Thus, our estimates of value may actually be lower than perceived values. In other cases, however, the reverse may be true. We have used expected values as certainty equivalents throughout the book as a simplifying assumption. In practice, adjustments can be made for the risk profile of decision makers.

Expected values are also used to refine a decision maker's guess by gauging his or her assurance that the estimate is accurate. For example, a decision maker might estimate that the OA tools increased profits by at least $2,000. We then ask what the chances are of that estimate being true; the decision maker might respond "I believe that estimate with two-thirds (67 per cent) assurance." We then ask him or her "how much" he or she believes that the tools will contribute at least $1,000; we might get an answer of 90 per cent. Going the other direction, we ask the chances of the contribution to profits being at least $3,000, and we might get an answer of approximately 40 per cent. The expected value of this probability distribution ($1,970) is generally a more accurate forecast than the decision maker's first estimate ($2,000).

Notes

1. The authors thank Richard A. Rossi for his significant contribution to this appendix.

2. The least biased approach would assume a geometric drop-off; that is, the probability of exactly three more sales is P, the probability of four is P^2, and the probability of five is P^3 where the probability P is such that the series adds up to 40 per cent. In this case, P would be 30 per cent. Thus, the probability of three is 30 per cent; the probability of four is 9 per cent, and the remaining probability of five is 1 per cent. In the case of a continuous (rather than a discrete) set of outcomes, the least biased curve would be an exponential (e^{-kx}). However, these calculations may be difficult for management to understand, and the subjective probabilities are not sufficiently accurate to support such accurate statistics. Thus, we use the simpler and more conservative assumption and ignore the probability of more than three sales.

3. If we had calculated the geometric distribution to take into account the possibility of four or five additional sales, the result would have been $2,080. The slight difference errs on the side of conservatism.

Tools Index

Industry Index

Key Word Index